Who You Are

and

Why You Are Here

Who You Are

and

Why You Are Here

———

Find Your Life Purpose and
Personality Type

Ruth Mierswa

RAINBOW GATEWAY
New York

WHO YOU ARE & WHY YOU ARE HERE: Find Your Life Purpose
& Personality Type

Copyright © 1998 by Ruth Mierswa B.A.

Published by
Rainbow Gateway
1092 Turk Hill Road
Fairport, NY 14450

Library of Congress Catalog Card Number: 97-92639
ISBN: 0-9661080-0-0

Mierswa, Ruth.
        Who you are and why you are here : find your life purpose and
    personality type / Ruth Mierswa.— 1st ed.
        p. cm.
        Includes index.
        Preassigned LCCN: 97-92639
        ISBN: 0-9661080-0-0

        1. Seven rays (Occultism) 2. Self-actualization (Psychology) 3.
    Typology (Psychology) I. Title

        BF1442.S49M54 1997   133
                                    QBI97-41500

Who You Are & Why You Are Here: Find Your Life Purpose and Personality
Type. An original method to find one's unique life purpose and personality type
with many proofs of its validity, and how this system can optimally change many
disciplines. Also detailed information for upliftment, especially for overcoming
anger and guilt, which has worked for author and clients.

Designed and composed by Sans Serif Inc., Saline, Michigan.
Printed in the United States of America

*To all who are searching for truth, for answers
to the meaning of life
who have found that riches, sex, drugs, alcohol, fame or honors
cannot bring true happiness and joy*

*Especially to readers of my first book who requested
a second in which no knowlege of
astrology is necessary to understand and benefit
from each chapter*

You came into this life for two reasons—one is to help people and the other is to change your weaknesses into strengths.

No one else can help humankind as well as you in your own unique capacity. You can find your unique Life Purpose in the pages of this book.

The kind of guidance not found anywhere else is given to eliminate your character flaws. Such concepts as why it is not only unnecessary but unwise to forgive anyone, and how to eradicate all anger and guilt are explained fully.

Numerous other original ideas to raise your level of consciousness are detailed. When these concepts become a part of your essence, you will have more joy, success and better health than you can ever imagine.

Irene Bouchard said that before she knew of these concepts and made them a part of herself, she was so unhappy that she felt she could not go on any longer. Now she is happier than she has ever been. Her life has turned completely around. She is spending all available time uplifting others.

Nancy Piccarreto ended up in a hospital because of unwarranted guilt. Since making these concepts a part of her being she, too, has evolved to a much higher level. Her health has improved and she is devoting her life aiding others in the ways she has been helped.

Contents

Charts and Graphs

FOREWORD

As Bob Dylan sang, "The times they are a-changin'." We now stand on the cusp between two great astronomical Ages, the Piscean and Aquarian. We can't go back to where we were. The boundaries between countries are coming down. The U.S.S.R. is gone. So is the Berlin Wall. The Yuppie lifestyle, characterized by the conspicuous spending typical of Ages on the wane and old orders on the brink of decline, has vanished. Even the so-called "New Age Movement" is not what it once was. A lot of those would-be gurus promising instant salvation and enlightenment are back at work at 9-to-5 jobs, or in therapy to figure out what went wrong.

In these confusing times, the questions of "Who am I?", "Why am I here?" and "What is my life's work?" are becoming increasingly frequent. It's not that people have become less interested in love, or money, or travel or any of those mundane concerns. These interests will always be with us, as they are part of life on Earth. More and more people are discovering that materialism doesn't bring peace. It may bring happiness for a time, but it may also bring pain. Spouses and lovers can leave. Jobs can be lost. Cars rust out and have to be replaced. Bodies, despite the best care from the best professionals, age.

So if the lover can go and the job title can go and the guru you thought was your salvation turns out to have mortal needs, what's left? Where is it? How do you find it? The answer has been the same over the Ages, but the path to the answer has varied in terms of the speed at which it can be traveled and the clarity of the road signs.

In the Piscean Age, the path was said to center around finding a Savior. Hence, Christ died for our sins. Love Jesus and you'll be saved. Let Jesus do the work. There's much truth in these statements, but there's also much missing. This is because in the Piscean Age, truth was veiled. When many souls were younger, they needed protection lest they confuse the Well of Truth with materialism. Only those deemed worthy were allowed to partake of the Well, which was guarded by the various Mystery Schools. Those admitted to these schools first had to pass the Initiations, which involved going through various experiences in life and reaching a point beyond which they could not pass unless they knew the passwords which were "Is this all there is?", "Is this all I am?" and "Is this all I can be?" The initiates protected the young souls from Truth that might have been too potent for them to handle. The hidden truth was this: We are *all* sparks of divinity with our own contributions to make to our own evolution and the world's. Christ, the Buddha and Krishna were Self-actualized, which means they knew and practiced this Truth. They were symbols of what we can do. They came to serve, to inspire and to teach. That was their work. They did not come to do our work for us. Their work was to serve as examples of the ways in which work *can* be done. They had not come as saviors, though, in the process of doing their work, they did save lives. But this was because they were doing their work—not because they were doing other people's work. They were merely being who they were and in doing so, allowing and inspiring others in turn be who they were. They have not done our work. They can't. And that's the truth that was veiled—the fact that we all have a great work to do because we all carry the spark of divinity within.

In the Aquarian Age, the path to Truth is the path of individualization. We must go from seeing others as saviors to seeing ourselves as capable of saving ourselves. This doesn't mean that we can't see others as helpers or can't help others. While others and externals can make a difference in our lives, they cannot save us or define us. We have to do that for ourselves.

According to tradition, the unveiling would come when the souls were ready to accept rather than fear the responsibility of being a spark of divinity. It's always been said that when the Age of Aquarius dawned, the symbols would be unveiled. This book is part of the process. Ruth Mierswa has taken the veiled hints and archaic language and obscure profundities of Alice Bailey's channeled texts and made them accessible to most, if not all. Those who will read will find answers.

No one could have written this book but Ruth. This is Ruth's work. The result of Ruth having the courage to "be" who she is. The system of Ray-Centered Astrology presented here is a tool for going within. It can help you discover who you are and why you are here. It will speak to your soul, clearly and simply, and in plain English rather than riddles. All you have to do is be prepared to listen to the answers that come from deep inside of you and act on them.

Easier said than done? Perhaps, but also easier done than not done. In the chapters that follow, Ruth provides a map to the well of Truth that's as clear as any I've ever seen. All you have to do is follow it. Your life's work awaits you. And the world awaits your life's work. Enough with this Foreword stuff; get on with the *real* food for thought! And by the way, I hope you enjoy this book as much as I did.

Donna Van Toen
astrologer, author, world lecturer

Acknowledgments

To the Master Djwal Khul and Alice Bailey for their
24 volumes of the Ageless Wisdom

To Lucis Trust for still making these books available

To my late husband, Richard, who supported my
beliefs that this work could uplift humankind
and eliminate the suffering of many
and who taught me much about the written word

INTRODUCTION

WHY I WROTE THIS BOOK

You are a divine being who has all the power within you to be who you are. You are here on earth to find out who you really are —your unique capacity in which no one else can help others as well as you. You are here also to find and eradicate your flaws, especially all anger and guilt both on a conscious and unconscious level. Guidance for this and much else is found in the following pages. But first, why I wrote this book:

What do you do when some readers say that while parts of your first book, *Ray-Centered Astrology*, helped them enormously in their upliftment, but other sections are beyond their comprehension because they have never studied astrology? And when some professional astrologers tell you they would like to use your pioneering work in their practices but that it would take too much time to digest your new concepts and calculations? And when some readers say your book has turned their lives completely around and you are strongly impressed to help more people in their Soul evolvement?

You write another book! You take your innovative concepts and calculations from your first book and simplify them so that no knowledge of astrology is necessary for readers to benefit from the entire book. You also add ideas and answers that have helped in your own evolvement since writing your first book. Further, you spend much time proving the efficacy of your work to satisfy both right and left brain oriented people. For example, several studies with bar graphs showing significant correlation of successful persons' careers and your system for discovering one's Purpose in life are in this book.

Whenever I become aware of a newly created work in any discipline, I am always intrigued to know why and how that new work came about. It is only fair that I divulge this same information about my book on the pioneering of a new astrology which can show one's unique life Purpose and help rid one of flaws, especially anger and guilt.

Ever since I was a child, I often wondered why we are here on earth, what the meaning of life is, especially for each individual. I asked these questions to whoever would listen to me, but the answers always fell into one of two categories—"don't ask such silly questions" and "who knows?" To be haunted by unanswered questions from childhood can be frustrating, yet my frustrations were the impetus for a persistent search for answers. Unaware at the time, I was somehow being led step by step through the years to find answers that finally satisfied me to the depths of my being.

The first step in my search was the study of psychology and mathematics at the University of Wisconsin, followed by postgraduate work in counseling at Northwestern University. Although these studies did not answer my questions, they did give me background that I would later need.

My second step was two years of high school teaching which gave me the opportunity to meet my future husband who played an important role in my life Purpose.

While bringing up three sons, I read psychology books from Freud to Maslow and all Spiritual books I could find which do not pertain to a specific religion. After my sons no longer needed my care, I decided to spend full time searching for answers. But I didn't know where to turn. I felt frustrated, helpless and depressed.

My confusion in Spiritual matters also caused me great mental suffering. Brought up as a Catholic, I was taught that God is loving, fair and wise. Yet conditions around me taught me the exact apposite. Why did my mother die when I was just four years old? Why did God give me a father who was unloving? Why do many children come into this world with physical, mental or emotional incapacities while some are born with good health and a high level of intelligence? The God I knew was far from loving, fair and wise. My frustration precipitated a definite lack of interest in living as I became occupied with these thoughts. What disturbed me the most was that I had found no answers to why we are here on earth. Aware that I had time for searching, but not knowing how to go about it, devastated me.

My husband, Richard, tried to ignite in me a spark of interest in life but it seemed I had no spark left. He suggested I go to the book store to "pick out just one book that interests you." At that time I was interested in nothing, but because he was trying to help me, I went to the store and reached for a book but with my eyes closed. It was *There is a River* by Thomas Sugrue, an Edgar Cayce book. When I arrived home, I tried to read it. I used all the will power I possessed to concentrate on its words. I had no sooner read to the bottom of the third page when a spark of interest ignited my whole being. I couldn't put the book down! I stayed up until the wee hours of the morning to finish it and as soon as the book store opened, I was there buying copies of all other Edgar Cayce books.

These books, along with several conferences on this work, taught me many things. They opened up for me a beautiful new world that I had never known existed—a world of justice, order, beauty, love and knowledge. Suddenly, the unloving, unjust and unwise God I had known all my life became the most loving, just and wise Deity beyond my wildest imagination. The Edgar Cayce readings on Reincarnation and Karma brought immense changes to my way of thinking. A heavy weight fell off my shoulders as I

was beginning to understand the workings of the universe. While
these teachings did not answer my question of how to find the
unique Life Purpose for each individual, they taught me the
meaning of life as it applies to all people. I wanted to give to others which was given me, but I didn't know how to go about it. I
asked God to show me the way.

Two days later, I came upon a statement in one of Edgar
Cayce's readings which said astrology is a superb tool for helping
people evolve Spiritually and that much astrological knowledge
has been published, but the greater knowledge has not yet been
written. I knew at that instant that astrology would be my life
work and that through it I would somehow find answers to my
life-long questions. I also knew then that my work would be a catalyst in the Spiritual evolvement of myself and many others. All
this went through my mind in a split second. This was indeed a
peak experience, after which I shouted to my husband, "That's
it!" He replied, "What's it?" I told him I was going to be an astrologer.

I was not surprised that he, having spent a lifetime in scientific research, was not only shocked but severely disappointed.
"Astrology is unscientific and superstitious. It is for the gullible
and uneducated;" he said, "you have a brilliant mind—don't
waste it on astrology." When I told him that I hoped for his moral
support, but that I would pursue this study regardless, he coun-
tered, "Remember, I will have nothing to do with astrology."

After studying for a year, and desiring to know at least one
other person interested in astrology, I noted that instructions
were offered in my area. I asked my husband to accompany me to
these classes, but he didn't want to show his face among "people
with such unscientific interests." Two friends agreed to go with
me, but later were unable to go. My husband then said reluc-
tantly, "I'll go with you under two conditions: that you realize that
the only reason I'm going is that I love you and that you will go

alone after the second class." Little did he know that he would later become an astrologer himself.

On the way home from the first class, he said, "There may be something to astrology after all." Coming back from the second class, he sheepishly muttered, "You won't have to go alone to any classes. I've decided to go with you."

The study of astrology opened up for me doors to knowledge siphoned down from the heavens to humankind, to each individual as different from all others, to be given by astrologers with understanding and love. The wisdom of the Universe made indelible imprints on my consciousness. I became aware that the interpretation of the placement and relationships of planets and important indices of one's horoscope, found by these positions in the heavens when one takes his or her first breath, to be aligned with one's abilities, strengths and weaknesses. I scrutinized my own horoscope and those of all my relatives and friends I knew well and found in every case that the interpretations were the same as what I knew to be true. After years of intense study and contemplation, I became a successful professional astrologer.

The final step in my search was the study of the twenty four volumes of the Alice Bailey books, nineteen which were dictated by the Master Djwal Khul. The many years of this study were interspersed with the taking and graduation of two metaphysical correspondence courses. At last, I found what I had searched for! I knew then why we are here on earth and that each of us has a special mission that no one else can perform as well. These books gave me glimpses of Ageless Wisdom to be meditated on and used to uplift those who want to know who they are and why they are here. I knew then I could create a system of finding one's unique Soul's Purpose. When I came across in one Alice Bailey book that before the end of the century there would be an astrology of the Rays, I instantly knew that my Soul's Purpose was to originate this new astrology.

When I told my husband what I planned to do, he was not only amazed but couldn't believe what I was saying. He told me there was no question in his mind as to my ability to accomplish a task of this magnitude, but that I would never finish it. He said, "You have so little self-confidence in your abilities." I told him, "That was the past. This is the present and I will work on it until it is finished." He did not believe me and remarked, "I don't want to see you hurt, but if you decide to go ahead with this project, remember that I want nothing to do with it." This was his left brain speaking. Having earned a living as a scientist, he was skeptical of everything until he had some semblance of proof—in this case proof of my potential success.

But he also had an enhanced right brain. He was unusually intuitive and psychic, often seeing entities in the spirit realm and hearing them speak. There is scientific research proving that one's facial features indicate certain capacities. My husband looked so much like the late renowned psychic Edgar Cayce that on one occasion when we visited the Association of Research and Enlightenment (The Edgar Cayce Institute), a person who knew Edgar Cayce approached my husband asking, "Who are you?" He later apologized explaining that he thought my husband was Edgar Cayce materialized.

As is always the case, when one has both superior left and right hemispheres, the right brain which houses the higher mind (abstract, intuitive, psychic) gives greater credence than the left lower mind (concrete, scientific, rational). So it was with Richard. Only two days after he said he would have nothing to do with my project, he completely changed his stance. After meditation this particular evening, he said, "I want you to know that I will do everything in my power to help you accomplish your task." This time, I couldn't believe what *he* was saying.

He went on, "An entity appeared to me who is your Spiritual teacher. He said the reason you have so much confidence in your ability is that he put that thought strongly in your mind when you read that the astrology of the Rays would find its rightful place in human thought before the end of the century. He added that a council had been formed in the higher Spiritual planes and he was chosen to find an earthling to write a book on the astrology of the Seven Rays. He studied horoscopes of astrologers and looked into their minds and hearts and gave you first choice."

I began writing my first manuscript in 1977, the same year that Chiron was discovered. It is a fact that every heavenly body and every new phase of any discipline is discovered when humanity is ready to benefit from its energies. Chiron, found between Saturn (materialism and the personality) and Uranus (the Soul and its urges), is a Rainbow Bridge from the personality to the Soul. Ray-Centered Astrology is a new phase of astrology (also a Rainbow Bridge from the personality to the Soul) which can tune in to everyone's life Purpose through a detailed knowledge of the Seven Rays.

With this, my second book, one's unique Purpose of Life can be revealed to all—from those who have never opened an astrology book to dedicated practicing astrologers. It is the result of requests from readers, both astrologers and non-astrologers, of my scholarly published book, *Ray-Centered Astrology*, for a simplified version of finding one's unique Soul's Purpose and guidelines for manifesting it. Also, to satisfy my own Soul yearnings.

Astrology is now reaching mainstream. It is becoming less concerned with the self-centered personality and more with the Soul. The beautiful cover of *Life* magazine, July, 1997, gave full coverage to this divine science with zodiacal symbols and these words: "Why So Many Of Us Now Believe The Stars Reflect the Soul. ASTROLOGY RISING" Kenneth Miller writes, page 40, 44, "Astrology is experiencing its biggest boom in 400 years. According to a recent poll, just 20 percent of Americans are flat-out believers; 48 percent say astrology is probably or definitely valid...Twenty years ago there were an estimated 1,000 professional astrologers in the United States; today there are something like 5,000. In 1968, when Linda Goodman's *Sun Signs* became the first astrological best-seller, the annual market for astrology books was around five million. Today, it is closer to 20 million . . . Astrology has changed. Today a tough planetary aspect is regarded as a challenge to personal growth, not a portent of doom."

The change in astrology is definitely a shift from personality to Soul focus. Humankind is now ready for this new astrology of the Soul. Proofs of its validity are given at the end of Chapters One through Seven and in the last Chapter including four bar graphs.

THE MEANING OF LIFE

Who am I? Why am I here? What is the Purpose of my life? If you have ever asked yourself these questions, you are not alone. Thinkers have asked themselves these same questions for centuries and have been searching ever since for answers that satisfy.

The general public also wants to know what life is all about. Ever-increasing numbers of people are looking for answers. It has been found that 80 per cent of American adults are seeking meaning and Purpose in their lives.[1]

Did you ever wonder why, at this time in history, it is not only the deep thinkers who are hungry for answers but also the general population? It is because of the advancement of the human race. It is the nature of humanity to progress as time goes on. (Humankind evolves to a higher level as the result of its experiences.) With each earth life that we experience (see Chapter IX on Reincarnation and Karma), we learn certain lessons, and having learned these lessons, we become more evolved, changing our interests and focus.

The interests and focus of humanity change appreciably every 2160 years when our Sun and its planets enter a new zodiacal constellation. That time is now (see Chapter X, The Dawning of a New Age). The earth is entering the constellation Aquarius whose energies induce swift changes, especially in enhancing the minds of humankind. Because the mind is the bridge to the Soul, humanity now is urged to focus on its Spiritual essence. Most of us, in our past lives in the Piscean Age, strove for riches, fame and honors. Having received them, we found they did not bring happiness. Now we are looking beyond the material. We are searching for something that can make life worthwhile. We want to know the true meaning of life. We want to know why we are here.

The only reason we are here on earth is to become divine beings. This is our heritage. It is only through the experience of earth lives that we can attain divinity.

The way we can become closer to our divine potential is serving others. It is not just any kind of service. It is a very special kind. Each of us has unique talents and abilities that no one else possesses, a special niche to fill in the scheme of things that no one else can fill as well. That is the Soul's Purpose of every individual.

"You have designed your body and your energy system to perform your life task," states scientist/healer/therapist Barbara Ann Brennan. "It is made up of a combination of energy consciousness that best suits what you have been incarnated to do. No one else has that combination . . . You are unique. The first principle to maintain your health is maintaining a deep connection to yourself and your purpose in life, both on the personal level and the world level. This means self-love and self-respect."[2]

It is sad that many people suffer from low self-esteem, resulting in depression, drug abuse, alcoholism and crime because they feel worthless. They do not know who they are! Jesus said, "Ye are gods." There is a spark of God within each of us. Some day, whether in this life or a future one, that spark will be ignited into a beautiful flame. Even though our physical bodies will be discarded in the process called death, our true essence will live forever. We will incarnate on this earth plane again and again at the proper times and places needed for our evolvement to best manifest our unique Soul's Purpose. Until our Soul's Purpose is found and manifested, frustration, unhappiness and even ill health can result.

Dr. Bernie states, "If you follow your Path, you will achieve your full growth and full potential . . . and if you don't, you will become psychologically and spiritually troubled, and if that doesn't call your attention back to your Path, your body will become physically ill."

Charles Garfield, Ph.D. has not only found better physical health in those who are working with a mission but, in his six year's work with cancer survivors discovered that each spontaneous remission was attributed to manifesting one's special Purpose in Life.

"I don't know what your destiny will be," said Albert Schweister, "but one thing I know: the only ones among you who will be truly happy are those who will have sought and found how to serve."

Greater benefits than physical health and happiness appear when we actually do what we were put here on earth to do. We then attain self-fulfillment, that feeling of joy that stretches to the core of our beings. I cannot think of anything better than filling that niche that was reserved for each of us.

When one finds and manifests his or her Soul's Purpose, all else is magnetically drawn to that person, including good health, happiness, self-fulfillment, peace, true prosperity and joy.

U Thant, who was unanimously appointed as secretary to the United Nations General Assembly November 30, 1962, believes that once you find your unique Purpose of Life, then love, understanding, compassion and peaceful relations with others automatically follow.

Willis Harmon, president of the Institute of Noetic Sciences, said, "Every person has a deep sense of purpose of being here to achieve some particular destiny . . . As we become aware of our own sense of purpose and consciously align our lives with that, we begin to prosper in the truest sense."

The late best-selling author, mythologist Joseph Campbell said that if your follow your "bliss," the world of fulfillment will open up to you—doors will swing wide open.

Even though the human Spirit is capable of great accomplishments, we cannot successfully serve others in a career that is not our Soul's Purpose.

"Inspirational speakers these days are fond of making the circuit of slum schools and depressed neighborhoods with the uplifting message, 'You can become whatever you want to be.' This is nothing less than . . . nonsense. You can become only what your . . . capacities permit," wrote the late Sydney Harris, newspaper columnist.

How do we know what our innate capacities permit, what our Soul's Purpose is, the true meaning of our life? How do we find what it is? Has science given us the answer?

Astronaut Edgar Mitchell doesn't think so. He said, "We want to understand the meaning of life; science doesn't provide that meaning."

"Big new questions present themselves, ones that can't be answered in the old ways—questions of purpose of life," stated Charles M. Johnston, MD.

Richard Kieninger says, "There has always been the questioning person who searches for reality and truth in order to avoid being misled by ignorance and authoritarian lies. Yet we are all conditioned by traditional values and conventional thinking, so break-throughs in knowledge proceed slowly . . . We each have a built-in impulse to fulfill our potential. The tension between what we could be and the evident failure of our institutions to hasten our attainment of human completeness urges us to seek better ways."[3]

What are the better ways? How can we find that unique Purpose for which we came into this life? A hint to the answer if given by Goswarmi Kriyananda who has been teaching and practicing astrology for 40 years, "Astrology . . . insists that you can know the meaning of life, the nature of life, even the purpose of life."

John D. Rea gives an added hint: "What is the destiny of our Souls? It is a gift of the stars to know the truth of these guardians of our lives on earth."[4]

It is truly a gift of the stars that one's unique Purpose in Life can now be found. From deep study of psychology, metaphysics and astrology, I became aware that one's special Purpose in Life is found in the identification and interpretation of his or her Soul and Personality Rays, Ascendant and Sun Sign derived from astrology, detailed in the following chapters.

HOW TO FIND YOUR SOUL'S PURPOSE

No knowledge of astrology is necessary to find your Soul's Purpose. This book was written with the sole intent of reaching everyone. It simplifies the material in my scholarly first book, *Ray-Centered Astrology*. To find your Soul's Purpose, you must know foremost what your Soul and Personality Rays are.

To find your Personality Ray, all you need to know is your month and day of birth, giving your Sun Sign.

To find your Soul Ray, you must know your Ascendant—the zodiacal Sign on the eastern horizon at birth. It is found from your natal horoscope which can be set up by an astrologer or an astrological computer service by knowing your year, month, day, clock-time and place of birth.

Even if you do not know your Ascendant, this book will give you a wealth of information and guidance on your personality type from your Personality Ray and Sun Sign.

We are not left in the dark to find that unique Purpose in Life that belongs to each of us. God, the universe, divine guidance—whatever you wish to call the Powers That Be—has given us clues, found in the cosmos, which have been released through certain Masters of the Ageless Wisdom.

These clues resulted in a system to find your Purpose in Life by knowing which Ray energies entered your consciousness as your Soul and Personality Rays, what your Sun Sign is and what zodiacal Sign was on the eastern horizon (Ascendant) when you took your first breath.

Finding Your Personality Ray

Your Personality Ray shows the type of personality you have to carry out your Purpose in Life. Please read the designated chapter for details of your Personality Ray with your Sun Sign:

BIRTH	SUN SIGN	PERSONALITY RAY	CHAPTER
March 21 to April 20	Aries	4	4
April 21 to May 20	Taurus	1	1
May 21 to June 20	Gemini	5	5
June 21 to July 22	Cancer	6	6
July 23 to Aug. 22	Leo	2	2
Aug. 23 to Sept. 22	Virgo	4	4
Sept. 23 to Oct. 23	Libra	7	7
Oct. 24 to Nov. 22	Scorpio	6	6
Nov. 23 to Dec. 21	Sagittarius	3	3
Dec. 22 to Jan. 20	Capricorn	3	3
Jan. 21 to Feb. 20	Aquarius	2	2
Feb. 21 to March 20	Pisces	1	1

The above chart shows the average day throughout the years when the Sun changed Signs. The day the Sun changes Signs varies within a day or two from year to year, so if your birthday falls near the changing days listed above, you may want an astrologer or computer service find your Sun Sign. However, you might intuitively know which Personality Ray is yours by reading both chapters.

Finding Your Soul Ray

To find your Soul Ray, you must know your Ascendant Sign found in your Natal Horoscope which can be set up by an astrologer or a computer service.

Five Ascendants With Given Soul Rays:

ASCENDANT	SOUL RAY	CHAPTER
Taurus	4	4
Gemini	2	2
Libra	3	3
Scorpio	4	4
Aquarius	5	5

If your Ascendant is not one of the five above, your Soul Ray is one of the two or three as shown below:

ASCENDANT	SOUL RAY	CHAP.		SOUL RAY	CHAP		SOUL RAY	CHAP.
Aries	1	1	or	7	7			
Cancer	3	3	or	7	7			
Leo	1	1	or	5	5			
Virgo	2	2	or	6	6			
Sagittarius	4	4	or	5	5	or	6	6
Capricorn	1	1	or	3	3	or	7	7
Pisces	2	2	or	6	6			

If your Ascendant falls in the above chart, you have two choices. One is to read the two or three possible chapters indicated, in a relaxed contemplative state to intuitively know which Ray fits you best. The other choice is to have a Ray-Centered Astrologer do necessary calculations. If you are an astrologer, my first book, *Ray-Centered Astrology*, (See Appendix) will show you how to calculate Soul Rays and more.

Your Soul Ray tells your Purpose in Life. It is important to find that special niche for each of us to shine and to serve in the scheme of things. Your Personality Ray indicates the type of personality you have to carry out your Soul's Purpose.

Although your Soul and Personality Ray energies are most indicative in finding your Soul's Purpose, your Ascendant and Sun Sign add detail.

Each Ray chapter gives a thorough explanation of both Soul and Personality Rays. The first section relays information of the Soul and Personality Rays and helps determine which Ray energies you are using unwisely. It also gives guidance for transmuting character weaknesses into strengths, affording rewarding Karma.

The second section is detailed Soul Ray information, followed by (1) the combination of the Soul Ray with each of the three possible Ascendant Signs and (2) a general meaning of the Soul Ray with each of the Seven Ray personalities.

The third section is an explanation of the Personality Ray, followed by either one or two Sun Signs, depending on whether that particular Ray has one or two ruling planets. Also, information is given on the average, advanced and very advanced person of each Sun Sign to help you determine which category you fall in and what changes to make if you wish to advance to a higher one.

Before you read the chapters for details of your Soul's Purpose and your Personality to carry it out, you may want an over-all idea. Following are the general meanings of the Seven Rays and twelve zodiacal Signs. Please read in this order—your Soul Ray, Ascendant, Personality Ray, Sun Sign:

General Meanings for Soul & Personality Rays

RAY 1
Power to make desired changes in government, education, science, healing, psychiatry, astrology and other disciplines

RAY 2
Capacity to heal physically, mentally and/or Spiritually or teach

RAY 3
Ability for creativity, such as found in inventions, theories and hypotheses

RAY 4
Helping others attain harmony through artistic ability (music, writing, painting and so on) and/or counseling

RAY 5
Aiding others in practical living through reason and logic, such as in scientific research and statistics

RAY 6
Uplifting others through such avenues as religion, writing and music

RAY 7
Helping others attain rhythm and order through capacity to excel in organizational work

General Meanings for Ascendants & Sun Signs

ARIES
Pioneering capacity, breaking new ground, especially in divine ideas with enthusiasm and integrity

TAURUS
Spiritual illumination, stability and determination to follow through what you decide to do

GEMINI
Ability to fluently, interestingly and charmingly communicate in various channels, such as writing, speaking and so on

CANCER
Nurturing capacity and ability to sense what others need

LEO
Self-confidence and awareness of what you and others are capable of becoming

VIRGO
Superb analytical and discriminative ability

LIBRA
Capacity to see both sides of a problem or issue

SCORPIO
Power to penetrate to the very depth of a problem or issue

SAGITTARIUS
Energy, optimism and enthusiasm directed on goal after goal

CAPRICORN
Self-discipline and persistence to accomplish what you want

AQUARIUS
Unconditional love toward all, freedom to be who you are and capacity to aid others in these attainments

PISCES
Excellent ability to contact Soul, and compassion toward the suffering

Using only these general meanings can give unusual guidance for your Soul's Purpose. Details can be added later from the chapters on your Soul and Personality Rays, but these general meanings can give an accurate big picture. For example, I have a Ray 2 Soul—capacity to teach and/or heal others with love and wisdom, a Pisces Ascendant—compassion and kindness toward the suffering and an excellent ability to contact my Soul, a Ray 4 Personality—helping others attain harmony through writing and counseling, and an Aries Sun Sign—breaking new ground with divine ideas, enthusiasm and integrity.

It is interesting and validating to both Ray-Centered Astrology and to the work of the renowned astrologer Philip Sedgwich that, while both are innovative, they dovetail. Yet he and I have had no correspondence of any kind.

He envisioned the kinds of energies which the Galactic Center, Galaxies and Pulsars emit to a person when conjuncting (are close) a planet or important point in one's chart.

The energies Sedgwick gives to those cosmic bodies which are significant in my horoscope coincide with the energies described above shown by Ray-Centered Astrology. It is no surprise that my life work is helping others find their unique Soul's Purpose because of my powerful Ascendant, which is the major indicator of one's Soul's Purpose. My Ascendant is conjunct Nuclear Galaxy BL Lac, "which holds a strong radio variability with the intensity of two billion suns. It helps one to blow out old theories and to plant the seeds of new concepts and abstractions to progress into the coming times with clarity of vision and illumined thoughts."[5]

My Ascendant is extremely powerful for other reasons. One is that it is the same degree as Chiron. Comet Chiron, when significantly placed in one's horoscope, urges one to quest for his or her unique Soul's Purpose in rapport with the Ageless Wisdoms, is an indicator of being ahead of one's time, and bestows a healing capacity by precipitating crises, followed by learning the lessons they are meant to teach. Chiron was discovered in 1977 (the year I began writing *Ray-Centered Astrology*) whose energies induced me to communicate my findings to others.

Another reason that my Ascendant/Chiron is powerful is that it relates beneficially to both my Saturn (the personality) and Uranus (the Soul). My Uranus also beneficially aspects my Sun and Mercury in Aries, showing intuitive creative capacity in pioneering work for the Aquarian Age. This gives me energy for manifesting my Soul's Purpose through helping others uplift their consciousness from the personality to the Soul.

The cusp (beginning) of my Career House is conjunct the Galactic Center. Of this, Sedgwick says, "The insight is precisely valid. it gives additional responsibilities, perspectives and insights through cosmic knowledge—provides knowledge that individuals seem to have no way of knowing. They hold the potential to make massive changes in the direction of human affairs . . . personally, for other individuals and within collective situations. These natives may be forerunners in innovative thought . . . They become instrumental in bringing about change, transitions and adjustments in the way that things are designed, implemented and completed." The cusp of my Career House also conjuncts a certain Pulsar whose energies give "communications from the essence of truth." Of another Pulsar conjunct my Neptune, Sedgwick says, "A sense of Divine Will."

After you have a good handle on the big picture of your Soul's Purpose, it is time to fill in the details by contemplating the two chapters of your Soul and Personality Rays which include material on your Ascendant and Sun Sign. Notice especially the wise and unwise use of your two Ray energies. You have the power to change the unwise use of any trait by often visualizing its wise use. Since energy follows thought, you will be building strong thought forms to help you attain what you want, lessening the self-discipline that must follow. To know which energies you are using unwisely, it is advisable to go into the silence. This is done by using your mind to relax every part of your body, breathing deeply a few times, visualizing the White Lights of Christ surrounding you, and asking your Soul for help. Greater success can be attained if you meditate when your right brain is activated by your breath. We breathe through only one nostril at a time except during short intervals when an exchange from one nostril to the other takes place. When you breathe through your right nostril, the left brain is activated—the optimal time for masculine Ray energies to manifest, such as logical mental activity, physical energy and courage. When the breath is ready to change to the left nostril, a brief period of breathing through both nostrils occurs which is a time of balance, harmony and joy. Then when your breath switches to the left nostril, the right brain is activated. This is the time to optimally engage in quiet activity, such as meditation, using your higher intuitive mind and contacting your Soul. Studies have shown that breathing from one nostril to the other changes on an average of every 90 minutes, but can vary from 40 minutes to 3 hours.

Even though each Ray energy is unique, different from the other six, all the odd-numbered ones have much in common, as do the even-numbered. The odd-numbered—1, 3, 5, 7—are masculine and are concerned with power, intellect, energy, courage, leadership and extroversion. The even-numbered Rays—2, 4, 6—are feminine, giving sensitivity, love, concern for others, intuition, wisdom and introversion. The degree of the above traits given any individual is consonant with his or her level of Soul evolvement. Even though you have both Soul and Personality Rays in the odd or even numbers, it does not mean you are lacking in balance, as each Ray has sub-rays of all seven Rays.

Even though two or more people, organizations or countries have the same Soul and Personality Rays which randomly happens in one out of 49 horoscopes, it is extremely unusual for these same entities to have identical Ascendant and Sun Signs. In this very rare case, which almost never would happen, the entire horoscopes must be delineated to obtain the detailed uniqueness of each.

Ray-Centered Astrology speaks to the entelechy in each individual. Entelechy is the Greek derived word which means the pattern of one's Purpose in Life. It is the entelechy of an acorn to be an oak tree. It is the entelechy of you to be what you came on earth this time around to be—your Soul's Purpose in this life.

When you find your Life's Purpose and begin to manifest it, you will feel in tune with the universe, having found that special niche designated for you and you alone. The universe will then give you what you deserve—success, joy and better health.

The next seven chapters give detailed guidance for your Soul's Purpose and your Personality Type to carry it out. Also supplied are names of self-realized people (manifesting their Souls' Purposes) showing how interpretation of their Soul and Personality Rays are consonant with their contributions to humankind.

Notes

1 *New Realities*, Daniel Yankilovitch

2 *Hands of Light*, Barbara Ann Brennan, Bantam 1987

3 *The Ultimate Disaster*, Richard Kieninger

4 *Patterns of the Whole*, John D. Rea

5 *The Astrology of Deep Space*, Philip Sedgwick, Seek-it Publications, 1984

I

RAY I SOULS AND PERSONALITIES OF WILL AND POWER

—◦◦◦—

Great Changes in Various Disciplines
Color—White
Taurus or Pisces Sun Sign—Ray 1 Personality
See Introduction for Possible Ray 1 Soul
for Aries, Leo or Capricorn Ascendant

Ray 1 is the most powerful of all Rays, and its rulers, Pluto and Vulcan, are the most powerful of all planets. The optimal use of Ray 1 energy is destroying outworn concepts, ideas and structures which delay the progress of humankind, and replace them with higher ones that humanity is now ready for. Yet Ray I energy can also preserve and maintain those concepts, ideas and structures that are still valuable for human evolvement.

Ray 1 energy is sharp and brilliant. Its brilliance, among other attributes, gives capacity to see the whole picture—to know what needs destroying and what needs preserving.

You can easily see the futility of continuing to manifest your character flaws with the resulting difficult karmic experiences and have wisdom and power to transmute weaknesses into strengths and thus reap rewards.

Ray 1 gives global vision which helps you see the big picture of a problem in any discipline. Government officials who have Ray 1 Souls or Personalities can easily understand that needs and abilities of other nations, as well as one's own, must be taken into account before just and wise decisions can be made. This says what is best for any other country is also best for one's own because the Law of Karma works for nations as well as individuals (see Chapter IX).

The colors of Ray 1 are red and white. While red's vibration bestows more energy than white, it is inadvisable at this stage of evolvement of the human race to use red profusely. Unless one's thoughts, words and deeds are always for the good of others, the use of red often provokes feelings of irritability, nervousness, anger and violence. However, red used for stop lights is wise because its energy is immediate and hits one between they eyes. White, the combination of all colors of the spectrum which are the colors of all Rays, vibrates intelligence, intuition, wisdom, love and self-confidence. Ray 1 Souls and Personalities can benefit by choosing white in clothes, linens, home furnishings, cars and so on.

The Monad (Spirit) is associated with Ray 1. Its Lord is Master Morya who is the former Saint Peter. The sense of Ray 1 is touch. The stone is the diamond, symbolizing sharpness and brilliance to the mind. The element is Akasha which is the storehouse of Universal Mind. Ray 1 has affinity with the Great Bear Constellation and with Shambala (those extremely highly evolved Spiritual entities who form God's Plan for earth). The most common symbol is the Eye of Shiva—the All-Seeing Eye, the Universal Eye—which directs the will of God. The most ancient symbol is the Angel with the Flaming Sword who lovingly in the after-life turns away those seeking admittance to the higher planes who are undeserving—thus protecting them from dangers they would encounter because of the difference in their vibrations and those of the higher planes.

Ray 1 energy is synonymous with power, clear vision, sense of time, singleness of purpose and detachment.

As Ray 1 Souls and Personalities, you can perform a great service now at the dawning of this New Age, a time when many changes are being made. Clear vision is badly needed to differentiate between what needs saving and what should be destroyed. Power is required to either preserve or destroy to produce liberation. You possess powerful energy, strong wills and clear vision urgently needed to make necessary changes in rapport with the New Aquarian energies.

Every Ray energy can be used unwisely or wisely—you have free will. The more wisely you use its energies, the better you can help humanity and therefore incur rewarding Karma and Soul evolvement for yourself. Because Ray 1 is the most powerful of all Rays, it will either greatly harm or help humanity and yourself.

Ray 1 energy is the most difficult of all Ray energies to use wisely—its sharpness, one-pointedness and brilliance in its ability to quickly attain its goal are all plus attributes if no others are concerned, but we live in a world of people, animals, plants and minerals—all having certain needs. You may have a tendency to brook no interference with others so that you can quickly actualize your ideas which are usually brilliant, but if you lack concern and love for others, many enemies result. This scenario brings much lesson-teaching Karma, often causing your brilliant projects to initially fail.

Thus you suffer greatly and learn quickly to combine your innate power and brilliance with love and concern for the needs of others. Now, instead of forcing your will on others, you invite their ideas in a cooperative fashion. Instead of believing that only your ideas of a project can be successful, you become aware that others, too, have helpful thoughts that can be fused with yours for more success. Instead of becoming angry and irritable toward those who offer suggestions, you welcome with understanding and love all who want and are able to add to the project's success. You no longer feel that your ideas and only your ideas will work, but develop a sort of humility in knowing that those of certain others are even sometimes better than your own.

When you have attained this level, you will find yourself so much in rhythm with the whole, profiting greatly in better physical, emotional, mental and Spiritual health. You will no longer feel isolated, alone and aloof. Yet you are able, because of your power, strength, courage, steadfastness, truthfulness, singleness of purpose, force of will, vision, power-to-do-good and leadership to use your energy dynamically in furthering God's Plan on earth. You can then, at the beginning of this New Age, make the necessary changes in any discipline—having the foresight of knowing which concepts, ideas and structures need to be destroyed, which should optimally be substituted and which ones should be allowed to exist, all for the good of humankind, not for your self-centered desires.

The greatest challenge of Ray 1 Souls and Personalities is to develop as much love and concern for others as for self.

Following is a list of character weaknesses you are prone to and the strengths you have or can have through transmutation. Although self-discipline is necessary to overcome your flaws, it is unwise to repress them as that would cause problems from your unconscious mind. Instead, because energy follows thought, transmute the energy of your weaknesses into specific strengths by visualizing often the following strengths, along with self-discipline. As you transmute your character weaknesses into strengths, your life will become more successful, enjoyable and fulfilled.

RAY I SOUL AND PERSONALITY ENERGIES

UNWISE USE	WISE USE
Lack of understanding and love	Unattached love for all
Power used for self-centered desires	Power used for the common good
Intolerance	Cooperation
Isolation and loneliness	Seeing the Oneness of All
Domination of others	Respecting freedom of others
Fearlessness yet creating fear in others	Fearlessness and helping others attain it
Pride and arrogance	Knowing that a humble person is strong
Impatience	Patience
Destroying for self-centered reasons	Destroying when needed and replacing
Insisting on your way, right or wrong	Capacity to take a stand on principle
Blaming others for your failures	Knowing you create your own reality
Destroying with anger	Destroying with love if not needed
Cruelty	Defending the weak

RAY I SOUL OF WILL AND POWER

An Aries, Leo or Capricorn Ascendant may give a Ray 1 Soul (see Introduction)

Your Soul's Purpose is to use your brilliant mind to make needed changes in a certain discipline. Your greatest challenge is to activate new ideas and structures in rapport with Aquarian energies. This is accomplished by changing those parts of a discipline that are no longer needed which are preventing humanity to progress, substituting higher ones, yet keeping those parts that are still helpful.

At the dawning of a New Age which happens every 2160 years, new energies of that Age ever-increasingly reach the consciousness of humankind while the Old Age energies gradually decrease. The disciplines that served humanity in the past must change if they are to survive. Outworn concepts, ideas and structures of the past Piscean Age must be replaced by those of the New Aquarian Age so humanity can continue to evolve.

As a Ray 1 Soul, you are well equipped with the power, the will and the ability to see clearly the greater whole, the big picture and courageously make necessary changes in a discipline of your choice and capability consonant with your Ascendant, Personality Ray and Sun Sign energy. Following are some disciplines in which you can excel:

Government

Because government officials wield more power than leaders in any other discipline and because global vision is necessary for success, more Ray 1 Souls are found in government than in any other field.

You have the ability to see the big picture on a national scale and understand its ramifications—that unless the government is run for the good of all people with primary requisites of food, clothing, shelter, health care and education for everyone, it cannot be successful. That means, among many other things, getting rid of lobbying by special interest groups and settling international disputes by sitting down at the table rather than going to war which not only kills people and creates hatred, but uses money that should be directed to those in need.

Your global vision enables you to see and understand what each country including your own can give other countries and what it needs from them. You can well understand the Universal Laws of Reincarnation and Karma (see Chapter IX)—knowing that nations operate the same as individuals. Just as individuals who care about no one but themselves have difficult karmic experiences, so do nations. From this understanding, you know that what is right and good for another nation, is ultimately good for your nation. Looking back through history, you can easily see that when a government leader through devious means has obtained an initial unfair advantage over another country, it has always later ended in a serious disadvantage for his or her own country.

With these insights, you are capable of getting your own house (nation) in order which will prompt other nations to do likewise.

Just as persons have Soul Rays, so do nations. The United States has a Ray 2 Soul of Love and Wisdom whose Soul's Purpose is to teach and/or heal other countries who are in need. It cannot be done with war which only brings more problems and more hatred. It can be accomplished by understanding and concern for all peoples in the world. We are a global community with every nation affecting every other nation. The key words of the future will be universality, not nationality; cooperation, not isolation; understanding and love, not war and hate. You have the power, will, intelligence and courage to bring these key words into actuality. It is through aligning yourself with the Soul's Purpose of your nation in making the necessary changes in government so urgently needed at this period in the history of the race.

Education

If your talents are used in education, you have an enormous but very soul-gratifying task.

The present educational system does indeed need overhauling.

So many intelligent youngsters quit school and get caught up in street gangs, violence, drugs, alcohol and so on because they don't know who they are and why they are here. You can bring them knowledge of the real Self, its divine heritage and its unique Soul's Purpose.

You have the ever-increasing Aquarian Age energies on your side which are inducing all of us to be our true Selves—to serve others consonant with the special reason for which we came into this life. Present education stifles this uniqueness. It says all students must learn certain things to progress to the next level or fail. It does not speak to the special potential of each child.

You have the ability to change this system so that all children know who they are, why they are here on earth. Then they can become aware of their unique capacities, leading them to find their Purpose in Life and thus taught the necessary subjects to attain it. It is sad to see the lives of many children being thrown away when they have so much to contribute to the evolvement of the race and to their own Soul progress.

It is imperative for the Spiritual, emotional and physical health of each student and for the contributions each can make to society, that each in the lower grades will know what his or her Soul's Purpose is. This should be followed throughout future education by the specific study necessary, customized to each child's Purpose in Life.

Ray-Centered astrologers working with teachers and parents can bring this condition into fruition, but it takes your expertise to bring this scenario about. You have the power, the will, the intelligence and the courage to make the changes in our school system so urgently needed at this period in the history of the race.

Psychology

If your talents lead you to psychology, you, like the Ray 1 Soul in education, have an enormous task but one of great Soul satisfaction.

One of the most prevalent methods of mainstream psychologists is often referred to as the "Child Within Theory." It holds that if clients are taken back to childhood to relive their difficult experiences, which these therapists believe caused their problems, they will be cured. What happens is that these people must again suffer what they originally did as children, adding to the anger they feel toward those who wronged them or even toward God who gave them their parents in the first place.

This cruel and unsuccessful method can be changed by Ray 1 Souls through understanding the Universal Laws of Reincarnation and Karma (see Chapters IX and XII). With this understanding, you can explain these Universal Laws so that your clients become responsible for where they find themselves with the knowledge that their Souls chose their parents because of certain lessons they need to learn. They can be taught how taking responsibility for their problems does not mean suffering guilt (See Chapter XII).

With your clear vision, you are able to see that we are all on different levels of evolvement and that wisdom tells us to accept and love ourselves and others wherever we and they are.

There is still another important change needed in psychology to help patients attain optimum physical, emotional, mental and Spiritual health that you are capable of bringing about. It is in finding and manifesting one's unique Soul's Purpose for service. You are able to link Psychology with Ray-Centered Astrology to make this possible. Each one of us has much to offer and until we know why we came back to earth this time and begin to study toward manifesting it, life cannot seem worthwhile.

You have the power, the will, the intelligence and the courage to make these necessary changes in psychology so badly needed at this period in the history of the race.

Religion

If your Ray 1 Soul leads you into the Spiritual field, your task is to change the religious thought forms of the past Piscean Age of some 2000 years to that of the dawning Aquarian Age. This is no easy task, but you are up to it.

There are two strong religious thought forms which served

humanity well in the past, but are now holding many people back and making their lives miserable. It is time for all humanity to release these worn-out concepts to make way for higher ones.

One is that those who pass away with serious imperfections will be damned forever in hell. This fear must be eradicated by substituting the fact that it is the heritage of each of us to become divine, no matter how many lifetimes it takes. There is both a transcendent loving God (entities in the higher planes) and an immanent God within each of us (our Higher Self) to help us evolve.

The other strong thought form that must be dissolved is intolerance for religions different from one's own. In speaking to Christians, Christ said, "Other sheep have I which are not of this fold." There are many paths to God—when people are no longer happy with the religion or Spiritual path they espouse, it is time to search for one with higher principles—a higher level of Spirituality. This may or may not be a group but might be meditation in the privacy of their homes. One's level of Soul evolvement determines what religion or path of Spirituality is right (see Chapters IX and XIV).

As a Ray 1 Soul choosing Spirituality as your mode of expression, you have the power, the will, the intelligence and the courage to bring about these and other needed changes of Spirituality from the Piscean to the Aquarian Age so needed in this period of the history of the race.

Science

If your Ray 1 Soul leads you to science, you have great challenges and, when met, can affect advantageously every discipline including your own.

The greatest change you can make is to eradicate the theory that stars, planets and people came into existence for no special purpose and that when their physical bodies die, that is the end to them. You can replace this fallacy with the concept that Spirit (God) is in all physical forms—stars, planets and people, down to the consciousness of the atom and sub-atom, and that the essence of each will last forever (see Chapters IX and XV). There has been some work done in this area, but it awaits Ray 1 Souls to elaborate on these findings and bring these thoughts into the minds of the population at large.

Another change you can bring about is stressing to the masses who have blind faith in the statements of scientists that there are some areas of life that scientists cannot, with present research methods, prove or disprove. Science, at present, is a priori in the minds of most people because of success it has had in materialistic research. So what scientists declare, no matter how accurate or inaccurate, is more easily accepted by society than what leaders in any other discipline find.

You, as a Ray 1 Soul scientist, have the power, the will, the intelligence, and the courage to bring about needed changes in science and society so needed now.

Astrology

As a Ray 1 Soul choosing astrology for your Soul's Purpose, you will find a deeper understanding of why great changes are occurring all over, especially in every discipline.

As you study astrology, you will not only find that humankind is going through an enormous change in all areas of life, but you will know the reasons. The most important is the shift of the Age of Pisces into that of Aquarius. You will know the types of energies of each Age and how they affect the minds of humanity. You will be aware that Pisces energy leads to blind faith in leaders of government, religion and other disciplines so necessary in the past, while Aquarius energy induces freedom of the individual to think and act by contacting his or her conscience. You will also know that Pisces energy equates with communism in which the state takes preference over the individual, versus Aquarian energy which stresses social democracy—the freedom and rights of the individual to be who he or she is, along with sharing the world's goods with all those in need. You have much cosmic help to accomplish this task. The Piscean Age energies were mainly emotional and personality-focused. The present Aquarius Age energies are predominately mental, and because the mind is the bridge to the Soul, the Aquarian energies are Spiritual. Therefore personality-focused Traditional Astrology needs changing to Soul-focused Ray-Centered Astrology (see Chapter XI).

A second reason for monumental changes taking place is the present relationship of certain planets, such as the conjunction of Neptune and Uranus and the relationship of Pluto and Saturn, depicting revolutionary changes from past self-centered desires to transformational Spiritual aspirations.

Another reason for astronomical changes on earth today is the recent discovery of the Comet Chiron in 1977. Its energies equate with those of Ray-Centered Astrology in that both are considered a Rainbow Bridge from the personality to the Soul. Chiron is found between materialistic Saturn and Spiritual Uranus, and Ray-Centered Astrology uses energies of the Seven Rays for Soul evolvement. The characteristics of both are results of Ageless Wisdoms. Both are pioneering energies welcoming in the New Age. Both stress wounded healing properties—ability to help others, having suffered much and learning the lessons the suffering is meant to teach. The salient energy of both is to help every person find his or her Purpose in Life.

Because Ray-Centered Astrology, which is the astrology of the Aquarian Age, is the tool for astrologers to help people know who they are and why they are here, one of the changes you can make is to bring Ray-Centered Astrology more into mainstream astrology and to link it with psychology.

You have the power, the vision, the will, the intelligence and the courage to not only give astrology the credence it deserves and to bring Ray-Centered Astrology more into mainstream and link it with psychology, but to convey its value into the minds and hearts of practitioners of all other disciplines and of the public.

RAY 1 SOUL AND YOUR ASCENDANT

Because your have a Ray 1 Soul, your Ascendant is Aries, Capricorn or Leo. Following is an interpretation of the coloring of your Ray 1 Soul's Purpose with subsidiary energies of your Ascendant:

Ray I Soul with Aries Ascendant

Aries is the most powerful of the three possible Ascendants of Ray 1 Souls in its capacity to pioneer and trail-blaze with divine ideas. It is not difficult for you to make the present needed changes in the discipline of your choice. Each planet has exoteric, esoteric and hierarchical rulers which help to identify its energies. The exoteric ruler applies to all, while the esoteric and hierarchical rulers' energy can only be received when one is more highly evolved. Mars, the exoteric ruler of Aries, gives enthusiasm and bubbling energy to start something. As a ruler of Ray 6, Mars grants idealism and devotion to one's cause in uplifting humankind.

When you begin to eradicate your character flaws and prepare for your Soul's Purpose, you also receive the energies of Mercury, the esoteric ruler of Aries, giving you a keen, quick mind. As a ruler of Ray 4, Mercury helps you attain harmony in working out conflicts with self and others through understanding the Universal Laws of Reincarnation and Karma (see chapter IX).

When you are ready to serve others consonant with your Soul's Purpose, you also receive the energies of Uranus, the hierarchical ruler of Aries, which induces you to contemplate, receiving original ideas. Because Uranus is the ruler of Ray 7 of Order and Rhythm, you also have superb organizational leadership abilities.

Ray 1 Soul with Leo Ascendant

Your finesse in relating to others is an important adjunct in having people accept your ideas for change. Your self-confidence in knowing your accomplishment capabilities, coupled with strong will and determination to attain them, are added advantages. The Sun, the exoteric ruler of Leo, gives a sunny disposition and a positive outlook. As a ruler of Ray 2 of Love and Wisdom, the Sun bestows a capacity to teach and/or heal.

When you begin to eradicate your character flaws and prepare for your Soul's Purpose, you also receive the energies of Neptune, which the Sun veils, giving you exceptional capacities for inspirational divine ideas when you go into the silence. As a ruler of Ray 6, Neptune allots idealism and devotion to your cause.

When you are ready to serve others consonant with your Soul's Purpose, you also receive the energies of Uranus, which the Sun veils, urging you to meditate to receive intuitive original divine ideas. Uranus, as a ruler of Ray 7 of Order and Rhythm, gives great organization and leadership abilities.

Ray 1 Soul with Capricorn Ascendant

Your ability to discipline self and engage in persistent hard work, even when it seems that you have a lost cause, will often bring success. These same traits are a priori in changing character weaknesses into strengths which make Capricorn the Sign of Initiation—giving optimal help to raise your level of consciousness. Saturn, the exoteric ruler of Capricorn and a ruler of Ray 3 of Creative Intelligence, gives you an enhanced abstract mind capable of creating theories, original concepts and inventions.

When you begin to eradicate your character flaws and prepare for your Soul's Purpose, you receive the energies of the esoteric ruler of Capricorn which is also Saturn. Here, Saturn gives, in addition to original ideas of the average person, a greater dedication and almost instant feedback (Karma) to the steps you make in your life work so that you know whether to keep those steps or substitute better ones.

When you are ready to serve others consonant with your Soul's Purpose, you also receive the energies of Venus, the hierarchical ruler of Capricorn, instilling in you a love of your life work—one of the most important indices to success. As the Rule of Ray 5, Venus also enhances your concrete mind, increasing your capabilities for logic, reason and scientific research.

RAY 1 SOUL WITH YOUR PERSONALITY RAY

Your Personality Ray shows the kind of energy you have to carry out your Ray 1 Soul's Purpose. Details of your Personality Ray are found in the chapter designating that Ray—Ray 1 Personality in Chapter I, Ray 2 Personality in Chapter II and so on. Following are general meanings of your Personality Ray as it aligns with your Soul Ray. This is only an over-view:

With a Ray 1 Personality, you are in rapport with your Ray 1 Soul's Purpose, giving you untold power, not only to will your Soul's Purpose strongly into your mind but to actually carry it out.

If you have a Ray 2 Personality of Love and Wisdom, you can make the necessary changes in the discipline of your choice by teaching and/or healing others physically, mentally and/or Spiritually with love and wisdom.

With a Ray 3 Personality of Creative Intelligence, changes will be made in a very original fashion.

A Ray 4 Personality of Harmony through Conflict will make

the changes through counseling or a form of art, such as writing, music and so on.

With a Ray 5 Personality of the Concrete Mind, you will make changes with logic, reason and possibly research.

A Ray 6 Personality of Idealism and Devotion will make changes with strong motivation of uplifting humankind in a devoted, idealistic manner.

If you have a Ray 7 Personality of Order and Rhythm, the changes your Soul urges you to make will be done in an organized, leadership capacity.

RAY I PERSONALITY OF WILL AND POWER

Pisces or Taurus Sun Sign gives a Ray 1 Personality

You have a powerful, strong-willed personality, coupled with courage to carry out your Soul's Purpose, whatever it is. You have the capacity to see the whole picture of any problem or issue.

Your greatest challenge is to develop love and concern for others. Your innate capacity for determination can be successfully used in trying to fill the needs of others. You have a tendency to quickly attain what you want, often hurting others. Unless you give equal energy to others' needs and your own, you will find that your powerful personality will backfire in giving you lesson-teaching instant Karma, impeding the manifestation of your life work.

RAY 1 PERSONALITY AND YOUR SUN SIGN

Because you have a Ray 1 Personality, you have either a Taurus or Pisces Sun Sign, the interpretation of which colors your Ray 1 Personality.

Please read the following three categories for your Sun Sign to identify yourself as average, advanced or very advanced in carrying out your Soul's Purpose, and what you can do to pull yourself up to the next phase. The more advanced you are, the better you can help others and the greater your success, health, happiness and joy.

Average Taurus Sun Sign Person

You are governed by Venus, the exoteric ruler of Taurus and the ruler of Ray 5 of the Concrete Mind. Your powerful personality is used in materialistic concerns, such as riches, fame, honor, self-centeredness and over-sexuality, often with a stubbornness that brooks no interference. As a Ruler of Ray 5 of the Concrete Mind, Venus also enhances your logical mind. Your intention to do whatever you set out to do is accented by your powerful nature and can be seen by others in your facial expression, your walk, your speech and your actions.

You often have brilliant ideas because you are able to see the whole picture and put all parts in their proper perspective, but if it is done in a dictatorial, uncooperative, prideful fashion without recognizing that others may have equally good or better ideas, it will backfire.

You have the most strong-willed, yet most stable personality of all Sun Signs. Because of your immense power, you may initially get any project to first base, but because you must deal with people, your project often does not endure, no matter how brilliant.

Your primary motivation in carrying out your Life Plan must always be love and concern for others if your wish your work to last. What good does it do if you antagonize people by your indifference to their needs while trying to get a project of your creation off the ground? Projects can never take preference over peoples' needs—you will only put yourself and your project in limbo because of undesirable thoughts, words and actions you send out.

Even though you may hurt many people in a short span of time, you learn more quickly than any other Sun Sign because of the Law of Karma—the resulting difficult lesson-teaching experiences prompt you to change your focus from self-centered desires to concern for others, putting you in the advanced category.

Advanced Taurus Sun Sign Person

Your primary motivation is serving others. You have great stamina, determination and power to carry out your Soul's Purpose, whatever it is. You receive the energy of Vulcan, which is a ruler of Ray 1 of Will and Power and esoteric ruler of Taurus. An astronomer recently found that Vulcan must be within eight and one-half degrees of the Sun.

Vulcan helps you in meditation to bring from the unconscious to the conscious mind, repressions, guilt feelings and wrong attitudes, stored from this life and past lives. Then you can rid yourself of them through understanding (see Chapter IX).

You also receive much energy from Venus, but on a higher level than the average Taurus Sun Sign person in that Venus now gives power to use your mind in controlling undesirable emotions. Desire for materialistic concerns has now changed to desire for Spiritual aspirations and illumination.

Very Advanced Taurus Sun Sign Person

You receive the energy of Vulcan on even a higher level than in the advanced state. Vulcan here gives the power not only to destroy character weaknesses, but transmutes some or all of your sexual energy from a lower chakra into the throat chakra, giving you astounding talent for creativity (See Chapter XIII). You also receive abundant energy from Venus, but even on a higher level than in the advanced category. This enhances your logical, reasoning mind and, because Venus is the hierarchical ruler of Capricorn, a capacity for immense self-discipline and persistence. Your passwords are the change from stubbornness and self-centered desires to determination in serving humanity with love.

Average Pisces Sun Sign Person

Your Pisces Sun Sign gives you enormous power to carry out your Soul's Purpose consonant with your Soul Ray, whatever it is, as does the Taurus Sun Sign person. But while he or she goes about it in a way that the world can see, your method is altogether different. Your power and will is as strong as a Taurus Sun Sign person, yet very few others are aware of this because of the subtlety of your powerful will, a decided advantage.

Your way is inward—you seldom speak of your intentions, but think and meditate about them deeply. Your sensitive nature gives you the capacity to often know what is in the minds of those concerned with your desired project, helping you decide what your next step should be. Also your strong thoughts have power in actualizing your work.

It may be difficult for you to manifest your Soul's Purpose because of a lack of self-confidence in your abilities. Your greatest challenge is to use your intense sensitivity to find how you can best help humankind through your Soul's Purpose.

You are ruled by Neptune, the exoteric ruler of Pisces and a ruler of Ray 6 of Idealism and Devotion, giving you great sensitivity, idealism and devotion to a cause. You are very aware of thoughts and feelings of others. Unless you have understanding and compassion for those with undesirable thoughts, you will suffer much because like attracts like.

When you feel or think on a low level, you strongly attract thoughts and feelings of others on the same level. Sometimes it seems this is too much to bear, and you may try to cop out through alcoholism, drug addiction or mental illness, thus distancing you from those who love you and making it impossible to manifest your Soul's Purpose.

Become aware that we are all on different levels of evolvement. Understanding and love toward those whose thoughts are undesirable is more important for you than for any other Sun Sign because of your sensitivity.

When you know that none of us is perfect and that we create our own environment (see Chapter IX), you will be able to show compassion and kindness toward the suffering which will give you self-confidence so that you can carry out your Soul's Purpose with power, courage and brilliance, thus putting you in the advanced category.

Advanced Pisces Sun Sign Person

Pluto, the esoteric ruler of Pisces and a ruler of Ray 1 of Power and Will, gives you immense power to regenerate Spiritually—to rid yourself of character weaknesses. Pluto's energy, coupled with Neptune's on a higher level than the average Pisces Sun Sign person receives, gives you astounding inspiration, vision and power to carry out your Soul's Purpose, whatever it is.

Neptune's energy gives vision and where there is no vision, humankind is diminished. Neptune here helps you become aligned with what is real—the immortal Self—and to help others accept their real Selves. You are beginning to feel at One with all life.

Very Advanced Pisces Sun Sign Person

You are influenced mainly by Pluto, the hierarchical ruler of Pisces and a ruler of Ray 1 of Will and Power, the same planet influencing the advanced Sun Sign person. Here, Pluto's energies come on a higher level in which you have the power to change your will to the Divine Will.

You also receive abundantly the energies of Neptune, but on a higher level than even the advanced Pisces Sun Sign person. Its energies inspire you with God's Plan for earth, and how, in carrying out your special contribution, you fit into it. You are capable of manifesting your Soul's Purpose with a personality of clear vision in seeing the whole picture with understanding, power and courage.

More information for Ray 1 Souls and Personalities is found in Chapters IX, X and XIV.

SUCCESSFUL RAY ONE SOULS

Ray 1 Souls have power to make great needed changes in various disciplines. Following are examples of Ray 1 Souls who have made immense changes in government, astronomy, religion, astrology, psychology and the arts:

Ray 1 Souls with Ray 1 Personalities of Will and Power

They not only have powerful inner drives but equally powerful Personalities to manifest their drives.

Mikchail Gorbachev, former president of the Soviet Republic, instigated desired revolutionary changes affecting all the world. His Ray 1 Soul indicates his Life Purpose is making radical changes and his Leo Ascendant shows these changes would be to allow individuals the freedom for self-realization—manifesting one's Soul's Purpose. His Ray 1 Personality gives him much power to carry out his Soul's Purpose with compassion and kindness for the suffering (Pisces Sun), helping millions in their Spiritual evolvement.

George Washington, with both a Ray 1 Soul and Personality, initiated enormous changes, being the first President of the

United States (Aries Ascendant), and used his powerful Ray 1 Personality to carry these changes out.

Edward Kennedy also has both a Ray 1 Soul and Personality. He has the power to institute greatly needed changes and an equally powerful Personality to carry them out.

King Edward IV had a Ray 1 Soul and Personality, affording him power for his position.

Galileo's Ray 1 Soul and Personality enabled him to make gigantic changes in astronomy.

One does not always use his or her Ray energy wisely. Machiavelli also had Ray 1 Soul and Personality with a Capricorn Ascendant and Taurus Sun. In his book, he wrote that the end justifies the means which caused many conflicts in various governments and more problems for himself.

It is not only individuals that have Soul and Personality Rays—nations, organizations, and groups also do. The American Federation of Astrologers has both a Ray 1 Soul and Personality, giving it immense power to institute and carry out needed changes in the astrological community and in the outside world. But it must be done with love and wisdom, which Machiavelli lacked, to be successful.

Ray 1 Souls with Ray 2 Personalities of Love and Wisdom

They have great power to make needed changes in any discipline to be carried out in a teaching and/or healing capacity.

Spiritual Leader Sri Auribindo used his Ray 1 Soul energy by changing outworn religious concepts. His success in healing many people with his Ray 2 Personality of Love and Wisdom helped him carry out his Soul's Purpose in convincing many that the concepts he introduced are valid.

Psychologist Helen Wamback changed deeply the thinking of many with her Ray 1 Soul energy through her esoteric work. She carried out her Soul's Purpose with her Ray 2 Personality by healing clients through helping them understand the Law of Reincarnation.

Alex Haley, a Ray 1 Soul, whose Purpose was changing wrong attitudes concerning the African-American population, used his Ray 2 Personality of Love and Wisdom to heal millions Spiritually and emotionally.

Ray 1 Souls with Ray 3 Personalities of Creative Intelligence

Their Souls' Purposes are to make great needed changes in any discipline with Personalities that can bring about these changes in original ways.

Yogananda instituted many changes in Spiritual concepts in the West when he founded the Self-Realization Movement with his Ray 1 Soul energy. His Ray 3 Personality of Creative Intelligence supplied him with original ideas for his mission.

Ray 1 Souls and Ray 4 Personalities of Harmony Through Conflict

They have the power to make great needed changes in any discipline with Personalities to help others attain harmony, such as in counseling or art.

Grandma Moses, whose powerful Ray 1 Soul demonstrated to humankind that age has no barriers, found her Soul's Purpose was to greatly change the thinking of many. At age 78 she began her successful painting career and at age 92 had her first book published. Her Ray 4 Personality of Harmony through Conflict gave her the ability to portray beauty in carrying out her Soul's Purpose.

Edmond G. Brown also has a Ray 1 Soul whose Purpose in Life is to use power to make needed governmental changes which he did as Governor of California. He had help in carrying out his Soul's Purpose with his Ray 4 Personality of Harmony through Conflict which prompted him to engage in many Spiritual studies.

Otto von Bismarck, the 19th century Prussian statesman who founded the German Empire and became its first Chancellor, had a Ray 1 Soul. With the energy of his Ray 4 Personality of Harmony through Conflict, he united the German people under one government.

Ray 1 Souls with Ray 5 Personalities of the Concrete Mind

They have the power to make great needed changes in any discipline and the ability to actualize this in a practical, useful way.

His Holiness, Acharya Sushil Kumarji Maharahj, had a Ray 1 Soul which gave him the power to found the World Fellowship of Religions. His Ray 5 Personality of the Concrete Mind helped him carry out his Soul's Purpose through the logical reasons he gave others for working on Spiritual evolvement.

The Ray 1 Soul of Walt Whitman, an American poet, gave him the impetus for his powerful writings helping democracy. His Ray 5 Personality of the Concrete Mind enabled him to write in a manner that seemed reasonable, logical and practical to his many readers.

Ray 1 Souls with Ray 6 Personalities of Idealism and Devotion

They have the power to make great needed changes in any discipline which are carried out with devoted personalities.

Joan Campbell with her Ray 1 Soul (and Aries Ascendant,

giving pioneering capacity) became the first female General Secretary of the National Council of Churches. Her Ray 6 Personality and Scorpio Sun indicate idealism and devotion in carrying out her Soul's Purpose.

Ray 1 Souls with Ray 7 Personalities of Rhythm and Order

They have the power to make great needed changes in any discipline which are carried out in an organized way with powerful Personalities.

Psychiatrist R. D. Laing with his Ray 1 Soul introduced desirable changes in psychiatry, and worked diligently in an organized fashion, in tune with his Ray 7 Personality, for these changes to be accepted.

II

RAY 2 SOULS AND PERSONALITIES OF LOVE AND WISDOM

―――*◊◊◊*―――

Teach and Heal
Color—Pastel Blue
Leo or Aquarius Sun Sign—Ray 2 Personality
Gemini Ascendant—Ray 2 Soul
See Introduction for Possible Ray 2 Soul
for Pisces or Virgo Ascendant

As a Ray 2 Soul or Personality, your essence equips you for teaching and/or healing others physically, emotionally and/or Spiritually.

The color of Ray 2 is pastel blue and has affinity with the Soul, which is associated with the Hierarchy—those extremely highly evolved entities who help us become closer to our Souls. It is suggested that Ray 2 people often use light blue in their clothes, bed linen, house furnishings and so on to become better attuned to their Souls or Personalities. Every color vibrates at a different frequency, causing the energies of each to be different.

The Lord of Ray 2 is the Master Koot Humi who was the former Saint John in the Bible and is the teacher of the Master Djwal Kuhl who dictated the voluminous books to Alice Bailey.

Of the five senses, Ray 2 correlates with vision. It has affinity with the right eye, which stands for wisdom. The element symbolic of Ray 2 is ether; the stone is sapphire; the star is Sirius. Ray 2 energy reaches the physical body through the heart, circulatory system and nervous system. The method of approaching the Spiritual path for Ray 2 Souls and Personalities is intense and earnest study of Spiritual teachings to become a part of their consciousness and daily living.

Ray 2, as all even-numbered Rays, is feminine and magnetic, concerned with the inner life. Its energy enhances one's intuition, sensitivity, love and wisdom. It has a strong connection with everyone's Soul because it is the Soul Ray of our Sun, the center of our little universe. That is why the level of attainment of love and wisdom determines one's degree of Soul evolvement. All Ray energies induce one to become more Spiritual, but the feminine Rays—2, 4 and 6— impress the conscious and unconscious minds more strongly to work on Soul evolvement than do the masculine Rays, with Ray 2 energy taking the lead.

For this reason, certain so-called nervous breakdowns (see Chapter XII) are found more in Ray 2 Souls and Personalities than in any other Rays. These are caused by a change-over from a focus on material desires to Spiritual aspirations. It is a difficult crisis and although help may be needed, few therapists are aware of reasons for this suffering. To the detriment of clients, most counselors try to eliminate the crisis by working with the personality, instead of the Soul. This treatment which relieves the problem only temporarily and may lead to a bigger crisis later. Whether reaching out for Soul contact is done on a conscious or unconscious (more probable) level, it represents a strong need that must be met for the individual to feel at peace.

An analogy to this situation involves children who are proficient at creeping but desire and are ready to walk. As they try to walk, they fall often, but it does more harm than good to encourage them to go back to creeping just because they are more proficient in that infantile manner of locomotion. Continuing to creep is not only frustrating but denies them the next step in the natural maturation process at the time they are ready for it. Likewise, it is unwise for therapists to lead those clients back to personality desires, thus arresting Soul development. Instead of recognizing and treating this difficulty as a sign of Spiritual progress indicating a highly evolved level—a high point in the evolutionary scale thus giving clients the encouragement they deserve—most therapists treat the condition as a malfunction of the mind and personality. Although this is a time of pain and distress, as it is for infants who keep falling as they try to walk, it is also a time of great opportunity. Clients can be brought through this crisis by recognizing that they are ready for the Soul and its aspirations to take preference over selfish concerns of the personality. Ray-Centered astrologers can help counselors find their clients' character weaknesses and Souls' Purposes for service to others (see Chapter XII).

Because of your love of truth and enhanced intuitive capacities, you often become earnest seekers of wisdom. You are usually empathetic and understand people well. You do not have to look for those you can help, but attract them because of your magnetic qualities and radiance.

When you meditate on how to best serve others, you often receive new ideas of God's Plan. You have the capacity to grasp details in meticulous entirety of the sensed whole, the big picture. Ray 2 is often called the Ray of Detailed Knowledge. It is also referred to as the Ray of Detailed Unity because of synthetic comprehension of details in expressing ideas as they relate to the whole, while comprehending cause and effect simultaneously.

Your greatest challenge is to live without fear. Ray 2 induces sensitivity which is a desirable and helpful trait, but when used in an undesirable way as Ray 2 Souls and Personalities sometimes do, it often brings fear in its path. Understanding followed by love can get rid of fear.

The energies of all Rays can be used unwisely or wisely. You have free will—the choice is yours.

Following is a list of character strengths, some of which you have or can have through transmutation, and weaknesses you are prone to. It is unwise to repress flaws because this energy will then cause problems from your unconscious mind. Instead, because energy follows thought, transmute the energy of your weaknesses into specific strengths as though you possess them by visualizing often the following strengths that you do not have, followed by self-discipline. The more you work at this, the more will be your success, good health and joy.

RAY 2 SOUL AND PERSONALITY ENERGIES

UNWISE USE	WISE USE
Fear from hypersensitivity and selfishness	Understanding and thus loving others
Sensing the whole and yet remaining apart	A feeling of Oneness toward All
Using only the left brain (logic)	Using predominately the right brain
Acquiring knowledge for self only	Using knowledge for all
Self pity	Knowing we create our own reality
Lack of will power	Positive thinking
Conflict between selfishness and the Soul	Choosing Soul for greater benefits
Strong attachment of certain persons	Unattached love for all
Contempt for mental limitations of others	Awareness of uniqueness of all
Impracticality	Knowing practicality is needed
Lack of trust	Accepting each where he or she is

RAY 2 SOUL OF LOVE AND WISDOM

If you have a Gemini Ascendant, you have a Ray 2 Soul
With a Pisces or Virgo Ascendant, you may have
a Ray 2 Soul (see Introduction)

Your greatest challenge is to overcome fear. A great help is understanding the Laws of Reincarnation ad Karma discussed later. All even-numbered Rays are receptive and sensitive, both of which tend to promote fear until one is able to experience unconditional love toward all.

Your Soul's Purpose is to teach and/or heal others physically, emotionally and/or Spiritually.

Ray 2 Souls and Personalities should know that each person has, besides the physical body which can be seen with the physical eyes, certain bodies that can be seen only psychically—an emotional body, a mental body and a Soul body. Each of these bodies is of a higher vibration than the one listed previously.

There are times when it is difficult for a healer to reach the client's Soul, mind and emotions, such as in severe accidents, in which the best treatment is usually through the physical body with surgery and medicine. But generally, the higher the vibrational body the healer works with, the greater the success.

Although the degree of success of every practitioner is measured by his or her level of evolvement, those who can reach the patient's Soul body, with the help of the Wisdoms of the present Aquarian Age, have the potential of greatest success. Ray-Centered Astrology has been the catalyst in bringing many to a Soul-infused personality: a teen-ager who was in a bad crowd and gave it up completely; a woman who was ill because of guilt feelings not only overcame her guilt and regained her health, but began to manifest her Soul's Purpose; and a woman who was so unhappy that she felt she couldn't go on any longer, but whose life turned completely around, after which she said she no longer blames her husband for her problems nor feels guilty, but eventually focuses all her energy overcoming her weaknesses and serving others consonant with her Soul's Purpose.

Both Ray-Centered astrologers and many Transpersonal psychologists working primarily with Soul are finding excellent results of uplifting clients. These practitioners believe that, for one to be healthy, he or she must find and manifest the reason for coming into this life—the Soul's Purpose. A link is now being made between Ray-Centered Astrology and Transpersonal Psychology.

Second in effectiveness for healing the physical body is working with the mental body. Perhaps we can say there is a tie with the Soul and mental bodies for success in physical healing because the Soul is reached through the mind.

Working on a high level with the mental body affects the Soul body, the emotional body and then heals the physical body through the chakras, glandular system and hormones.

Many healers of the physical body who began serving with allopathic medicine in which drugs and surgery are the main methods, combine, as they begin to understand the Universal Laws, their allopathic knowledge with the power of the client's mind, with astounding success. Some are Endocrinologist Doctor Deepak Chopra, Surgeon Doctor Bernie Siegel, Cardiologist Doctor Dean Ornish and Oncologist Doctor Simonton. The success of healers as these is beginning to reach mainstream—there are now a government agency for Alternate Healing and a company which insures patients of Doctor Ornish.

To become self-realized and in tune with your own Souls, not only you who are healers but who teach must use the Universal Laws of Reincarnation and Karma to help others attain wisdom and unconditional love.

Teaching at the elementary and secondary level, you can weave into the fabric of every subject the reasons for such traits as honesty, persistent work, self discipline and unconditional love. You can help students know why it is advisable to attain these characteristics by acquainting them with Universal Laws of Reincarnation and Karma. You can explain how health, success and happiness are found to the extent one acquires these traits (See Chapter IX).

A priori for Ray 2 Souls who teach on any level is helping students find their unique Soul's Purpose and guiding them to their proper studies. When one knows that he or she was put on earth for a special Purpose and is working on preparing for manifesting it, transmuting weaknesses into strengths comes much easier. This is where Ray-Centered Astrologers can be a great help.

RAY 2 SOUL AND YOUR ASCENDANT

Your Ascendant which colors your Ray 2 Soul is Gemini, Virgo or Pisces

Ray 2 Soul with Gemini Ascendant

Gemini is the Sign par excellence for communication. You have an ability to relate well with others—in fact, you are able to relate better with others than any other Sign, helping you attain success in one or more avenues of communication. This is a great plus to your Soul's Purpose in teaching and/or healing. Mercury, the exoteric ruler of Gemini, indicates your interest in becoming acquainted with many people and with diverse kinds of knowledge. As a ruler of Ray 4 of Harmony through Conflict, Mercury helps you attain peace in giving you many lesson-teaching experiences to work out conflicts.

When you begin to eradicate your character flaws and prepare for your Soul's Purpose, you will also receive the energy of Venus, the esoteric ruler of Gemini and ruler of Ray 5 of Science and the Concrete Mind, inducing you to also use logic and reason in your work and perhaps engage in research.

When you are ready to serve others consonant with your Soul's Purpose, you will also receive the energies of Planet Earth, the hierarchical ruler of Gemini and a ruler of Ray 3 of the Creative Mind. This gives energy for inspirational, original ideas and many experiences to enhance your Soul's Purpose in teaching and/or healing.

Ray 2 Soul with Virgo Ascendant

You have superb capacity for discrimination, detailed analytical work and the ability, with a strong urge, to make more perfect whatever and whomever you work with. This is a positive adjunct to your Soul's Purpose of teaching and/or healing if you make a special effort to avoid any unkind criticism which could hurt others. Mercury, as the exoteric ruler of Virgo and a ruler of Ray 4 of Harmony through Conflict, indicates the possibility for much lesson-teaching Karma when you think, say or do anything to hurt another.

When you begin to eradicate your character flaws and prepare for your Soul's Purpose, you will also receive the energies of the Moon which is the esoteric ruler of Virgo and a ruler of Ray 4 of Harmony through Conflict. This helps you feel what others are feeling, thus minimizing your tendency to criticize them.

When you are ready to serve others consonant with your Soul's Purpose, you will also receive the energies of Jupiter, the hierarchical ruler of Virgo and a Ruler of Ray 2. You are aided to use wisdom, which is a combination of knowledge and love, along with optimism and enthusiasm. No longer having critical thoughts, you now accept and love yourself and others wherever you and they are.

Ray 2 Soul with Pisces Ascendant

When you manifest your innate compassion and kindness toward the suffering as your primary motivation for your Soul's Purpose of teaching and/or healing, others are helped immensely. They know how much you have helped them, but often you have difficulty believing that your service actually did help—you need more self-confidence, more self-esteem. Neptune, as the exoteric ruler of Pisces and a ruler of Ray 6 of Idealism and Devotion, often leads you on an idealistic journey of uplifting others. Your heightened sensitivity enables you to reach their conscious and often unconscious minds.

When you begin to eradicate your character flaws and prepare for your Soul's Purpose, you will also receive the energies of Pluto, the esoteric ruler of Pisces and a ruler of Ray 1 of Will and Power, giving you the ability for Spiritual regeneration—raising yourself and others to a much higher level of consciousness.

When you are ready to serve others consonant with your Soul's Purpose, you will also receive the energies of Pluto, the hierarchical ruler of Pisces. Here it gives you the will and power to align yourself with God's Plan for earth, resulting in your Ray 2 Soul's Purpose of teaching and/or healing to take place on an extremely high level to large numbers of people.

RAY 2 SOUL WITH YOUR PERSONALITY RAY

Your Personality Ray shows the kind of energy you have to carry out your Ray 2 Soul's Purpose, colored by your Ascendant Sign. Details of your Personality Ray are found in the chapter designating that Ray—Ray 1 Personality in chapter I, Ray 2 Personality in chapter II and so on. Following are only one-liners of your Personality Ray as it aligns with your Ray 2 Soul. This is only an overview:

With a Ray 1 Personality of Will and Power, your Soul's Purpose of teaching and/or healing will be carried out with a powerful personality which can make many needed changes in the discipline of your choice.

If you have a Ray 2 Personality of Love and Wisdom, your Soul's Purpose and your Personality to carry it out are in rapport, making it somewhat easy to manifest your Soul's Purpose.

With a Ray 3 Personality of Creative Intelligence, you will teach and/or heal in an original creative fashion, using the Universal Laws as your basis.

As a Ray 4 Personality of Harmony through Conflict, your teaching and/or healing will be, most likely, in counseling or in an artistic form such as writing, music and so on.

If you have a Ray 5 Personality of the Concrete Mind, your teaching and/or healing will be carried out in a logical, practical way, perhaps through research.

With a Ray 6 Personality of Idealism and Devotion, your teaching and/or healing will be performed with a strong motivation of uplifting others in an idealistic and devoted manner.

A Ray 7 Personality of Order and Rhythm shows your teaching and/or healing will be achieved in an organized leadership capacity.

No matter what your Personality Ray, having a Ray 2 Soul, you can impart with love those sections of the Ageless Wisdoms that the Aquarian age energies are now releasing, such as the understanding of Reincarnation, Karma and Ray-Centered Astrology.

RAY 2 PERSONALITY OF LOVE AND WISDOM
Leo or Aquarius Sun Sign gives a Ray 2 Personality

Whatever your Soul's Purpose as shown by your Soul Ray, it should be carried out by your Personality in teaching and/or healing others physically, emotionally, mentally and/or Spiritually in tune with Aquarius Age wisdoms and with love.

RAY 2 PERSONALITY AND YOUR SUN SIGN

Because you have a Ray 2 Personality, you have either a Leo or Aquarius Sun Sign, the interpretation of which colors your Ray 2 Personality.

Please read the following three categories of your Sun Sign to identify yourself as average, advanced or very advanced in carrying out your Soul's Purpose and what you can do to pull yourself up to the next phase. The more advanced you are, the better is the help you give others and the greater your success, health, happiness and joy.

Average Leo Sun Sign Person

You are more aware of who you and others are capable of becoming than any other Sun Sign in the average category. Your greatest challenge is to develop humility.

Your Ray 2 Personality of Love and Wisdom indicates that your Soul's Purpose, whatever it is, should be carried out through teaching and/or healing. It should be colored in a subsidiary fashion with a focus of helping students/clients/patients attain self-realization—an awareness of what they are capable of becoming. Here Ray-Centered astrological delineations are a tremendous help.

You have great self-confidence, courage, enthusiasm and determination, but tend to use these traits in self-centered desires. Humility is not one of your virtues—you take pride in dominating others.

The Sun, the exoteric ruler of Leo, wants you to shine by sharing your sunny disposition with others, but you often misinterpret this and try to shine by being the center of attraction. While you have many leadership qualities which originally give you an interested audience, their interest will only be fleeting because in time they will perceive that your motivation is not to help them but to get admiration and praise for self. This is a difficult lesson for anyone to learn, but you can bounce back quickly and become aware that true joy can only be attained in serving others. Once this karmic lesson is learned, you have progressed into the next category.

Advanced Leo Sun Sign Person

Your Ray 2 Personality of Love and Wisdom gives you the capacity to carry out your Soul's Purpose, whatever it is, through teaching and/or healing others. But unlike the average Leo Sun Sign person, you are guided by the esoteric ruler of Leo which is Neptune, veiled by the Sun, a ruler of Ray 6 of Idealism and Devotion.

You thus have much contact with your Soul through Neptune's capacity for inspiration and idealistic, devoted behavior. You no longer are concerned primarily with self-centered desires, but are more interested in serving others, having learned through difficult karmic experiences that it is unwise to be motivated only by selfish desires. Neptune's energy increases your capacity to help others—one of the many ways is your awareness of what you are capable of becoming, leading to helping others become aware of what they are capable of.

You are also affected by the Sun, the exoteric ruler of Leo, but on a higher level than the average Leo Sun Sign person. Here the Sun gives self-confidence, courage and awareness of the Spirit within each individual, all of this shining through your work.

Very Advanced Leo Sun Sign Person

You receive the energies of the Sun and Neptune, giving you more vitality, self-confidence, courage and enthusiasm even than the advanced Leo Sun Sign person. You also are influenced by Uranus, veiled by the Sun, as the hierarchical ruler of Leo which is also the ruler of Ray 7 of Order and Rhythm. This brings a high degree of leadership capacity along with conception of original ideas.

Together, the three rulers of Leo—the Sun, Neptune and Uranus—enable your Personality to really shine in the best way possible because there is no vestige left of pride and self-centered desires. There is only a primary motivation of helping others through your intuitive ideas and the rhythmic and orderly way you help people become self-realized, true to their Souls' Purposes.

Average Aquarian Sun Sign Person

Your energy is in rapport with the New Aquarian Age so it should not be difficult for you to understand and feel at home with everything Aquarius stands for—such as the freedom to be who you are, unattached love toward all peoples and the understanding of Reincarnation and Karma. Your keyword is either stubbornness or determination, depending on your level of evolvement.

Your Ray 2 Personality of Love and Wisdom gives you capacity to carry out your Soul's Purpose, whatever it is, through teaching and/or healing others, physically, emotionally and/or Spiritually.

You are influenced by Uranus, the exoteric ruler of Aquarius and the ruler of Ray 7 of Order and Rhythm. This induces you to seek the freedom to do what you want to do, often regardless of your responsibilities. You have the urge to change people's attitudes which you sometimes do in a harmful way.

You can be erratic and rebellious and definitely opposed to the status quo. You want no one, including the government, telling you what to do and what not to do. Laws, rules and regulations are foreign to your way of thinking. You believe you have the right to do what you want to do. You are motivated to satisfying your self-centered desires, regardless of the concerns and needs of others.

If you do not accede to the regulations of your employment, you will never make it to the top where you have the chance to change that which you feel is unfair. Your greatest challenge is the accomplishing of a long term perspective—using self-discipline in following laws, rules and regulations so that you can be in a position to make changes later to benefit humankind. If you disobey government laws, you might end up in jail. If you do not follow the rules and regulations of the school or college you attend, it is very likely that you will not graduate.

Advanced Aquarius Sun Sign Person

Your Ray 2 Personality of Love and Wisdom gives you the capacity to carry out your Soul's Purpose, whatever it is, through teaching and/or healing others physically, emotionally and/or Spiritually.

You are influenced by Uranus, the exoteric ruler of Aquarius and the ruler of Ray 7 of Order and Rhythm, but on a higher level than the average Aquarius Sun Sign person. Having suffered many lesson-teaching karmic experiences from doing exactly what you want to do, regardless of your responsibilities and concerns and needs of others, you now are using your intuition and urges which Uranus supplies to assess what others need that you are equipped to give.

You are influenced mostly by Jupiter, the esoteric ruler of Aquarius and a ruler of Ray 2 of Love and Wisdom, which gives you a capacity for deep understanding of the Ageless Wisdoms. You are willing to use self-discipline to put your creative ideas on the back burner until you are in a position to activate them successfully.

Very Advanced Aquarius Sun Sign Person

You are much in tune with the New Aquarian Age whose concepts you can easily understand and implement as you carry out your Soul's Purpose, whatever it is, through teaching and/or healing others physically, emotionally and/or Spiritually. You believe in the freedom of the individual to think, speak and act in line with his or her conscience and that each of us can become what we came on earth to be.

You honor the rights of others to do their own thing. Unattached, unconditional love and an independent, yet generous spirit, are relatively easy for you to attain. Many of you remain single as it may be difficult to attract a mate who does not require closely attached love. Attached to people or possessions, many people feel that they can't survive without them. With your unattached attitude, you have wants but you feel it is all right if you don't get them. You are aware that your higher Self will get you what you want only if it is for your ultimate good.

You are influenced by Uranus, the exoteric ruler of Aquarius, but now employ its energies in desirable ways. No longer erratic and rebellious, you now use the intuitive original thoughts and leadership capacities Uranus gives you, coupled with the energy of Jupiter, the esoteric ruler of Aquarius and a ruler of Ray 2 of Love and Wisdom. Even on a higher level than the advanced Aquarian Sun Sign person, these energies grant you rhythm, order, wisdom and enthusiasm.

You are ruled mostly by Vulcan, veiled by the Moon, a ruler of Ray 1 of Power and Will and the hierarchical ruler of Aquarius. This gives you the power to help others crystallize in the unconscious mind any repressions, guilt feelings, wrong attitudes or out-grown concepts and bring them to the conscious mind for eradication through understanding Universal Laws.

Together, the Moon veiling Vulcan, Uranus and Jupiter induce creative ideas which you can share with wisdom and unattached love. This enables you to rid people of problems stored in their unconscious minds in order to experience the freedom to be who they are supposed to be, consonant with their Souls' Purposes.

More information for Ray 2 Souls and Personalities is found in Chapters IX, X, XIII and XIV.

SUCCESSFUL RAY 2 SOULS

Following are examples of Ray 2 Souls who have taught and/or healed others physically, emotionally and/or Spiritually through music, research, government, writing, astronomy, astrology, making esoteric books available, teaching preparation of nutritious food and various healing techniques:

Ray 2 Souls and Ray 2 Personalities of Love and Wisdom

They not only have as their Souls' Purposes teaching and/or healing with love and wisdom, but Personalities with similar abilities to carry out their life plans.

Ellen Yoakum had both a Ray 2 Soul and Personality. Her Soul's Purpose was to heal people physically in an unorthodox manner. Her Ray 2 Personality helped her carry out her Purpose as she healed hundreds a day by passing her hands over their bodies.

Julia Child's Purpose is to physically heal others through teaching them to prepare and eat delicious, nutritious food. Her Ray 2 Personality helps carry out her Soul's Purpose through TV shows and books on cooking.

Thomas Merton had both a Ray 2 Soul and Personality whose Soul's Purpose was to heal others Spiritually. His Ray 2 Personality supplied him with love and wisdom which definitely helped him carry out his Soul's Purpose.

Like Thomas Merton, Andrew Greely also has a Ray 2 Soul and Personality whose Soul's Purpose is to heal others Spiritually and whose Ray 2 Personality helps carry out his Soul's Purpose easily.

Ray 2 Souls and Ray 1 Personalities of Will and Power

Their Souls' Purposes are teaching and/or healing and their powerful Personalities can make needed changes in various disciplines.

Shirley MacLaine's Ray 2 Soul's Purpose is Spiritual teaching and healing of others. This she is accomplishing through her powerful Ray 1 Personality by explaining certain Universal Laws on TV interviews and a miniseries, and lecturing throughout the United States.

The late Neil Michelsen had a Ray 2 Soul, showing that his Purpose was to heal and/or teach others. This he did admirably with his powerful Ray 1 Personality in pioneering astrological computer technology. He published the first computer-generated ephemerides which aided astrologers world-wide to be of help to clients.

Edna St. Vincent Millay's Ray 2 Soul's Purpose was healing others Spiritually. Her Ray 1 Personality gave her power as a world-wide traveler to lecture and appear on radio.

William Jennings Bryan's Ray 2 Soul's Purpose was to heal others. His Ray 1 Personality gave him much power to carry out his Soul's Purpose through being a member of the House of Representatives and leader of the Democratic party with the opportunity of enacting just laws.

Pope John Paul II, a Ray 2 Soul, found his Soul's Purpose is teaching and healing others Spiritually. His Ray 1 Personality of Will and Power helps him carry out his Purpose magnificently.

The Purpose of William Shakespeare, a Ray 2 Soul, was teaching and healing others. His Ray 1 Personality aided him to carry it out through his powerful writing by teaching humankind many lessons.

John Foster Dulles had a Ray 2 Soul whose Purpose was to teach and heal others with the help of his powerful Ray 1 Personality as a statesman.

Elizabeth Barrett Browning whose Ray 2 Soul's Purpose was to teach and/or heal, manifested it magnificently through her powerful Ray 1 Personality. She expressed her strong feelings through poetry, helping people in many ways, including her part in bringing about independence and unification of Italy.

Ray 2 Souls with Ray 3 Personalities of the Concrete Mind

Their Souls' Purposes are teaching and/or healing and their Personalities give creative, original ways of serving.

The Purpose of Saint Bernadette, a Ray 2 Soul born in 1844, was the physical healing of many. Her Ray 3 Personality gave her the ability to heal in a manner different from the status quo. In meditation, she saw visions of the Holy Mother at Lourdes, France where a spring of healing waters bubbled forth which she was directed to use for healing.

Johannes Kepler manifested his Ray 2 Soul energy in both teaching and healing through his Ray 3 Personality by discovering laws of planetary motion and astrological planetary influences. His teachings and healings reached millions through astronomers who make it possible for astrologers to heal many.

Philosopher Baruch Spinoza's Purpose was healing and teaching. His Ray 3 Personality gave him the capacity to manifest his Soul's Purpose in a manner so different from the mass consciousness that it upset many Christians and Jews, yet his ideas benefited many.

Ray 2 Souls and Ray 4 Personalities of
Harmony Through Conflict

Their Souls' Purposes are teaching and/or healing and their Personalities carry this out in harmonious ways, such as in counseling or art.

Karl Bohm had a Ray 2 Soul whose Purpose was healing others emotionally and Spiritually. His Ray 4 Personality of Harmony through Conflict helped carry out his Soul's Purpose by uplifting the thoughts and feelings of those who listen to his music. He was noted as a conductor for beautiful interpretations of Mozart, Wagner and Straus.

Max Ernst, whose Ray 2 Soul's Purpose was healing, carried it out with his Ray 4 Personality by paintings which uplifted viewers.

Franz Joseph Hayden's Ray 2 Soul's Purpose was healing. With his Ray 4 Personality of Harmony through Conflict, he healed many who listened to his musical compositions by raising their level of consciousness.

Ray 2 Souls with Ray 5 Personalities of
the Concrete Mind

Their Souls' Purposes are teaching and/or healing and their Personalities manifest their Purposes in practical, useful ways, such as in research and statistics.

The Soul's Purpose of Francoise Gauquelin, a Ray 2 Soul, was teaching and healing others, having a degree in psychology. Her Ray 5 Personality of the Concrete Mind helped carry out her Soul's Purpose. With a degree in statistics, she set out to prove that astrology is invalid, but after years of painstaking research in collaboration with her late husband, Michel, proved its validity.

Vivian E. Robson, famous astrologer born 1890, whose Ray 2 Soul was teaching and whose Ray 5 Personality stressed practicality illustrated both her Ray 2 and Ray 5 energies by this quote, "The first seed of astrology is accuracy and definition, not pseudo religious speculation, and it is only by concentrating on the practical and scientific side that one can really make astrology of service and obtain for it the recognition it deserves."

Elias Ashmole, a Ray 2 Soul born 1817 in England, whose Soul's Purpose was teaching and healing accomplished it with his Ray 5 Personality of the Concrete Mind in a practical way. He collected astrology and other esoteric books and left them to Oxford University where many had the opportunity to benefit from his enormous collection, which knowledge resulted in their healing themselves and others.

French poet and critic Charles Baudelaire, a Ray 2 Soul whose Purpose was teaching, accomplished it with his Ray 5 Personality of the Concrete Mind. He taught perfection of artistic form through his writing.

Engineer Samuel Harwick found his Soul's Purpose was to teach, and his Ray 5 Personality of Logic and Science helped students accept his teaching.

Ray 2 Souls and Ray 6 Personalities of Idealism and Devotion

Their Souls' Purposes are teaching and/or healing and their Personalities can idealistically and devotedly carry out their Purposes.

First Lady Hillary Clinton has the identical Soul and Personality Rays of the United States, allowing her great attunement with its Soul's Purpose and its Personality in carrying it out. She is using her Ray 2 Soul of Love and Wisdom to both teach and heal others with her superb work in trying to make health care available to all citizens. Her Ray 6 Personality of Idealism and Devotion indicates her dedication to this idealistic work.

Both Charles and William Mayo, sons of William Worrall

Mayo who started the Mayo Clinic, have Ray 2 Souls and Ray 6 Personalities. Their Souls' Purposes were to heal others physically and to teach. Charles was famous for reducing death rate in goiter surgery and William for skill in gallstones, cancer and stomach surgery. Their Ray 6 Personalities gave them idealistic behavior devoted to their causes.

III

RAY 3 SOULS AND PERSONALITIES OF CREATIVE INTELLIGENCE

═══◦∅∅◦═══

Original Ideas
Color—Yellow
Capricorn or Sagittarius Sun Sign—
Ray 3 Personality
Libra Ascendant—Ray 3 Soul
See Introduction for Possible Ray 3 Soul
for Capricorn or Cancer Ascendant

Ray 3 energy enhances the abstract mind, paving the way for brilliant ideas, leading to original concepts, theories, hypotheses and inventions.

Rays 1, 2 and 3 are considered the most divine and are the primary Rays from which Rays 4 through 7 are attributes. It is no coincidence that the colors of the first three Rays are the primary colors from which all other colors result.

It is advantageous to use yellow, the color of Ray 3, profusely in clothes, bed linens, house furnishings and so forth so that its vibration will help you better tune into your Souls' Purposes or Personalities. Yet it is to any one's advantage to use it when needing optimal functioning of the mind, either for mental pursuits or for controlling emotions.

Ray 3 correlates with God, the Holy Spirit, which gives life to the mind, physical body and personality. The Lords of Ray 3 are the Masters R and Hilarion; the divine principle is the Universal Mind from which all knowledge comes; the sense is sight; the symbol is the left eye, standing for the personality; the element is fire by friction; the stone is the emerald; the physical body processes are assimilation and elimination; the heavenly affinity is the Pleiades consisting of seven sister stars.

Your way to approach the Spiritual path is to think deeply on philosophical and Spiritual ideas until you know that God is within them.

Because Ray 3 energy enhances the abstract mind, it helps to understand Universal Laws such as Reincarnation, Karma and the concept that we create our own environment (see Chapter IX).

While Ray 1 and Ray 2 Souls and Personalities are interested primarily in proven truths, the a priori position for Ray 3 people is a wide range of possibilities for the truth—creative imagination are the key words.

You can stimulate, sharpen and inspire the intellect of humankind by manipulating ideas so that most people can understand them. You are often referred to as weavers because you put all your ideas together on one subject to form a unified whole. You often waste energy by weaving for the future, not aware that circumstances change with time. The awareness of your misuse of energy when weaving for the future is often a time of crisis. The great opportunity here is to release those ideas and begin weaving for the present to meet needs that exist.

Although Ray 3 energy gives one wise views with many ideas to see every side of a problem clearly, it does not bestow practicality. However, if you have both a Ray 3 and Ray 5 in your Ray makeup, you not only receive brilliant ideas, but are able to use them in a practical way. Ray 3 energy induces deep contemplation to receive original ideas, concepts and theories in most any subject or discipline. Ray 5 correlates with science and the concrete mind and gives excellent research capacities to prove or disprove the efficacy of concepts, inventions and scientific theories of Ray 3 energy.

Because of your clear and forceful thinking, you may impose your views on others and often with manipulation.

You are often highly critical of those whose intellect is not as developed as yours. To overcome this attitude, you need to be aware of the uniqueness of every individual—that many, who are not as intelligent as you, could be more highly evolved having acquired more understanding and love, and that those who are both less intelligent and less highly evolved than you, may be Souls who have had very few earth lives for Spiritual growth. Also, you must realize that it takes a very highly evolved Soul to rightly judge another, which very few people on earth are capable of.

The pride that you often engender, because of the awareness of your brilliant ideas, can be mitigated by the thought that all ideas come from the Universal Mind, made up of minds more advanced than yours.

Following is a list of character weaknesses you are prone to and the strengths, some of which you now have or can have through transmutation. It is unwise to repress your flaws because this energy will then cause problems from your unconscious mind. Instead, because energy follows thought, transmute the energy of your weaknesses into specific strengths by visualizing often the following strengths, along with self-discipline. As you transmute your character weaknesses into strengths, your lives will become more successful, enjoyable and fulfilled.

RAY 3 SOUL & PERSONALITY ENERGIES

UNWISE USE	WISE USE
Intellectual pride	Knowing ideas come from Universal Mind
Criticism	Aware that none of us is perfect
Impracticality	Leaving practical use of ideas to others
Inaccuracy in details	Having wide views on abstract questions
Coldness and stubbornness	Using mind to control emotions
Love of own thoughts	Love of truth and beauty
Imposing ideas on others	Knowing others also have good ideas
Manipulation because of selfish desires	Aware that helping others is helping you
Absent-mindedness	Absence of worry
Isolation and separateness	Self-confidence
Wasting energy on tasks not helpful	Solving problems which exist

RAY 3 SOUL OF CREATIVE INTELLIGENCE

If you have a Libra Ascendant, you have a Ray 3 Soul.

With a Cancer or Capricorn Ascendant, you may have a Ray 3 Soul (see Introduction).

Your Soul's Purpose is creating original ideas, concepts and theories to help humankind.

Your greatest challenge is to overcome intellectual pride and criticism toward others through understanding and love. The Universal Laws, especially Reincarnation and Karma, can be a great help (see Chapter IX).

A high level of intelligence is definitely a plus in your make-up, but it is imperative that you use it for the common good of all people. If it is used for selfish reasons, you will be the loser because of the Law of Karma. It is so easy to fall in this way because you have superb manipulative capacities. However, your manipulative abilities can be harnessed to work in benefiting everyone and ultimately bringing you success, happiness and joy.

Your motivation for your work is of utmost importance because if it is not to serve others, your precious time and capabilities might be wasted in some theory whose resolution is not needed at present or in an idea whose selfish desire is the instigator. In either case, this waste of superior intellect not only robs humanity of much good but brings you difficult lesson-teaching Karma.

RAY 3 SOUL AND YOUR ASCENDANT

Your Ascendant which colors your Ray 3 Soul is Libra, Cancer or Capricorn

Ray 3 Soul with Libra Ascendant

Your innate ability to see both sides of a problem or issue urges you to use your creative abstract mind in helping individuals and organizations to solve problems in a fair and unique way. Your original ideas can be extremely beneficial, not only to individuals with conflicts, but also various groups such as strikers versus entrepreneurs and one manufacturer versus another. You are a born mediator and therapist. Venus, the exoteric ruler of Libra, gives you enjoyment in socializing and relationships. As a ruler of Ray 5 of the Concrete Mind, Venus also increases your logical reasoning capacity.

When you begin to eradicate your character flaws and prepare for your Soul's Purpose, you will also receive the energies of Uranus, the esoteric ruler of Libra, enhancing your intuitive ability for original ideas, concepts, theories and unusual solutions to problems. As the ruler of Ray 7 of Rhythm and Order, Uranus also bestows great organizational and leadership ability.

When you are ready to serve others consonant with your Soul's Purpose, Saturn, as the hierarchical ruler of Libra and a ruler of Ray 3 of Creative Intelligence, is also released to you, enhancing your creative capacity. This also gives self-discipline and persistence to work diligently on your Soul's Purpose of serving others and on transmuting your character weaknesses into strengths. Be aware that the quality of your service correlates with your level of Soul evolvement, thus with the caliber of your original thoughts that you easily receive in meditation.

Ray 3 Soul with Cancer Ascendant

Your ability, because of your psychic sensitivity to know just what humanity needs, allows you to use your creative abstract mind, not for what might be future needs which may change, but for what is actually needed now. The Moon, the exoteric ruler of Cancer and a ruler of Ray 4 of Harmony through Conflict, gives you strong emotions which can make you miserable (often ill) or bring you to the very heights of joy and good health, depending on the type and strength of emotions you allow in your mind.

When you begin to eradicate your character flaws and prepare for your Soul's Purpose, you will also receive the energies of Neptune, the esoteric ruler of Cancer and a ruler of Ray 6 of Idealism and Devotion. This gives added sensitivity in meditation to reach your higher Self and entities in the higher Spiritual planes. You can easily receive idealistic original ideas to uplift yourself and others, especially those who need nurturing.

When you are ready to serve others consonant with your Soul's Purpose, Neptune, on a higher vibration than even in the advanced category, gives you a feeling of Oneness toward all creation, and as a ruler of Ray 6 indicates your unattached, unconditional love for all beings.

Ray 3 Soul with Capricorn Ascendant

Your dedication, shown by sustained effort and self-discipline in your work, allows good use of your creative abstract mind in whatever your project is at the time. Saturn, the exoteric ruler of Capricorn, urges you to work diligently on every project you begin. As a ruler of Ray 3, Saturn's energy induces you to meditate for creative ideas.

When you begin to eradicate your character flaws and prepare for you Soul's Purpose, you will also receive the energies of Saturn but on a higher level. In addition to working diligently on serving others, you will also use admirable self-discipline in transmuting weaknesses into strengths.

When you are ready to serve others consonant with your Soul's Purpose, you will also receive the energies of Venus, the hierarchical ruler of Capricorn and the ruler of Ray 5 of the Concrete Mind. You are urged, now that you have attained a high Initiation by raising your level of consciousness, to come down from the mountain top and help, in a very down-to-earth way, those who have not yet attained your heights.

Ray 3 Soul with Your Personality Ray

Although your Soul's Purpose of creating ideas, theories and concepts can be manifested in many fields, the specific ones may be denoted by your Personality Ray. Some of the disciplines that are a natural for you are philosophy, writing, architecture, psychology, astrology, metaphysics and mathematics.

If your Ray 3 Soul's Purpose is creative writing, a Ray 1, 2, 4, 5 or 7 Personality would help you excel: A Ray 1 Personality would make you a powerful writer—using words and ideas in a way that really hits readers straight on; a Ray 2 Personality leads you in writing original ideas to heal readers physically, emotionally, mentally and/or Spiritually; with a Ray 4 Personality, your writing would help the reader solve his or her conflicts; with a Ray 7 Personality, your brilliant ideas would be structured in an organized form; lastly, a Ray 5 Personality could make you a master of the pen because you would not only have original ideas, but would be able to express them in detail with logic and accuracy.

The following paragraphs show ways that your Ray 3 Soul's Purpose, whether it is writing or any other Ray 3 career, can be carried out according to what your Personality Ray is. These are only generalities—details are given for Ray 1 Personality in Chapter I, Ray 2 Personality in Chapter II and so on:

If you have a Ray 1 Personality of Power and Will, you can easily take your creative ideas to proper channels and see that they are manifested so that needed changes can be made in your discipline.

With a Ray 2 Personality of Love and Wisdom, you could teach and/or heal others physically, emotionally and/or Spiritually with your creative ideas.

With a Ray 3 Personality of Creative Intelligence, you are capable of excellent original ideas, but need someone with Ray 5 energy to make your work practical.

If you have a Ray 4 Personality, your brilliant ideas can be used in counseling or in artistic expression.

With a Ray 5 Personality, your chances of success are great because you can easily prove or disprove your own creative ideas through research. Famous scientists and mathematicians often are in this category.

As a Ray 6 Personality, you are able to uplift others through writing, lecturing or any type of communication or service using your original ideas.

If you have a Ray 7 Personality, you can use your creative ideas in a leadership capacity, such as the president of a business or a government official.

RAY 3 PERSONALITY
OF CREATIVE INTELLIGENCE

Sagittarius or Capricorn Sun Sign gives a
Ray 3 Personality

Your Personality carries out your Soul's Purpose, whatever it is as shown by your Soul Ray, in an original, creative fashion with new ideas, concepts or theories.

Your greatest challenge is to search for truth. Although your methods may be valid and also enticing to you and those you serve, if you don't have a Ray 5 Soul, it would be wise to have a statistician or scientist do your research.

You have a vivid imagination and many times come up with ideas which later prove useful, but that is not always so. You are a dreamer and often your ideas, though theoretically right, are impractical.

RAY 3 PERSONALITY AND YOUR SUN SIGN

Because you have a Ray 3 Personality, you have either a Sagittarius or Capricorn Sun Sign, the interpretation of which colors your Ray 3 Personality.

Read the following three categories for your Sun Sign to identify the status of your Personality—either average, advanced or very advanced. The more advanced it is, the better you will serve others and the greater will be your success, happiness, health and joy. Suggestions are presented to aid you in reaching the next category.

Average Sagittarius Sun Sign Person

Your Ray 3 Personality with your enhanced abstract mind, giving opportunities for creativity, is colored by your optimism, enthusiasm and goal-orientation.

Your greatest challenge is attaining humility, knowing that what you receive in contemplation comes from minds more advanced than yours, and that each person is unique. While your mind may be more advanced than some, their love of humankind may be on a higher level.

You receive the energy of Jupiter, the exoteric rule of Sagittarius and a ruler of Ray 2 of Love and Wisdom. There is a tendency for you to believe things are a lot better than they are. While positive thinking which you brought from a past life is extremely helpful in most instances, you sometimes carry it too far in disregarding reality. When you have problems, do not pretend they do not exist. If you do, you only add to repressions in your unconscious mind which can create nervousness and other difficulties. When you have lesson-teaching karmic experiences, accept them in a responsible manner. Don't run from them or you will meet them later in a more difficult form. You have not yet become interested in your Soul evolvement so your main goal is career advancement for prestige, fame and more income.

Truth and its search is becoming very important to you, yet you can be somewhat tactless in speaking. You can still be honest and yet abstain from saying the truth to someone who is not ready to benefit.

Advanced Sagittarius Sun Sign Person

You are subject primarily by Earth, the esoteric ruler of Sagittarius and a ruler of Ray 3 of Creative Intelligence, giving opportunities for varied experiences and many original ideas. You have tasted riches, fame and honors, either in a past life or this one, and found they do not give the happiness you seek.

You are now searching for that joy you know is your heritage and are beginning to realize it is found through Soul evolvement by overcoming character weaknesses and serving others consonant with your Soul's Purpose. You are finding the Bible quotation, "Seek ye first the Kingdom of God and all else will come to you" to be true.

You also receive the energies of Jupiter, but on a higher level than the average Sagittarius Sun Sign person. You use Jupiter's enthusiasm and optimism in working on your Spiritual progress.

Very Advanced Sagittarius Sun Sign Person

Mars as the hierarchical ruler of Sagittarius gives you courage and energy to transmute your character weaknesses into strengths and to serve others consonant with your Soul's Purpose. Because Mars is a ruler of Ray 6 of Idealism and Devotion, it gives energy and courage to refrain from talking about Spiritual concepts to those who are not ready to hear.

Mars, along with Jupiter and Earth, gives you much energy and courage for many experiences, whether karmic lesson-teaching or rewarding, to accept with enthusiasm, optimism and wisdom in seeing each new vision clearly.

Average Capricorn Sun Sign Person

Your Ray 3 Personality of Creative Intelligence, with your enhanced abstract mind giving you opportunities for creativity, is colored by self-discipline and persistence to work on each project as long as it takes to accomplish what you are capable of. Capricorn is the Sign of great opportunities for Initiation in raising your level of consciousness. It is considered an ideal path to the mountain top (Spiritual heights) because of Capricorn's qualities of hard persistent work and self-discipline.

You receive energies of Saturn, the exoteric ruler of Capricorn and a ruler of Ray 3 of Creative Intelligence. You may have a decided lack of concern and love toward others. Although you are ambitious and work hard in your career, your motivation is riches, fame and honors which in time you usually receive, however fleeting. The symbol here is the goat—the greedy seeker for satisfaction of desires.

When you find no happiness in these materialistic things and feel lonely because of your coldness toward others, you are ready to climb the mountain a little higher and become an advanced Capricorn Sun Sign person through meditation afforded by your Saturn.

Advanced Capricorn Sun Sign Person

You also receive the energies of Saturn but on a higher level than the average Capricorn Sun Sign person. Your self-discipline and hard work is no longer in acquiring selfish desires but now primarily in serving others.

Having experienced, whether in this life or a past one, difficult karmic lessons from selfish concerns, you begin to turn your attention outward in concern and love for others.

Your symbol is the crocodile which lives both in water and land. The water symbolizes your desire for wealth and high position with no concern for others while the land symbolizes discipline in changing materialistic desires to Spiritual aspirations. Like the crocodile, you go back and forth from water of selfish desires to land of concern and love for others. Having tasted both and noting the difficult karmic experiences resulting from the former and the rewarding ones from the latter, you are now a candidate for the very advanced Capricorn Sun Sign person.

Very Advanced Capricorn Sun Sign Person

Like the average and the advanced Capricorn Sun Sign person, you also have a Ray 3 Personality and receive very creative ideas. And like them, you also receive the energies of Saturn, but on a higher level. Here Saturn's energies give your abstract mind even greater creative capacity. Unlike the average and advanced Capricorn Sun Sign person, you receive the energies of Venus, the hierarchical ruler of Capricorn and the ruler of Ray 5 of the Concrete Mind. This enables you to bring down to earth in a practical and useful form any original ideas that Saturn's energies relay to you, along with a joy and a love of work. Your symbol is the unicorn, its one horn like a spear upon its brow, indicating one-pointedness toward Soul evolvement—the climb to the mountain top.

More information on Ray 3 Souls and Personalities is found in Chapters IX, X and XIV.

SUCCESSFUL RAY 3 SOULS

Following are examples of Ray 3 Souls who have developed new theories, brilliant ideas and original inventions in Spirituality, government, philosophy, mathematics, writing, music, film-making, chemistry, bacteriology, painting, oceanography, esotericism, physics, meteorology, medicine, microbiology, geology, conservation, astronomy, astrology, economics, ontology, chemistry, hypnotism, singing, dancing and acting:

Ray 3 Souls and Ray 3 Personalities of Creative Intelligence

They not only have creative projects as their Souls' Purposes, but Personalities which carry out their life plans in creative ways.

Astrologer Robert Hand, with a Ray 3 Soul, conceived many brilliant ideas, such as the Composite Chart showing how two or more people operate as a unit and also developed astrology software programs. His Ray 3 Personality showed itself in his creative lecturing and writing.

The very highly evolved Dalai lama uses his Ray 3 Soul in creating Spiritual concepts and his Ray 3 Personality imparting knowledge in an original manner focusing on love and respect for all.

George Gurdjief, a Ray 3 Soul, developed original Spiritual ideas to help humankind. His Ray 3 Personality helped carry out his Soul's Purpose by uplifting many in an unorthodox way.

Winston Churchill, a Ray 3 Soul, had brilliant thoughts to combat invasion as England's Prime Minister. With his Ray 3 Personality, he devised original ways to enlist the cooperation of foreign governments and thus led England to victory.

John Edgar Hoover used his magnificent creative capacity by not only developing, with his Ray 3 Soul, the world's most efficient law enforcement agency when he was director of FBI, but also by putting his ideas into practice in an original fashion attuned with his Ray 3 Personality.

Albert Schweitzer, a philosopher which is a natural for a Ray 3 Soul, lived his creative ideas with his Ray 3 Personality by greatly helping humankind in a pioneering way.

John Candies, a mathematical genius, also had both a Ray 3 Soul and Personality. His methods were certainly different from mainstream mathematicians.

Thomas Carlyle, considered a genius, used his Ray 3 Soul contemplating original ideas and his Ray 3 Personality in writing about them.

Steven Spielberg's Ray 3 Soul's Purpose is conceiving original ideas, and his Ray 3 Personality enables him to produce excellent science fiction films. He is unusually successful because all his planets are below the horizon but Uranus in the 12th House which supplies immense energy for his inner life. He also receives much help from the far-out cosmos as his Sun is conjunct our Galactic Center.

The following singers have Ray 3 Souls and Personalities who not only have original ideas for singing, but have Personalities to express their singing in unusual ways: Frank Sinatra, Francis Sinatra, Burton Cummings, Catarina Valente and Johnny Ray.

The second group with both Ray 3 Souls and Personalities are writers whose purposes are to create ideas in diverse subjects and have Personalities which help put their ideas on paper in original ways. Some are: Susan Watkins, Maria Fida Moro, Alexander Petofi, Chrinta Rossetti, Sir Lawrence Van der Post, Ross Mac-Donald, and poets Kenneth Pathen and Charles Guerin.

Musicians who have both Ray 3 Souls and Personalities often compose or change compositions as their Souls' Purposes. Their Personalities have the capacity to bring their pieces or arrangements to humankind in original ways. Some are: Hector Berlioz, Scott Walker and Michael Thomas.

The last group of Ray 3 Souls and Personalities are scientists with enhanced abstract minds having creative ideas, not to be confused with scientists with enhanced concrete minds (researchers who are Ray 5 Souls bringing the original ideas of Ray 3 Souls down to earth to use practically). Some are: chemist W. Lysscomb, scientist I. Newton, professor of economics G. Stigler, geophysicists A. Cox and L. Pasteur. As their Souls' Purposes, they discover processes, methods or any new ideas. Their Ray 3 Personalities can introduce their discoveries in original and fascinating ways which might induce Ray 5 people to make practical through research and statistics.

Ray 3 Souls and Ray 1 Personalities of Will and Power

Their Souls' Purposes are creative work whose powerful Personalities help make needed changes in certain fields:

United States president S. Truman had a Ray 3 Soul whose Purpose was to create original theories and ideas. His Ray 1 Personality gave him power to put his ideas into practice.

Oliver W. Holmes, a Ray 3 Soul whose purpose was creative ideas, manifested it through the power of his Ray 1 Personality as justice of the United States Supreme Court.

Orde Wingate, known for his genius true to his Ray 3 Soul, manifested his capacities as a major general with the power of his Ray 1 Personality.

Chemist G. Pimental and petrologist H. Yoder also had Ray 3 Souls who were able to express their original ideas powerfully through their Ray 1 Personalities.

Michaelangelo with his Ray 3 Soul's energy became an excellent artist, sculptor and painter. He used his Ray 1 Personality of Power and Will to express his talents through channels which reached many during his time and even today.

Leonardo Da Vinci, a Ray 3 Soul, became a noted architect, painter and sculptor who invented a musical instrument sounding like a lute and many labor-saving machines and also introduced a high sense of color in painting. With his Ray 1 Personality of Will and Power, he was able to reach the minds and hearts of the populace with his attainments.

One does not always use his or her energy wisely. Adolph Hitler with his Ray 3 Soul did have unusual ideas, but, as dictator of Germany during World War Two, used his Ray 1 Personality of Power and Will with his warped ideas to kill many, building a great deal of difficult lesson-teaching karmic experiences for the future.

Ray 3 Souls with Ray 2 Personalities of Love and Wisdom

Their Souls' Purposes are creative work which can benefit humankind through teaching and/or healing.

Helen Blavatsky used her Ray 3 Soul's energy with her superior abstract creative mind in writing the astoundingly deep and accurate metaphysical books, *Isis Unveiled* and *The Secret Doctrine*. With her Ray 2 Personality, she taught and is still teaching untold numbers of readers how to heal themselves and evolve Spiritually.

British bacteriologist Sir Alexander Fleming with his Ray 3 Soul discovered the mold from which penicillin was derived. His Ray 2 Personality energy allowed many to be healed through his discovery.

Engineer H. Eckner, scientists A. Piccard and R. Hooke, biochemist R. Holley and professor of chemistry R. Connick also had Ray 3 Souls and Ray 2 Personalities, each of whom taught and/or healed others with their original ideas.

Ray 3 Souls and Ray 4 Personalities of Harmony Through Conflict

Their Souls' Purposes are creative work which they can easily express harmoniously, such as through counseling or art.

Some are: actress and singer Janis Paige, dancer Linda Kan Henning, musician Accardo Salvator, composer Mason Williams, writer Paul Theroux and painter Marilyn Greenwood whose Ray

3 Souls supplied them with original ideas and whose Ray 4 Personalities, through their artistic expressions, helped many attain harmony.

Ray 3 Souls with Ray 5 Personalities of the Concrete Mind

Their Souls' Purposes are creative work which they can bring down to earth in a useful form, such as in research.

Blaise Pascal used his Ray 3 Soul energy as a philosopher, mathematician and creative scientist. His Ray 5 Personality energy gave him the ability to bring his ideas down to earth in a practical way.

Jacques Cousteau, oceanographer, invented many useful products with his Ray 3 Soul energy and aided scientific investigations with his Ray 5 Personality.

Others with Ray 3 Souls and Ray 5 Personalities are: hypnotist Messner, economists Staats and J. Sawhill, chemist J. Roberts, physicist B. McDaniel and meteorologist Robert Mill whose creative ideas of their Ray 3 Soul energies were made practical with logic afforded by their Ray 5 Personalities.

Ray 3 Souls with Ray 6 Personalities of Idealism and Devotion

Their Souls' Purposes are creative work with which they devotedly and idealistically can help humankind.

Jonas Salk, a Ray 3 Soul, successfully developed a polio vaccine. His Ray 6 Personality which showered him with devotion to his cause.

Saint Francesca Cabrini's Ray 3 Soul's Purpose was creating ideas. She expressed them with her Ray 6 Personality in devoted and idealistic work of setting up orphanages and missions and working in hospitals and jails.

Nobel Prize winner Andre Guide used his Ray 3 Soul energy in deep contemplation on philosophy, religion and ethics, and uplifted many with his Ray 6 Personality by putting his original thoughts on paper, especially on the psychology of creative artists.

Microbiologist Leeuvenlock, petroleum geologist A. Jacobson, entologist R. Metcalf, conservationist D. Brower and astronaut Don Eisele also had Ray 3 Souls and Ray 6 Personalities, all of whom used creative ideas, each in his unique capacity, with idealism and devotion.

Ray 3 Souls with Ray 7 Personalities of Order and Rhythm

Their Souls' Purposes are creative work reaching humankind in an organized fashion.

Chemist A. Nobel with his Ray 3 Soul invented dynamite and with his Ray 7 Personality of Rhythm and Order founded the Nobel Prize Organization.

Biophysicist T. Ruch, professor of physics M. Goldberger and biochemist L. Hepperry also have Ray 3 Souls and Ray 7 Personalities. Their Ray 3 Soul energy gave each original ideas which, through Ray 7 Personalities, were relayed to humankind through leadership capacities.

IV

RAY 4 SOULS AND PERSONALITIES OF HARMONY THROUGH CONFLICT

‹‹‹ ⚹⚹⚹ ››

Creating Harmony
Color—Green
Aries or Virgo Sun Sign—Ray 4 Personality
Scorpio or Taurus Ascendant—Ray 4 Soul
See Introduction for Possible Ray 4 Soul
for Sagittarius Ascendant

While all Ray energies, when used wisely, bring beauty to the Soul, Ray 4 is the precursor of the most beautiful. It brings harmony and when there is harmony, there is beauty on a deep level.

Harmony results from manifesting the Soul's Purpose and from transmuting character weaknesses into strengths. Ray 4 energy induces harmony by many difficult karmic lesson-teaching experiences which helps you evolve quickly.

The purpose of Ray 4 energy is to produce unity through understanding—understanding from becoming acquainted with the New Aquarian energies whose wise use brings love, beauty and much else. When employing these Ray energies with love and intelligence, you can find an unlimited source of help in counseling others and in artistic expression. A high vibration of color and

sound are found in Ray 4 energy which can easily produce colorful and beautiful writing, painting and other types of art. Highly
evolved Ray 4 persons often heal others through their voices.

The Lord of Ray 4 is the Master Serapis; the divine principle
is intuition; the sense is smell; the element is air; the stone is
jasper. The approach to the Path is by self-control, gaining equilibrium among the warring forces of one's mind.

The color of Ray 4 is green, the most relaxing color of the
spectrum, so necessary to help one contemplate and thus learn
quickly from the many difficult experiences encountered. Green
is the middle color of the spectrum and Ray 4 is the middle of all
Rays which connects Rays 5, 6 and 7 to the divine Rays of 1,2 and
3. It is the bridging Ray from the Personality to the Soul. The
planetary rulers of Ray 4 are Moon and Mercury. Moon gives re-
call of what happened in the recent as well as distant past which
is stored in the unconscious. Mercury enhances the conscious
mind in dealing with both desirable and undesirable thoughts in
attracting either rewarding or lesson-teaching experiences. Difficult karmic experiences are actually blessings in disguise as they
help one evolve quickly by affording opportunities for learning
lessons.

Although harmony and beauty are important key words of
Ray 4, others are conflicts and lesson-teaching experiences. Ray 4
is the most difficult of all Rays to work with, especially if it is one's
Personality Ray. Yet it is the one of greatest opportunities to grow
Spiritually from experiencing many difficult karmic lessons. It is
imperative that you have an understanding of Reincarnation and
Karma to help you progress, as you took on lot of lessons to learn
in this lifetime (see Chapter IX).

As time goes on in the history of the race, the cosmos supplies the energies needed in every Great Age for its continued
evolvement. We are now in a very difficult period which happens
every 2160 years as a new Age begins. The transfer of the Old
Piscean Age energies to those of the New Aquarian Age is not

easy until an understanding of the new energies reaches the minds and hearts of humanity (see Chapter X).

It is especially difficult for teen-agers who are also making the adjustment from childhood to adulthood. The reason for the increasing numbers of teen-age drug and alcohol addictions, suicides, violence and killings, which seldom happened in the past, is that few teen-agers have been exposed to the understanding of these new energies and how to use them wisely. Just as Aquarian energy can play havoc with young individuals and young Souls when there is a lack of understanding, it also can do much good when they know how to use this energy wisely and when they are aware that Aquarian energy is a step up from Piscean energy of the past.

Most teen-agers are ready and searching for answers to life's meaning. I did a Ray-Centered astrological delineation, explaining this information for a teen-ager, and received a letter from his mother. She said that her son had previously been a part of a gang and got into trouble, but has since left the gang and listens to the tape every night and is a completely different person.

It is hoped that those in a position to make changes in our school systems will supplement the curriculum with the understanding of these New Aquarian energies. With understanding comes love, and with love there is no violence, no cop-outs in alcohol and drug abuse. If this book becomes required reading in schools throughout our country to help students know who they are, why they are here, what their unique life Purpose is and what the consequences of one's thoughts and actions are, then undesirable happenings will very likely be a thing of the past.

Two symbols represent Ray 4. One is a golden bird on a rosy cross, standing for the sacrificing of selfish desires for the harmony and joy of Soul contact. The other is the Rainbow Bridge, which is the connective tissue from the Personality to the Soul.

While Ray 4 energy, Comet Chiron discovered in 1977 and Ray-Centered Astrology are each considered the Rainbow Bridge from the Personality to the Soul, yet unique in its contribution to humankind, all have much in common.

All three are in tune with the Aquarian energies, helping to accelerate and make easier the necessary journey of the Personality to the Soul. They induce humanity to transfer energies of outworn concepts of the past Piscean Age to those needed for the New Aquarian Age we are now entering.

All are in rapport with the Ageless Wisdoms—those being released at this exciting period of many changes precipitated by the New Aquarian Age.

All are concerned primarily with aiding individuals to find their unique Purpose for this Life: Ray 4 energy and Chiron through speeding up difficult lesson-teaching experiences to give people added energy for manifesting their Souls' Purposes, and Ray-Centered Astrology through helping them find and manifest their unique Souls' Purposes while also guiding them in awareness of and in overcoming weaknesses.

All three are "wounded healers." Ray 4 energy gives lesson-teaching experiences accumulated from many past lives. Chiron's energies quicken peoples' lesson-teaching experiences, enabling them to sooner help others who are suffering the way they suffered in the past. Ray-Centered Astrology is the tool for astrologers who have evolved from experiencing and learning from many difficult karmic lessons and thus able to help others.

None of these three are easy to handle, yet are given in excessive amounts to those ready to take the journey from Personality to the Soul in this lifetime.

It is no surprise that I chose to write this book. All three are strong components in my horoscope. I have a Ray 4 Personality, giving ability for writing and counseling; pioneered Ray-Centered Astrology (Aries Sun Sign); and have Chiron powerfully placed in the most significant part of my horoscope—the same degree as my Ascendant which is the most important indicator of the Soul's Purpose.

In 1988 as I was preparing a workshop in Ray-Centered Astrology and concentrating on Ray 4 Personalities, I was impressed to check the horoscopes in my file with Ray 4 Personalities to see if they had Chiron significantly placed near the Ascendant or at least in the First House which is the area of Soul expression. I felt that those who requested Ray-Centered delineations would apt to be highly interested in Soul evolvement because of the affinity of Ray 4, Ray-Centered Astrology and Chiron. I omitted all traditional delineations I had done in the 13 years previous to 1986 when I began Ray-Centered delineations.

Since Ray 4 Personalities have taken on much lesson-teaching Karma, I felt they would be the most likely candidates for walking Chiron's Rainbow Bridge to the Soul. Being wounded from suffering on the way and then learning the lessons the wounds are meant to teach, they could ultimately be excellent counselors and artists. Having walked this Bridge, they can show others how to walk it.

Since the most difficult Personality Ray is Ray 4 and the most difficult placement for Chiron is conjunct the Ascendant or at least in the First House, I felt that both, being indicative of many karmic difficulties and subsequent rapid Soul progress, would be found together in higher than average frequency.

I was not disappointed. In the first five months that I had done Ray-Centered delineations, 17 were for clients who had Ray 4 Personalities. It would be expected, because there are 12 Houses, that randomly ½ of them would have Chiron conjunct the Ascendant or in the First House which would be 1⅓ (1 or 2 clients) as the expected number. I was both delighted and amazed to find 9 of the 17 (more than half) had Chiron in the First House. Even more revealing is that 6 of the 9 were very close to the Ascendant and one was the exact degree of the Ascendant (mine).

Therefore it is likely that if you have a Ray 4 Personality, you have Chiron in your First House or at least significantly placed in your horoscope, giving you a double edge to help others attain harmony.

Ray 4 as an even number has feminine characteristics of sensitivity, intuition, love and introversion.

Your major weaknesses are fear and self-centeredness which may show in strong passions, worry, laziness, extravagance and a lack of moral courage. Your major strengths are quickness of perception, intuition, good judgment, physical courage, skill in action, generosity, love, sympathy and sensitivity.

Following is a list of character weaknesses you are prone to and the strengths, some of which you now have or can have through transmutation. It is unwise to repress your flaws because this energy will then cause nervousness and/or other problems from your unconscious mind. Instead, because energy follows thought, transmute the energy of your weaknesses into specific strengths by visualizing often the following strengths you lack, along with self-discipline. As you transmute your character weaknesses into strengths, your life becomes more successful, enjoyable and fulfilled.

RAY 4 SOUL & PERSONALITY ENERGIES

UNWISE USE	WISE USE
Fear and worry	Learning lessons quickly
Self-centeredness	Love and sympathy
Strong passions	Right judgment
Laziness	Synthesis of beauty
Extravagance	Generosity
Pessimism	Physical courage
Inaccuracy	Intellectual quickness
Failure of karmic tests	Vivid imagination
Criticism of others	Divine indifference to others' faults
Harboring guilt	Guiltless through understanding

RAY 4 SOUL OF HARMONY
THROUGH CONFLICT

Scorpio or Taurus Ascendant gives a Ray 4 Soul
Sagittarius Ascendant may give a Ray 4 Soul
(see Introduction)

Your Soul's Purpose is to help yourself and others attain harmony through resolving conflicts, that is transmuting character weaknesses into strengths.

One way to help people attain harmony is through artistic pursuits—uplifting others by helping them see the beauty in life through writing, music, painting, dancing, singing and so on. Art serves others in various ways—reading a soul-stirring book, hearing songs of a melodic voice, gazing at a superb painting, watching a mind-altering play or artistic performance and listening to beautiful classical music can raise one's consciousness to a much higher level.

The colors that a painter produces could be "out of this world" as the saying goes in that the beauty produced is magnificent and uplifting. Watching the precision and rhythm of dancers can give one a feeling of harmony for all that lives. As an architect, you can plan the building of cities, highways, churches and other structures so that beauty and usefulness are paramount, adding to the joy that millions receive from your work, lifting their level of consciousness. The oft quoted "Music is food for the Soul" could not be better illustrated than in its capacity to help others in their Spiritual progress. Or if you are a performer in a play which touches the chords of humanity on a deep level, you will probably never know how much your work has aided perhaps millions in their evolvement. You have the ability to not only move people, but change their lives completely around.

Another way to help others attain harmony is counseling. If this is your choice, it matters not whether it is through psychology, astrology or any other discipline. What does matter is that it be performed in tune with the New Aquarian Age energies which are ever-increasingly entering the hearts and minds of humanity (see Chapter X). Some practitioners of these disciplines who have not yet attuned themselves to these new energies are still offering a modicum of help to people, but as we are entering a New Age, the help available now in rapport with Aquarian energy is far superior for our present needs to that of the past Piscean Age. Most practitioners in rapport with the New Aquarian Age energies have benefited from Ray 4 energy as noted in the change in their disciplines—Psychology to Transpersonal Psychology, Astrology to Ray-Centered Astrology, Organized Religion to Spirituality or Metaphysics. All three weave the Universal Laws of Reincarnation and Karma into their practices.

By adding Reincarnation and Karma to their disciplines, these practitioners basically hasten Soul progress, success and better health for clients and parishioners by eliminating blame toward others and guilt. These practitioners also can explain how we and only we are responsible for where we find ourselves—that we create our own environment. This can lead to accepting and loving ourselves wherever we are on the scale of Soul evolvement and then accepting and loving all others wherever they are (see Chapters IX, X, XII and XIV).

Following are examples of people being helped by using Ray 4 energy wisely: Where there was once blame and hatred directed toward those who wronged us, there is now the understanding that we create our own reality; where there was once a need to want forgiveness from those who wronged us, we now know that forgiveness is superfluous because one's Soul attracts wrongdoers for its progress; where there was once guilt feelings from wrongs committed, there is now the awareness that none of us is perfect and that we grow Spiritually with every earth life; where there was once a defeatist pessimistic view of what life is all about, there is now a reason for living and an urge to find and activate one's unique Purpose in Life.

RAY 4 SOUL AND YOUR ASCENDANT

The energies of your Ascendant color the basic energies of your Soul Ray.   Because you have a Ray 4 Soul, your Ascendant must be either Taurus, Scorpio or Sagittarius.

Ray 4 Soul with Taurus Ascendant

Your Ray 4 Soul's Purpose in aiding people attain harmony, whether through art or counseling, finds its greatest help in your voice—singing, speaking, counseling, lecturing or acting. When you have evolved to a certain level, your voice can heal others. Stability and determination are your key words, helping you succeed quickly in manifesting the Purpose for which you came into this life. You are influenced by Venus, the exoteric ruler of Taurus and ruler of Ray 5 of the Concrete Mind, allowing you much enjoyment of ma-terialistic things such as food, money, possessions and sex.

When you begin to eradicate your character flaws and prepare for your Soul's Purpose, you are also influenced by Vulcan, the eso-teric ruler of Taurus and a ruler of Ray 1 of Will and Power. This gives the ability to crystallize repressions of anger, guilt and out-grown concepts in your unconscious mind and bring them into the conscious mind, eradicating them through the understanding of Reincarnation and Karma (see Chapters IX and XII).

Vulcan is found between the Sun and Mercury, and in the last few years word is that an astronomer has calculated Vulcan's posi-tion to be within 8½ degrees of the Sun. Although Vulcan's position in our solar system has not yet been officially recognized by astronomy, metaphysicians are aware of its presence. However, in the 19th century, some astronomers believed there was another planet near Mercury because it was determined that Mercury's rate of perihelion advanced 38 seconds of arc per century faster than theory would indicate. In 1849, in a note to the French Academy of Science, the astronomer Leverrier urged all colleagues to search for transits of an intramercurial planet during eclipses of the Sun. An amateur astronomer, Lescarbuilt, saw the transit of a small object across the Sun. After checking Lescarbuilt's instruments and observations, Leverrier was convinced that Vulcan had been sighted.

When you begin to serve others consonant with your Ray 4 Soul's Purpose and are successfully beginning to overcome character weaknesses, you will also be under the influence of Vulcan, a ruler of Ray 1 of Will and Power as the hierarchical ruler of Taurus. Here Vulcan not only gives power to eradicate your character flaws, but also helps you rid others of theirs.

Ray 4 Soul with Scorpio Ascendant

Your Ray 4 Soul's Purpose in helping others attain harmony, whether through art or counseling, finds its greatest help in your intense nature—your ability to go to the very depth of a problem or issue and to the unconscious minds of those you wish to heal. Likewise, in artistic expression you are capable of penetrating the depths of the psyche to reach others on a subtle level through music, painting, acting, singing, dancing and so on. You are influenced by Pluto, the exoteric ruler of Scorpio and a ruler of Ray 1 of Power and Will. This deep and intense power will either take you to the very depths of undesirable thoughts, words and actions or the very heights of your Soul. In the first case, all this testing will in time also bring much Soul progress because of Karma.

When you begin to eradicate your character weaknesses and

prepare yourself to serve others consonant with your Soul's Purpose, you will also be ruled by Mars. It is the esoteric ruler of Scorpio and a ruler of Ray 6 of Idealism and Devotion, giving extra energy and courage to do what your Soul asks of you.

When you are ready to serve others consonant with your Soul's Purpose, the energies of Mercury, the hierarchical ruler of Scorpio and a ruler of Ray 4 of Harmony through Conflict, is released to you. This increases your awareness of many things, including deep understanding of lesson-teaching and rewarding Karma, thus putting you in an advantageous position to raise your level of consciousness and that of many others.

Ray 4 Soul with Sagittarius Ascendant

Your Ray 4 Soul's Purpose in helping others attain harmony, whether through art or counseling, will be influenced by Jupiter, the exoteric ruler of Sagittarius and a ruler of Ray 2 of Love and Wisdom. This bestows enthusiasm, optimism and one-pointedness in teaching and/or healing others physically, emotionally and/or Spiritually. After attaining one goal, you immediately are impressed to start working toward another and then another, ad infinitum.

When you begin to eradicate your character flaws and prepare for your life service, you will also receive the energies of Earth, the esoteric ruler of Sagittarius and a ruler of Ray 3 of Creative Intelligence. This gives you brilliant ideas, received in contemplation, and many experiences which can be great opportunities for Soul growth.

When you are ready to serve others consonant with your Soul's Purpose, the energies of Mars, the hierarchical ruler of Sagittarius and a ruler of Ray 6 of Idealism and Devotion, will be released to you. This give immense energy and the courage to go ahead with your Soul's Purpose in spite of those who do not understand and who may give you a hard time. Integrity and honesty are a part of your make-up. You are a seeker of truth and thus may be impressed to become better acquainted with the Universal Laws to use as a facet of your Soul's Purpose (see Chapters IX and XII).

RAY 4 SOUL WITH YOUR PERSONALITY RAY

Your Soul's Purpose as found by your Ray 4 Soul and colored by your Ascendant receives the help of your Personality Ray energy to carry it out. See Introduction to find your Personality Ray and chapter number for a detailed interpretation. Following is only a general idea of how to use your Ray 4 Soul with each of the Personality Rays:

A Ray 1 Personality of Will and Power gives you what is necessary to make great desirable changes in counseling or some form of art.

With a Ray 2 Personality of Love and Wisdom, you will be urged to teach and/or heal in your particular Ray 4 discipline.

If you have a Ray 3 Personality of Creative Intelligence, you will carry out your Soul's Purpose in an original fashion.

With a Ray 4 Personality of Harmony through Conflict, you will find it fairly easy to manifest your Soul's Purpose because of the rapport between your Soul and Personality.

A Ray 5 Personality of the Concrete Mind will carry out your Soul's Purpose in a practical way with logic and possibly research.

With a Ray 6 Personality of Idealism and Devotion, you can carry out your Ray 4 Soul's Purpose with a strong motivation of uplifting humanity with idealism and devotion.

If you have a Ray 7 Personality of Rhythm and Order, you will be impressed to manifest your Ray 4 Soul's Purpose in an organized leadership capacity.

For example, suppose your Ray 4 Soul's Purpose is writing— your work could be intuitive and brilliant with colorful words. With a Ray 1 Personality your prose or poetry would also be powerful; with a Ray 2 Personality, much love and wisdom would also be expressed; with a Ray 3 Personality, it would also be composed of original ideas; with a Ray 4 Personality there would be enhancement of color, beauty and harmony; with a Ray 5 Personality, research could be interestingly written; with a Ray 6 Personality, your writing could also promote idealism; and with a Ray 7 Personality, you could also be a leader of a writers' group.

RAY 4 PERSONALITY OF HARMONY THROUGH CONFLICT

Virgo or Aries Sun Sign gives a Ray 4 Personality

Your Ray 4 Personality shows that you can best carry out your Soul's Purpose, whatever it is, through art such as writing, painting, sculpturing, architecture, music, performing or through counseling.

Your greatest challenge is to become aware that your Personality Ray is probably the most difficult of all Personality Rays in that it gives many lesson-teaching karmic experiences, but also is the one of greatest opportunity for Soul growth. You have chosen to come back with this Personality Ray because you wanted to progress a great deal in this life. It will not be an easy life until your karmic lessons are learned, but awareness of Universal Laws makes it less difficult (see Chapter IX). Were you not evolved enough to handle this many karmic experiences in one lifetime, you would not have been allowed to take over that body that was born at your time of birth.

You do not work optimally if there is too much authority over you, which sometimes results in anger or irritability. Being highly intuitive, you are capable of visualizing and synthesizing the whole picture, the whole problem and how to proceed. That is why you can be an excellent therapist or artist.

Highly sensitive to your surroundings is a plus for success in your career, but be careful that you are not hypersensitive in getting your feelings hurt when people wrong you. Be aware that none of us is perfect and that we attract people with certain flaws for lesson-teaching experiences (see Chapter IX).

Worry, fear and anxiety can sometimes take hold of you, but at those times, breathe deeply and relax every part of your body with your mind and visually put orange light around your kidneys and solar plexus, and then surround yourself with the White Light of Christ. Love your solar plexus, but in meditation, visually take it by the hand to the mountain top and ask a Master to help it evolve. Your emotions through your solar plexus are trying to help you the best way they know but a Master can help it find a way that is joyful instead of harsh.

Self-discipline is important for all Personality Rays, but is doubly important for you because Ray 4 is the midpoint of the Seven Rays—the energy between self-centered personality desires and Soul aspirations. You are blessed with good judgment which could be the catalyst for exercising discipline in choosing Soul aspirations with great future reward rather than self-centered desires with only momentary pleasure resulting in future difficult Karma.

There is a possibility, if you are highly evolved, that you may experience a crisis, coined a "spiritual emergency" by psychiatrists Stan and Christina Grof. Even though this is a difficult period in which you need emotional support of others, it is a time of great opportunity. In fact it is a time when your unconscious knows you are ready to overcome many flaws in your psyche and uses this crisis to make sure you do it (see Chapters XII and II).

RAY 4 PERSONALITY AND YOUR SUN SIGN

Because you have a Ray 4 Personality, you have either a Virgo or Aries Sun Sign, the interpretation of which colors your Ray 4 Personality. Just as your Soul Ray is colored by your Ascendant Sign, your Personality Ray is colored by your Sun Sign. Read the following three categories for your Sun Sign to identify the status of your personality—either average, advanced or very advanced. The more advanced it is, the better you will serve others and the greater will be your happiness, health and joy. Suggestions are presented to aid you in reaching the next category.

Average Virgo Sun Sign Person

Mercury, the exoteric ruler of Virgo, releases its energy to you through extensive mental wanderings with precise analyzing abilities, often resulting in critical thoughts and words regarding the imperfections of others. Because Mercury is a ruler of Ray 4, the same Ray as your Personality Ray, difficult karmic experiences will be many.

Your greatest challenge is to accept and love yourself and others where you and they are. You are helped by the Law of Karma which brings lesson-teaching experiences when you are critical of others in thoughts or words, helping you realize that none of us is perfect and that we have earth lives to learn needed lessons (see Chapter IX).

Advanced Virgo Sun Sign Person

Your Ray 4 Personality, which hands you many difficult karmic experiences, is colored by the energies of the esoteric ruler of Virgo, the Moon which is also a ruler of Ray 4 of Harmony though Conflict. This increases the lesson-teaching experiences you will encounter, but is a blessing in disguise because it is a period of great opportunities for Soul growth. The Moon veils Neptune, a ruler of Ray 6 of Idealism and Devotion, and Vulcan, a ruler of Ray 1 of Power and Will. When the Moon or Sun veils a planet, it means that the energies of that planet are received only by one who is advanced enough to use its energies wisely. These veilings make it somewhat easy for you to idealistically transmute weaknesses into strengths, especially through vulcanizing (crystallizing) your repressions of guilt, blame and other wrong attitudes from the unconscious and bringing them to the conscious mind. You can then eradicate them through understanding Aquarian Age principles (see Chapter IX).

You also receive the energies of Mercury but on a higher level than the average Virgo Sun Sign person. Here Mercury helps you understand more clearly the Universal Laws of Reincarnation and Karma.

Very Advanced Virgo Sun Sign Person

Your Ray 4 Personality which gives many difficult karmic experiences is colored by Jupiter, the hierarchical ruler of Virgo and a ruler of Ray 2 of Love and Wisdom. This bestows an ability to use knowledge wisely, especially in reference to your discriminative powers. Many questions and answers go through your mind such as:

Should we always trust others? Those who trust everyone are bound to get burned. Yet those who trust no one suffer more—they feel separate from all others and build a wall around themselves that no one can enter. As you use the energies of the very advanced Virgo person at a higher level, you will know whom and whom not to trust. The answer is cautious trust, but with no unkind criticism and always with love.

With your enhanced discriminative and analytic capacities, you are able to wisely assess those who come to you for help and to aid them in becoming more perfect.

You also receive the energies of the Moon veiling Neptune and Vulcan, and of Mercury, but on a higher vibration than even the advanced Virgo Sun Sign person. Here, these energies along with Jupiter help you understand God's Plan for Earth and give you the wisdom to do your part in manifesting your Soul's Purpose.

Average Aries Sun Sign Person

Your Ray 4 Personality of Harmony through Conflict which brings you may karmic lesson-teaching experiences is colored by Mars, the exoteric ruler of Aries and a ruler of Ray 6 of Idealism and Devotion. This gives you an independent spirit, much physical energy, a strong ego and an idealistic nature. You work hard at what interests you at the time, but when things or people do not go the way you would like, you have a tendency to become impatient, angry and irritable. When you realize you are your own worst enemy and begin to become truly concerned about others as well as self, you advance to the next category.

Advanced Aries Sun Sign Person

Your Ray 4 Personality of Harmony through Conflict which brings many lesson-teaching experiences is colored mainly by Mercury, the esoteric ruler of Aries and a ruler of Ray 4 of Harmony through Conflict. This helps to use your powerful mind instead of your emotions for guidance.

In this category you find that Aries is a very mental Sign. You are aware how the mind can make one ill as well as heal one. Your high level of intellectual activity shows you the results of self-centered desires versus Spiritual aspiration.

You also receive the energies of Mars but on a higher level than the average person. Here it gives energy for mental pursuits.

It is difficult even for an advanced Aries Sun Sign person to succeed if there is too much authority over him or her. Your highly independent spirit and your synthesizing ability to visualize the whole picture indicates it is wise for you to work more or less independently.

Very Advanced Aries Sun Sign Person

Your Ray 4 Personality of Harmony through Conflict which brings many lessons-teaching experiences is colored mainly by Uranus, the hierarchical ruler of Aries and the ruler of Ray 7 of Rhythm and Order. This gives you organizational and leadership abilities and a capacity for original ideas. Along with Mars and Mercury, Uranus gives immense physical energy, courage, integrity, mind power and capacity to create divine ideas and idealistic behavior to help yourself and others work out conflicts through organizational and leadership capacities. You are a pioneer and trail-blazer.

More information for Ray 4 Souls and Personalities is found in Chapters IX, X, XII and XIV.

SUCCESSFUL RAY 4 SOULS

Following are examples of Ray 4 Souls who help others attain harmony through music, poetry, mythology, the Woman's Movement, writing, singing, acting, painting, psychology, philosophy, occultism, astrology, government and Spirituality:

Ray 4 Souls and Ray 4 Personalities of
Harmony Through Conflict

Their Souls' Purposes are to help others attain harmony with Personalities in rapport with their Life Purposes.

Musician Antone Dvorak whose Ray 4 Soul's Purpose was to bring harmony to others, manifested it as a teacher, violinist and composer in writing nine symphonies.

Musician Joe Chambers' Ray 4 Soul's Purpose was helping

others attain harmony. He carried it out through his Ray 4 Personality in gospel and soul music and became internationally famous.

Poets Johann Goethe and Paul Verlaine discovered their Ray 4 Souls' Purposes were to help others solve problems. They used mythology with their Ray 4 Personality energies to aid people resolve conflicts.

Gloria Steinem found that her Ray 4 Soul's Purpose is to help women attain equality. Her Ray 4 Personality is enabling her to resolve conflicts between the sexes, thus promoting harmony.

Some writers with Ray 4 Souls and Personalities are: Washington Irving, Taylor Caldwell, Samuel Beckett, Nellie Wilson Parsons, John Sack, Sirkar Van Stolk, Ruth White and Marshal P. Wilder, all of whom used their writing to help readers attain harmony.

Some singers with Ray 4 Souls and Personalities are: Pearl Bailey, Thomas Stewart and Sarah Vaughan whose melodic voices helped listeners raise their consciousness level.

Some actresses/actors with Ray 4 Souls and Personalities are: Marlon Brando, Joel Grey and Diana Ross who with their performances helped many resolve their conflicts.

Gina Severini, whose paintings uplift many viewers, also has a Ray 4 Soul and Personality.

The late Dane Rudyhar is considered by many to be one of the greatest modern astrologers. With his Ray 4 Soul, he pioneered Person-Centered Astrology, stating that one can, because of free will, attain harmony through working out conflicts. His Ray 4 Personality enabled him to lecture and write voluminously on his astrological concepts.

Ray 4 Souls with Ray 1 Personalities of Will and Power

Their Souls' Purposes are helping themselves and others attain harmony with powerful Personalities to make great needed changes through government, psychology, religion, writing or any other field.

Sigmond Freud, with his Ray 4 Soul energy, worked to establish harmony in the psyches of patients, and with his Ray 1 Personality developed psychoanalysis, bringing a great change in methodology for mental patients.

Occultist/philosopher Rudolph Steiner's Life Purpose was helping people attain harmony. His Ray 1 Personality gave him power to found an organization and school to instigate needed changes in mainstream education.

Ulysses S. Grant also had a Ray 4 Soul whose purpose was to help others attain harmony. His Ray 1 Personality afforded him much power to carry out his Purpose as a president of the United States.

Nikolai Lenin's Ray 4 Soul showed his Purpose also was to help humankind attain harmony. With his powerful Ray 1 Personality, he put into practice in Russia the doctrine of Karl Marx.

Hugo Black, justice of the Supreme Court from 1937 to 1971, was called a "Militant Humanist"—the humanist referring to his Ray 4 Soul and the militant corresponding to his powerful Ray 1 Personality.

Diplomat John Foster Dulles, a Ray 4 Soul, found his Purpose was helping others attain harmony. He certainly had the power to accomplish this with his Ray 1 Personality.

Daniel Berrigan, a priest, also had a Ray 4 Soul whose Purpose is helping others attain harmony. He was an anti-war activist who destroyed draft cards with the energy of his powerful Ray 1 Personality.

Writer George Bernonos' Ray 4 Soul's Purpose was to help people attain harmony and was noted for his powerful writing from the energies of his Ray 1 Personality.

Ray 4 Souls with Ray 2 Personalities of Love and Wisdom

Their Souls' Purposes are to help themselves and others attain harmony whose Personalities bring this about through teaching and/or healing others physically, emotionally and/or Spiritually.

Psychiatrist Alfred Adler helped others attain harmony by healing them emotionally. He specialized in child guidance, true to his Ray 4 Soul's Purpose, and with his Ray 2 Personality, healed many through his work in child guidance, delinquency and inferiority complex cases.

Minister Troy Perry whose Ray 4 Soul's Purpose is helping others attain harmony, manifested it with his Ray 2 Personality energy in healing emotionally his mostly homosexual congregation by helping them work out conflicts.

Ray 4 Souls with Ray 3 Personalities of Creative Intelligence

Their Souls' Purposes are creating harmony to uplift others while their Personalities find original ways to do this.

Simone de Beauvoir had a Ray 4 Soul whose Purpose was helping people attain harmony through working out their conflicts. She accomplished this with her Ray 3 Personality through philosophy.

Some musicians who have Ray 4 Souls and Ray 3 Personalities are: Vincent Lopez, Ernest Chausson and Sam Most who brought harmony to others through their unique interpretations of music.

Some writers who have Ray 4 Souls and Ray 3 Personalities are: Kahil Gibran, Pierre John Jouvet and Francis Thompson. They help people resolve conflicts with their innovative writing.

Some composers who have Ray 4 Souls and Ray 3 Personalities are: Ludwig Beethoven, Manuel de Falla of Spain and Giovanni Pergolesi whose Souls' Purposes to bring harmony to humanity were carried out in original compositions.

Some singers who have Ray 4 Souls and Ray 3 Personalities are: Dianne Warwick, Heino, James McCracken and Austin O. Spare. Their Purposes for earth life this time around were to aid people in resolving conflicts by raising the consciousness level of listeners because of the beauty and unique expression of their voices.

Marv Myers also has a Ray 4 Soul and Ray 3 Personality who carried out his Soul's Purpose to help others attain harmony by the upliftment of viewers with original paintings.

Ray 4 Souls and Ray 6 Personalities of Idealism and Devotion

Their Souls' Purposes are helping others attain harmony with Personalities devotedly carrying out their missions.

Helen Keller, blind and deaf author, found her Soul's Purpose was to help herself and others so stricken to read and write. Her Ray 6 Personality induced a devotion to her cause in successfully carrying out her Soul's Purpose.

Evangelist Billy Sunday's Ray 4 Soul's Purpose was to help others attain harmony. He carried it out with his Ray 6 Personality in flamboyant pulpit preaching.

Cardinal John Krol also had a Ray 4 Soul whose Purpose was to help others attain harmony. His Ray 6 Personality helped him manifest it through idealism and devotion to a cause and was directed to Catholicism which is a Ray 6 religion.

Ray 4 Souls with Ray 7 Personalities of Order and Rhythm

Their Souls' Purposes are helping others attain harmony through Personalities in a leadership capacity.

Pope John Paul I with his Ray 4 Soul found his Purpose was to help humankind attain harmony and with a Ray 7 Personality of Order and Rhythm, became a religious leader.

Frances Willard, whose Purpose was to help others attain harmony, has a Ray 4 Soul. With her Ray 7 Personality of Order and Rhythm she organized and became president of the Temperance Movement which was the impetus for national prohibition.

V

RAY 5 SOULS AND PERSONALITIES OF THE CONCRETE MIND

―⟋⟋⟋―

Enhances Logic
Color—Indigo
Gemini Sun Sign—Ray 5 Personality
Aquarius Ascendant—Ray 5 Soul
See Introduction for Possible Ray 5 Soul
for Leo or Sagittarius Ascendant

Ray 5 energy enhances the left brain (the concrete mind), giving superb rational faculties. It uses "common sense"—the five senses. While Ray 5 energy can generate success in any work demanding a high level of logic and reason, its major use is scientific research—proving or disproving validity or efficacy. It is not the energy for inventors and creators of new ideas which is the province of Ray 3. However, if you have a Ray 3 Soul and a Ray 5 Personality, you have both creative capacity and research ability to bring your work down to earth to use in a practical way. Examples are given later.

The Lord is Master Hilarion who was the Biblical Paul; the stone is the topaz; the element is the flame of fire; the color is indigo which should be used in furnishings and so on to become more in rapport with Ray 5 energy.

Ray 5, being an odd number, is masculine concerned with the intellect, self-confidence, independence, and power in action.

The work of dedicated Ray 5 Souls and Personalities who choose research have not only made living easier and more enjoyable, but have saved many lives in proving through painstaking research that certain medicines, food, cars, appliances and various other materials and procedures are either beneficial or hazardous to one's health. Choosing this work, you can offer a much needed service to humankind in scientifically proving or disproving the validity of anything that is material, such as food, medicines, appliances, machines, surgeries, travel conveyances, materials for building structures and roads, and the positions and compositions of heavenly bodies as well as means to physically reach some.

But you must be careful that you do not get out of your areas of expertise. This is so easy for scientists because of the success they have attained in the material realm. That brings to mind the "Peter Principle" resulting from a book of the same name which proves that those who are highly successful in one particular field are very seldom successful in another. Ray-Centered Astrology says the same—that each of us has a special unique Purpose. Scientists have rightly deserved trust from humanity because of success they have had in valid research, but because of this trust many people tend to believe almost anything they publish. Some scientists have foolishly taken advantage of this by publishing erroneous statements in areas that are out of their bounds.

There is a real danger here when you venture into territory which you are not equipped to validate. This is a danger not only to those who believe you, but also to your profession because as the truth comes out, science will get a bad name which will destroy some of the trust rightfully built; therefore humankind may even disbelieve the good work continuing to be done in researching material realities.

Scientists do not presently have research tools and procedures for evaluating that which is not material, not a product of the concrete, rational mind—that which is intuitive, creative and Spiritual of the higher mind. Yet they published an ultimatum signed by 186 scientists that astrology is invalid. However, ultimately they did publish a retraction, but in smaller print.

The enhanced concrete mind loves the form—the material—which is good as long as it is put in proper perspective without overemphasizing it. The form must be known for what it is—the veiling of the Spirit which brought the physical body into the earth plane.

Some Ray 5 persons believe the Soul does not exist and that human beings are only matter and at their death will be totally annihilated. They often work with the form, unaware of the Spirit behind the form. Writer Jessica Murray asks, "How do we solve poverty? Count the homeless? How do we prepare for childbirth? Accumulate and record fetal measurements? How do we understand the biology of the frog? Kill it and dissect it? And if you can't find the living Soul under a microscope, it must not exist!"

Scientific research, when carried to its ultimate in materiality and finding an impasse, will induce scientists to develop their higher abstract/intuitive minds to explain what their concrete minds are unable to—leading to contact with the Soul. There is some work being done in this area. French Scientist Jean Charon, working with computers for eight years, proved mathematically that the Soul actually exists (see Chapters XIV and XV).

Even though most scientists believe the Soul does not exist as they begin their career, many, as they get deeper into scientific thought, do indeed become aware of it.

You have a brilliant mind which can easily control your emotions and because the mind is the bridge to the Soul, you can often reach your Soul through your work. True scientists are often closer to their Souls than most leaders of organized religions. The latter are ruled mostly by their emotions resulting in fanaticism and competition, while the former often share their knowledge globally.

Ray 5 energy is very much in tune with the New Aquarian Age energies because both are concerned more with the mind than the emotions. Understanding and enlightenment are hallmarks of both. When Ray 5 people come to an impasse with their well-developed concrete minds, they are candidates for wisdom that Aquarian energies offer. Such concepts as the Universal Laws of Reincarnation and Karma, if looked into, could be readily accepted because of the logic and reason of these Laws (see Chapter IX).

Scientists are discovering principles which metaphysicians have known for ages. One is that everything in the universe is energy. You may in the future be able to measure the rate of vibration of certain subtle energies, such as love and intelligence. If you are able to prove that love is the highest vibration humankind is capable of, you can develop it easily in your own psyche because true love is unattached, free from emotion, sentiment and personal emphasis, which sacrifices, understands and acts with strength and decision. True love is not in the interest of any one person but for all humankind. All of these qualities are part of your make-up, waiting to be activated to a soulful fashion on a large scale.

Your major strengths are the ability to mentally control undesirable emotions, tendency to be unaffected by flattery and favors, perseverance, stability and the capacity to attain a high level of knowledge which can lead to wisdom. Knowledge in its highest aspect is Oneness with All. Since it is impossible to feel the Oneness of all creation without love, when you have attained a high level of knowledge, love will be a part of your essence.

Your major weaknesses are lack of love, narrow and distorted view of the truth, harsh criticism, intense materialism and inability to see the whole picture.

You often criticize concepts and disciplines different from your own, having narrow, one-pointed minds, contra-indicative to good loving relationships and Soul evolvement. When the Law of Karma gives you many difficult experiences, it shouldn't take long with your enhanced logical mind to learn your lessons and become aware of others' needs and the benefits of disciplines other than your own.

Following is a list of character strengths, some of which you now have or can have through transmutation and weaknesses you are prone to. It is unwise to repress your faults because this energy will then cause serious problems from your unconscious mind. Instead, because energy follows thought, transmute the energy of your weaknesses into specific strengths by visualizing often the following strengths, along with self-discipline. As you transmute your character weaknesses into strengths, your life becomes more successful, enjoyable and fulfilled.

RAY 5 SOUL & PERSONALITY ENERGIES

UNWISE USE	WISE USE
Lack of love	Mental control of undesirable emotions
Harsh criticism and rationalization	Precise and accurate research capacities
Blaming others for your faults	Detailed analytical ability
Not relating well with others	Unattached love
Arrogant, prejudiced and opinionated	Self-confidence and independence
Narrowness of views	Intelligence, perseverance and stability

Too materialistic	Unaffected by flattery and favors
Using right brain pursuits with left brain	Truthful, just and fair
Wasting time on wrong emphasis	Proving materialistic ideas true or false
Inability to see the whole picture	Precision and accuracy
Belief that the material is all there is	Awareness of Soul and its importance

RAY 5 SOUL OF THE CONCRETE MIND

With an Aquarius Ascendant, you have a Ray 5 Soul
A Leo or Sagittarius Ascendant may give a Ray 5 Soul
(see Introduction)

Your greatest challenge is to use your enhanced concrete mind (left brain) in practical ways with logic and reason such as in scientific research, statistics, or any work with practical application. Making a better life for others in all material ways should be your livelihood. Research is the major career of Ray 5 persons—proving or disproving the validity of everything that can be examined by the five senses to ease one's day-to-day life in helping each accept practical inventions, ideas, concepts and theories of Ray 3 Souls.

If you choose science, it is normal to throw out Spirit as you begin your career because your well-developed concrete mind is focused on brilliance in things material. But later, as you become deeply engrossed in science, this same brilliant mind will bring

Spirit back to your consciousness in all its glory. A few scientists have proven that God is found within the atom (see Chapter XV). Dedicated seasoned scientists may soon prove that God is knowledge, power and love and that through wisdom (the wise use of knowledge), they will prove that the greatest of these is love and that with love all things are possible.

Some careers of Ray 5 individuals are research scientists, statisticians, chemists, surgeons, and practical electricians and engineers.

RAY 5 SOUL AND YOUR ASCENDANT SIGN

Your Ascendant is Leo, Aquarius or Sagittarius. Although the primary indicator of your Soul's Purpose is your Ray 5 Soul, a secondary indicator is your Ascendant Sign.

Ray 5 Soul with Leo Ascendant

You are influenced by the Sun, the exoteric ruler of Leo and a ruler of Ray 2 of Love and Wisdom. Your Ray 5 Soul's Purpose, using your enhanced concrete mind, will be accomplished with independence and the awareness of what you are capable of doing to attain self-realization.

When you acknowledge and begin to eradicate your character flaws and prepare for your life work, you are also ruled by Neptune which the Sun veils and is the esoteric ruler of Leo and a ruler of Ray 6 of Idealism and Devotion. This gives enhanced inspirational capacity to contact your Soul and entities in the higher Spiritual planes and an urge for Spiritual evolvement.

When you are ready to serve others consonant with your Ray 5 Soul's Purpose, the hierarchical ruler of Leo, veiled by the Sun, which is Uranus and the ruler of Ray 7 of Order and Rhythm, is also activated in your life. This gives you unusual capacity for organizational work as a leader.

Ray 5 Soul with Aquarius Ascendant

Your Ray 5 Soul's Purpose of using your enhanced left brain to serve in a practical way is coupled with your free Spirit. This induces you to go beyond the status quo which Uranus, the exoteric ruler of Aquarius, confers upon you. As the ruler of Ray 7 of Rhythm and Order, Uranus also gives you organizing and leadership ability.

When you acknowledge and begin to eradicate your character flaws and prepare for your life work, you also receive the energies of Jupiter, the esoteric ruler of Aquarius and a ruler of Ray 2 of Love and Wisdom. This helps you understand Universal Laws (see Chapter IX) and thus, coupled with energies of Uranus, enables you to use your leadership capacity with love and wisdom.

When you are ready to serve others consonant with your Ray 5 Soul's Purpose, the Moon, as hierarchical ruler of Aquarius and a ruler of Ray 4 of Harmony through Conflict, is activated in your life. The Moon here veils Vulcan, Neptune and Uranus which, along with Jupiter, supplies you with a strong sense of unconditional love toward all—giving when there is a need, regardless of race, color, sex, religion, or level of evolvement in order to help people be who they really are.

Ray 5 Soul with Sagittarius Ascendant

Your Ray 5 Soul's Purpose of using your enhanced left brain to supply humanity with practicalities is accomplished in a directed, one-pointed way with optimism and enthusiasm. When you have attained what others may think is the final result, you work on and on for greater answers. When you reach one goal, you immediately begin to work toward a higher one because you are ruled by Jupiter, the exoteric ruler of Sagittarius and a ruler of Ray 2 of Love and Wisdom.

When you acknowledge and begin to eradicate your character flaws and prepare for your life work, you are also influenced by Planet Earth, the esoteric ruler of Sagittarius and a ruler of Ray 3 of Creative Intelligence. This gives more experiences than the average person and an enhanced abstract mind to optimally benefit from them.

When you are ready to serve others consonant with your Ray 5 Soul's Purpose, Mars, the hierarchical ruler of Sagittarius and a ruler of Ray 6 of Idealism and Devotion, is also activated in your life. Mars here gives undaunted courage, strength, perseverance and idealism to start and finish any task you deem helpful to humankind.

RAY 5 SOUL WITH YOUR PERSONALITY RAY

Your Soul's Purpose as found by your Ray 5 Soul and colored by your Ascendant has help in carrying it out through your Personality Ray energies. See Introduction to find your Personality Ray and the chapter number of a detailed interpretation. The following gives only a general idea of how to use your Ray 5 Soul with each of the Personality Rays:

If you have a Ray 1 Personality of Power and Will, you can easily make great needed changes as a result of the findings of your concrete mind, which most likely is research. You can quickly take measures to make sure that people are no longer affected by that which you prove invalid and are quickly influenced by what you prove valid.

With a Ray 2 Personality of Love and Wisdom, you would be instrumental in teaching and/or healing others resulting from your research or other practical work. You could be a great surgeon.

As a Ray 3 Personality of Creative Intelligence, you could carry out your Soul's Purpose of research or another career of a practical nature in an original, creative fashion that could intrigue others.

With a Ray 4 Personality of Harmony through Conflict, the results of your enhanced concrete mind would be expressed as a therapist or in some form of artistic beauty, such as architecture, writing, acting, dancing, music or painting.

If you have both a Ray 5 Soul and Personality of the Concrete Mind, you would not only come up with logical results in the area of your expertise, but will express these results in an extremely logical, reasonable manner so that humankind will more easily accept them.

With a Ray 6 Personality of Idealism and Devotion, the logical results you have found can be expressed with feeling and devotion to your cause of idealistically desiring to uplift others.

As a Ray 7 Personality of Rhythm and Order, the results of research or some other practical career can help others through your superb sense of order. Perhaps you will be the president of an organization having its main thrust in what comes from your left brain of logic and reason.

RAY 5 PERSONALITY OF THE CONCRETE MIND
If you have a Gemini Sun Sign, you have a
Ray 5 Personality

Your Ray 5 Personality shows that you can best carry out your Soul's Purpose, whatever it is, through proving its validity by research or statistics or in some other practical way.

Your greatest challenge is to accept and love yourself wherever you are. Then you are better able to accept and love others wherever they are (see Chapter IX). You are capable of unattached love because praise means little to you.

A tendency to criticize other persons, groups or disciplines can be transmuted through the understanding that every individual or field of learning has a different background and each has something to contribute to humanity—unity in diversity. When you have arrived at this understanding, your former separative attitude can be changed to inclusiveness.

Just as your Soul Ray is colored by a Sign—the Ascendant Sign—so is your Personality Ray colored by a Sign—the Sun Sign.

Average Gemini Sun Sign Person

You are subject to Mercury, the exoteric ruler of Gemini and a ruler of Ray 4 of Harmony through Conflict. Here, Mercury accelerates your thoughts and speech. With this enormous inflow of thoughts, you sometimes aren't sure what you really think because some of your thoughts are antagonistic to others. Yet, you love to communicate and have a charming manner, but what you say and what you think are seldom the same—your speech and behavior are sometimes irresponsible.

Your are prone to nervous instability because your self-centered personality desires versus Soul urges are strongly accented in your mind. When you have suffered enough difficult karmic lesson teaching experiences from choosing self-centered desires over Soul aspirations, you change your focus to a predominance of the Spiritual, lifting you to the next category.

Advanced Gemini Sun Sign Person

Your Ray 5 Personality which gives a practical, logical outlook on life is colored by Venus, the esoteric ruler of Gemini and the ruler of Ray 5 of the Concrete Mind. Venus here gives you the opportunity for your mind to master your emotions with logic and reason and induces you to be honest in all your dealings, enabling you to gain respect among all those you contact.

You also receive energies of Mercury but on a higher level than the average Gemini Sun Sign person. Here Mercury, along with Venus, stabilizes your mind in that it helps you to refrain from saying anything you know to be untrue—this gives you a peace that you have never known before.

You now communicate fluently, not only with charm, but with truthfulness, logic and reason. Because of your honest dealings with others, coupled with your communicative ability, people are drawn to you, giving you an opportunity to help them.

Very Advanced Gemini Sun Sign Person

You are ruled mainly by the energies of Planet Earth, the hierarchical ruler of Gemini and a ruler of Ray 3 of Creative Intelligence, giving you many experiences and original ideas.

You also receive energies of Mercury and Venus but on a higher level even than the advanced Gemini Sun Sign person. Together, these planetary energies, which you have learned to use wisely in the advanced category, are now a relatively ingrained part of your essence. You can now manifest your Soul's Purpose, whatever it is, with your innate charm, yet not with criticism, but with accepting and loving others wherever they are, and with truthfulness, logic and reason.

With Rays 3, 4 and 5 strong in your Personality, you are able to manifest your Soul's Purpose with originality, logic and intuition aligned with God's Plan for Earth.

More information for Ray 5 Souls and Personalities is found in Chapters IX, X, XIV and XV.

SUCCESSFUL RAY 5 SOULS

Following are examples of Ray 5 Souls whose concrete logical minds serve others through psychology, astronomy, meteorology, engineering, astrology, surgery, communication, bacteriology, the psychic realm, UFO sightings and research of harmful products:

Ray 5 Souls with Ray 5 Personalities of the Concrete Mind

Their Souls' Purposes are not only helping humankind with logic and reason, but their Personalities carry out their careers in practical ways.

Famous astrologer Lois Rodden, with both a Ray 5 Soul and Personality, found her Soul's Purpose was to research birth data of untold numbers of individuals to help astrologers prove the validity of astrology. She is manifesting her Purpose magnificently through her Ray 5 Personality in painstaking research for finding accurate as possible birth times using five categories for range of accuracy, resulting in a number of books published and an ongoing newsletter to help her colleagues.

Broadcast journalist Bill Moyers' Ray 5 Soul's Purpose is research and with his Aquarius Ascendant, his research attuned to New Aquarian Age ideas. His Ray 5 Personality and Gemini Sun Sign shows how he carries out his Purpose with extensive research and superb communicative ability for TV programs and writing.

Physics professor Oliver Lodge's Ray 5 Soul's Purpose was also research. His Ray 5 Personality aided him to successfully accomplish this, not in physics, but in the psychic realm, proving its authenticity and practicality.

Ray 5 Souls with Ray 1 Personalities of Will and Power

Their Souls' Purposes are to help humankind better their material lives with powerful Personalities to make needed changes in disciplines of their choice.

Attorney Ralph Nader's Ray 5 Soul's Purpose is research, and his powerful Ray 1 Personality as Safety and Consumer Advocate helps millions by researching harmful and undesirable products and services.

Karl Marx, a Ray 5 Soul, believed his Purpose was to espouse dialectal materialism (logical discussion or argumentation). With his Ray 1 Personality energy of Will and Power, he made great changes in government and founded the Social Democratic Labor Party in Russia.

Ray 5 Souls with Ray 2 Personalities of Love and Wisdom

Their Souls' Purposes are helping humankind with logic and reason and their Personalities accomplish this with healing and/or teaching.

Nuclear physicist Stan Friedman proved with his Ray 5 Soul's energy that 10% of UFO sightings are valid. His Ray 2 Personality of Love and Wisdom brought a special kind of teaching and healing to many through a deeper understanding of the universe.

Surgeon Cooley and psychology researcher N. Miller also have Ray 5 Souls and Ray 2 Personalities whose Souls' Purposes were manifested in healing.

Ray 5 Souls with Ray 3 Personalities of Creative Intelligence

Their Souls' Purposes are to help humankind with logic and reason and their Personalities accomplish this in original ways.

Danish astronomer Tycho Braha used his Ray 5 Soul energy in systematic observations and his Ray 3 Personality of Creative Intelligence in discovering that the prevailing concept of no change ever occurring in the heavens is false.

Koch's Ray 5 Soul's Purpose was scientific research. He manifested it with his Ray 3 Personality of Creative Intelligence by his original ideas along with his research, resulting in successful techniques for fixing and staining bacteria.

Ray 5 Souls with Ray 6 Personalities of Idealism and Devotion

Their Souls' Purposes are helping humankind with logic and reason and their Personalities devotedly and idealistically can manifest their missions.

The late Michel Gauquelin found that his Ray 5 Soul's Purpose was to conduct research in astrology to either prove or disprove its validity. His Ray 6 Personality gave him devotion and idealism to his cause. Desiring to scientifically disprove astrology, he and his former wife, Francois (both with degrees in statistics and psychology) instead proved statistically its validity.

James E. Groppi, Catholic priest, also had a Ray 5 Soul and Ray 6 Personality. He led demonstrations and lectured against injustice. Leaders of organized religions often have Ray 6 in their structure because of their devotion, idealism and one-pointedness.

Mary Baker Eddy, in tune with her Ray 5 Soul's Purpose, chose to prove a certain religious concept. With the help of her

Ray 6 Personality of Idealism and Devotion, she founded the Christian Science Church.

Meteorologist Henry Morton Dickson and engineer George Washington Goethals also had Ray 5 Souls and Ray 6 Personalities whose research was carried out devotedly.

Astronomer/mathematician Edmond Halley used his Ray 5 Soul's energy in observing the heavens, devoted to his cause in accord with his Ray 6 Personality.

VI

RAY 6 SOULS AND PERSONALITIES OF IDEALISM AND DEVOTION

—◦◦◦◦—

Urges upliftment
Color—Silvery Pink
Cancer or Scorpio Sun Sign—Ray 6 Personality
See Introduction for Possible Ray 6 Soul for Pisces,
Virgo or Sagittarius Ascendant

Ray 6 energy is a catalyst for uplifting yourself and others because it induces strong emotions of idealism and devotion.

The color of Ray 6 is pink. Because Neptune is a ruler of Ray 6, it is no surprise that scientists have found Triton, the largest Moon of Neptune, to be pink. An example of the brilliance and love of those highly evolved entities who control the universe: Ray 6 is the most emotional of all seven Rays and because the Moon symbolizes emotion, and because pink is the color of love, it is the best color to help you transmute undesirable emotions into love. Yet, since each Ray has all Rays as sub-rays, pink is a color that could advantageously be used by all since very few, except those who came back to help the rest of us, have attained true unconditional love.

The Lord of Ray 6 is the Master Jesus whose teachings were the basis of the Christian churches founded almost 2000 years ago. While His immediate followers raised their level of consciousness by following His principles, leaders of most organized Christian religions through recent centuries have changed or misrepresented many statements He made, such as "Other sheep have I which are not of this fold." These Christian churches have served their purpose and Jesus is slowly withdrawing His energy from Ray 6 Ashram to Ray 2 of Love and Wisdom as we are moving from the Piscean to the Aquarian Age.

In the dawning of this New Age, ever-increasing numbers of people, having experienced many lives in the Piscean Age, are ready to be guided no longer by religious leaders but by the God within—their conscience. In meditation, they know what is right and wrong for them and they know that what is wrong for them may not be wrong for another. They know there are many Paths to the Mountain Top.

The divine principle of Ray 6 is the desire for physical sensation expressed as indulgence. This is a divine principle because the difficult karmic experience that follows is the impetus to uplift oneself for a happier and better life.

The sense of Ray 6 is taste. The gemstone is the ruby. The element is water, a symbol for emotions. Ray 6 has affinity with the pancreas gland and the solar plexus chakra—the seat of emotions in the physical and etheric bodies. The way of approaching the Path for you is prayer, meditation and faith in God.

Because Ray 6 is an even number, it is in rapport with the feminine part of one's psyche and in tune with sensitivity, love and intuition.

Ray 6 energy is decidedly one-pointed which can be either a difficulty or an attribute, depending on how it is used. In its higher use, it enables you to concentrate on truth to its utmost. In its lower use, it has tunnel vision where you see only one thing at a time, where everything is either right or wrong for all people disregarding circumstances and one's level of evolvement.

When using this energy unwisely, you often force your ideals and attitudes on others. You love the truth as you see it, not aware that your truth is narrow and not inclusive. You often direct hatred intensely toward those who do not think as you do. You see no point except your own and are suspicious of others' motives and have a tendency to make trouble with those who think differently. In your religious beliefs, you often come to the point of fanaticism—believing that your religion is the only right one and tend to idolize certain leaders instead of their messages. You often emphasize the personality which is sometimes separative and cruel. The Crusades were started by Ray 6 energy used unwisely. Also the religious wars of today—fighting in the name of religion—are caused by wrong use of Ray 6 energy.

Difficult karmic experiences are the lot of all of us, no matter what our Rays are—that is the catalyst for transmuting our weaknesses into strengths. So when you have suffered enough from using your intense emotions in the ways listed above, you are ready to make deep changes in your consciousness.

You will then begin to shift your separative attitudes to inclusive ones in all areas of life. In religion, you will become aware that there are many roads to God and what is right for one person may not be right for another. In relationships, you will realize that only in treating others the way you wish to be treated, because of the Law of Karma, will others treat you well (see Chapter IX). You will change your focus of thinking that everything is either good or bad into a more wise attitude—knowing that there are many grades of good and bad as there are different grades of evolvement. You also become more understanding to those committing crimes, knowing that the Law of Karma will teach criminals in difficult ways to change their behavior, but that understanding, not anger and hate, can help the criminals to sooner change and at the same time will bring you to a higher Soul level. You learn to hate the crime but understand and love the criminal.

Being intensely emotional, you could be a great preacher or orator and can be a source of help to many when they become attuned to the New Aquarian Age principles (see Chapters IX and X). Your former devotion to a leader has changed to devotion to the truths you have recently accepted. You can now help others recognize ideals which are blueprints of ideas to aid people and to desire the good, the true and the beautiful.

Your former narrow vision turns into a wider and more healthy acceptance of everyone and each one's place in the universe. Your fiery anger can be transmuted into sympathy, tenderness, intuition and love when you become aware that none of us is perfect and that we came back to earth to have certain experiences in order to grow Spiritually. By accepting this understanding, your innate idealism, devotion and single-mindedness that was formerly used in undesirable patterns can now be manifested in ways that can not only uplift you but also others. You will know that to be dedicated to help only your group, your city, your state or your nation and disregard the needs of others is contra-indicated. You will learn that the Law of Karma applies to groups and governments as well as individuals and when your former strong national attitudes change to universal ones, you find that what is best for all humanity is also best for your nation.

Following is a list of character strengths, some of which you now have or can have through transmutation, and the weaknesses you are prone to. It is unwise to repress your flaws because this energy will then cause serious problems from your unconscious mind. Instead, because energy follows thought, transmute the energy of your weaknesses into specific strengths by visualizing often the following strengths, along with self-discipline, so that your life will become more successful, enjoyable and fulfilled.

RAY 6 SOUL & PERSONALITY ENERGIES

UNWISE USE	WISE USE
Bewildered idealism of separativeness	Idealism of inclusiveness and reverence
Emotional devotion to personalities	Devotion to just causes and truths
Anger, arguments, hatred and violence	Peace by understanding Universal Laws
Fanaticism	Breadth of vision
Forcing one's opinions on others	Respect for others' viewpoints
Selfish possessive love	Unattached love and empathy
Jealous and suspicious of others' motives	Tenderness and capacity to uplift others
Unhealthy dependence on others	Awareness of the strength within you
Prejudice—lack of understanding others' views	Sensitivity to views of others
Impracticality and self-deception	Sincerity
One-pointed narrow vision	One-pointed concentration on truths
Superstition	Intuition
Short-sighted blindness	Visualization of the good and true
Interference in lives of others	Loyalty
Desires for power, fame and riches	Aspirations for Soul evolvement

RAY 6 SOUL OF IDEALISM & DEVOTION

Virgo, Pisces or Sagittarius Ascendant—
Possible Ray 6 Soul (see Introduction)

Your Soul's Purpose is to uplift others with idealistic thoughts, behavior and strong devotion to just causes. Some careers are Spiritual lecturing and counseling, psychology, nursing, volunteer work, inspirational writing and sacred music.

You have intense emotions and are idealistic, always trying to better yourself and others. Your greatest challenge is to use your intense feelings and thoughts, not in a separative angry way, but free from hatred in understanding, loving inclusiveness. Your success in uplifting others is consonant with your awareness of their contributions, even if a different view from yours.

When uplifting others, be aware of both the God Transcendent and the God Immanent. In the past Piscean Age, we have been informed of the God Transcendent—all those entities who have progressed Spiritually beyond us and from whom much help is given on our Path. Now in the Aquarian Age, we are being taught also of the God Immanent—that there is a spark of God within each one, waiting to be kindled in most, but flaming brightly in some, and that we are divine beings who will live forever. Also that eternal damnation is a falsehood, and our difficult karmic experiences teach us lessons, and that it is our heritage to become one with God.

Everything happens for our ultimate good should be your theme in uplifting self and others. No matter how difficult one's experiences, they are blessings in disguise (See Chapter IX). The main procedure for successfully enduring difficult karmic experiences is not in fighting or running from them, but in accepting them by carrying out your responsibilities the best way you can, at the same time learning the lessons these experiences are meant to teach.

RAY 6 SOUL AND YOUR ASCENDANT SIGN

You have a Virgo, Pisces or Sagittarius Ascendant. Although the primary indicator of your Soul's Purpose is Ray 6 energy, the secondary one is your Ascendant Sign.

Ray 6 Soul with Virgo Ascendant

Your Soul's Purpose to uplift others through idealism and devotion is helped by your innate desire to perfect yourself and others, your superb analyzing and discriminative capacities and your preciseness for detailed work. Mercury, the exoteric ruler of Virgo and a ruler of Ray 4 of Harmony through Conflict, enhances your left brain for superb discriminative work and detailed analysis.

When you acknowledge and begin to overcome your character flaws and prepare to serve others consonant with your Soul's Purpose, the energies of the Moon, veiling Vulcan and Neptune, are also released. This gives you power for inspiration and capacity to see into the unconscious mind of self and others enabling the emotions and mind to work in harmony.

When you are ready to manifest your Soul's Purpose, Jupiter, the hierarchical ruler of Virgo and a ruler of Ray 2 of Love and Wisdom, is also released to you—inducing optimism, positive thinking and wisdom from understanding the Universal Laws so that you can better help self and others evolve (see Chapter IX).

Ray 6 Soul with Pisces Ascendant

Your Soul's Purpose to uplift others through idealism and devotion is enhanced by your feeling of love and compassion for the suffering and your sense of the oneness of all humanity. Neptune, the exoteric ruler of Pisces and a ruler of Ray 6 of Idealism and

Devotion, gives you a sensitivity to know where you and others are and how you can best bring yourself and others a little higher.

The energies of the esoteric ruler of Pisces, Pluto which is a ruler of Ray 1 of Will and Power, are released to you when you acknowledge and begin to eradicate your character flaws and prepare for service consonant with your Soul's Purpose. The deep and intense power of Pluto leads to fast Spiritual evolvement.

Pluto is also the hierarchical ruler of Pisces whose higher energy is also released to you when you are ready to serve others consonant with your Soul's Purpose. Here it gives you power, coupled with love, to make desired changes in your own psyche and that of others, as well as making needed changes in rapport with Aquarian Age principles in a discipline of your choice.

Ray 6 Soul with Sagittarius Ascendant

Your Soul's Purpose to uplift others through idealism and devotion is aided by your enthusiasm, positive outlook, goal-directed activity and searching nature for metaphysical truths. Jupiter, the exoteric ruler of Sagittarius and a ruler of Ray 2 of Love and Wisdom, helps you establish a positive outlook on life, coupled with a high degree of enthusiasm. The symbol here is the centaur (half human and half horse), signifying a fused duality between your selfish animalistic nature and your human thoughts.

Planet Earth, the esoteric ruler of Sagittarius and a ruler of Ray 3 of Creative Intelligence, also enters your consciousness when you acknowledge and begin to overcome your character flaws and prepare yourself to serve others consonant with your Soul's Purpose. It gives many and varied needed experiences and original ideas to optimally benefit you in eradicating flaws. The symbol here is the archer where there is still duality, but your animalistic and thinking natures are in conflict and not attached to each other.

The energy of Mars, the hierarchical ruler of Sagittarius and a ruler of Ray 6 of Idealism and Devotion, is also released to you when you are ready to manifest your Soul's Purpose with love by giving you unusual courage and physical stamina to do what you came to do this time around. The third symbol is represented here—the bow and arrow signifying a one-pointed mind which is changing animalistic desires to Spiritual goals.

RAY 6 SOUL WITH YOUR PERSONALITY RAY

Your Soul's Purpose, as found by your Ray 6 Soul and colored by your Ascendant, has help in carrying it out through the energy of your Personality Ray. See Introduction to find your Personality Ray and chapter number for a detailed interpretation. Following are only a few remarks of your Ray 6 Soul with each of the Personality Rays:

If you have a Ray 1 Personality of Will and Power, your idealistic nature, coupled with your powerful Personality, can act as a catalyst to make necessary changes in the discipline of your choice.

With a Ray 2 Personality of Love and Wisdom, your Ray 6 Soul's Purpose of devoted work to uplift others can be carried out through teaching and/or healing.

A Ray 3 Personality of Creative Intelligence gives super capacity to receive original ideas in contemplation which can be aligned with your Ray 6 Soul's Purpose of idealistic work for humankind.

Your Ray 6 Soul's Purpose with a Ray 4 Personality of Harmony through Conflict indicates a capacity for counseling and artistic expression such as writing, singing, music, painting and so on to uplift others.

If you have a Ray 5 Personality of the Concrete Mind, your Ray 6 Soul's Purpose of uplifting others can be carried out in practical ways, for example, in explaining the logic of the Universal Laws of Reincarnation and Karma and helping people see how their lives will be happier as they evolve Spiritually.

With a Ray 6 Personality of Idealism and Devotion, your Ray 6 Soul's Purpose is in harmony with your Personality, allowing easy manifestation. If you become attuned to the New Aquarian Age teachings of Reincarnation, Karma and other insights, you can become a great Spiritual leader in lecturing and writing because of your sincerity and intense feelings.

Your Ray 6 Soul's Purpose with a Ray 7 Personality of Rhythm and Order indicates that your idealism and devotion to a cause is coupled with your superb leadership and organizational capacity in the discipline of your choice.

RAY 6 PERSONALITY OF IDEALISM AND DEVOTION

A Cancer or Scorpio Sun Sign gives a Ray 6 Personality

Your Ray 6 Personality shows that you can best carry out your Soul's Purpose, whatever it is, through intense feelings of idealism and devotion to uplift others.

Your greatest challenge is to change any separate feelings into loving inclusive ones as a result of deep meditation on Universal Laws (see Chapter IX).

Average Cancer Sun Sign Person

Your Ray 6 Personality of Idealism and Devotion is colored by the Moon, the exoteric ruler of Cancer and a ruler of Ray 4 of Harmony through conflict. You are very emotional and extremely sensitive. Because you have not yet been introduced to the teachings of the Universal Laws or not yet ready to accept them, you suffer greatly when others wrong you—often going into your shell because you cannot cope with others' flaws as your feelings get hurt very easily (see Chapter IX).

You have a tendency to withdraw and isolate yourself when your hypersensitive nature causes you suffering. Become aware that your Soul attracts to you people who wrong others the same way you have wronged someone so that you may know how it feels to be on the receiving end in order to learn that lesson. Then you will no longer isolate yourself but will be grateful for those difficult experiences.

Advanced Cancer Sun Sign Person

Your Ray 6 Personality of Idealism and Devotion is colored by Neptune, the esoteric ruler of Cancer and a ruler of Ray 6, giving inspirational capacities to contact your Soul with great devotion.

Neptune's energy, coupled with that of the Moon on a higher level than the average Sun Sign person, changes your instinctual reactions of undesirable emotions when you are wronged. You are now able to understand that each of us creates our own environment because of our thoughts, words and actions. You no longer go into your shell when someone wrongs you, but now know that you have a lesson to learn from each difficult karmic experience. You have a superb sensitive nature conducive to meditation and can easily find exactly what you need to change within for learning each lesson.

Very Advanced Cancer Sun Sign Person

Your Ray 6 Personality of Idealism and Devotion is colored primarily by Neptune which is also the hierarchical ruler of Cancer and a ruler of Ray 6 of Idealism and Devotion. Neptune here, along with the higher vibration of the Moon, gives you inspirational capacity par excellence and an urge to idealistically devote yourself to a just cause. That which guided you as an advanced person is now transmuted to an even higher level into instant knowing (intuition).

You can tune in to what others need for their evolvement, whether for individual or mass consciousness. You know what to say and when and to whom to say it to be of superb help to others, especially those who are down and out—unable to fend for themselves. You are the true nurturer of the zodiac.

Average Scorpio Sun Sign Person

You are endowed with the deepest and most powerful psychic sensitivity of all zodiacal Signs. For this reason, you have the potential of sinking to the very depths or raising yourself to the very heights of living. Your Sign gives many temptations and severe testing.

You have a tendency to be exceedingly vengeful when someone wrongs you. Strong desires for fame, honors and wealth are part of your make-up.

You are ruled by Pluto, the exoteric ruler of Scorpio and a ruler of Ray 1 of Power and Will. Your symbol is the scorpion which uses its tail to sting enemies to death or when unable to escape, stings itself to death.

You suffer severely from difficult karmic experiences as you often use your intense psychic power unwisely, inducing you to become quickly aware of the results of undesirable thoughts, words and actions. Your powerful wish to change them puts you in the next category.

Advanced Scorpio Sun Sign Person

Along with Pluto's energy on a higher level than the average Scorpio Sun Sign person, you receive energies of Mars, the esoteric ruler of Scorpio and a ruler of Ray 6 of Idealism and Devotion. This gives outstanding courage and intense power to transmute your character weaknesses into strengths by bringing hidden flaws from the unconscious to the conscious mind to eradicate through understanding Universal Laws. Since energy follows thought, remember to visualize often the character strengths you wish to acquire, thus lessening the discipline needed.

Your symbol is the eagle, which characterizes your ability to rise to a higher level, to fly above materialistic concerns and thus leave behind difficult karmic experiences as a result of lessons learned. You are now in a position to be of immense help to others who are going through that which you suffered and overcame. When you have the urge to uplift others as a result of your overcoming, you are ready for the next category.

Very Advanced Scorpio Sun Sign Person

You are subject primarily to Mercury, the hierarchical ruler of Scorpio and a ruler of Ray 4 of Harmony through Conflict. Along with the higher energies of Pluto and Mars, Mercury gives you ability to become aware of difficult karmic results when one uses energy unwisely and the rewarding results when energy is used wisely. It also gives courage and power to reach a very high level. Because we can only help others to the level we have reached and because you have gone through much and have come on top, you are an excellent candidate in helping others attain your level.

Your symbol is the phoenix. Its legend is that it gives up its life and from its ashes is born a better and noble being. You have given up your self-centered materialistic desires, substituting Spiritual aspirations and are a great source of help to many.

More information for Ray 6 Souls and Personalities is found in Chapters IX, X and XIV.

SUCCESSFUL RAY 6 SOULS

Following are examples of Ray 6 Souls who have uplifted others with idealism and devotion through Spirituality, physical culture, astronomy, physics, biology, psychology and writing:

Ray 6 Souls with Ray 6 Personalities of Idealism and Devotion

Their Souls' Purposes are the uplifting of humankind with idealism and devotion with Personalities in rapport.

Helen Coulthard, a minister in England, had both a Ray 6 Soul and Personality. Because she was so dedicated from both her Soul's prompting and her Personality urge, she preached her first sermon at age nine.

Physical culturist J. Delinger is devoted to his Ray 6 Soul's Purpose of helping people better their physical health. His Ray 6 Personality gives him added devotion and dedication in accomplishing his task.

Ray 6 Souls with Ray 1 Personalities of Will and Power

Their Souls' Purposes are uplifting humankind in devoted and idealistic ways and their powerful Personalities can make needed changes in disciplines.

Nicolas Copernicus had a Ray 6 Soul whose Purpose was to work with dedication as an astronomer to enlighten humankind. His Ray 1 Personality enabled him to change the view of many when he announced that the earth rotates on its axis and the planets revolve around the Sun.

The Ray 6 Soul's Purpose of minister Jimmy Swaggert is dedication to his idealistic concepts. His Ray 1 Personality gave him much power and energy which afforded him large TV audiences for fundamentalist preaching.

Ray 6 Souls with Ray 2 Personalities of
Love and Wisdom

Their Souls' Purposes are to uplift humankind in devoted idealistic ways through Personalities which teach and/or heal.

Physicist L. Branscomb has a Ray 6 Soul whose Purpose is dedication in science, and his Ray 2 Personality shows his ability to teach and heal others through his work.

Ray 6 Souls with Ray 3 Personalities of
Creative Intelligence

Their Souls' Purposes are to uplift humankind, devotedly and idealistically, through Personalities which uplift others in original ways.

William James whose Ray 6 Soul indicated his Purpose was dedication and devotion to a cause, manifested it through his Ray 3 Personality of Creative Ideas as philosopher and psychologist and was considered one of the most influential minds of his time.

Physical chemist F. Wall has a Ray 6 Soul whose Purpose is one-pointed dedication to his work. His Ray 3 Personality gives him ability for creating hypotheses and theories.

Edward Flanagan is a dedicated Ray 6 Soul whose Purpose is one-pointed energy to help the homeless. His Ray 3 Personality showered him with creative ideas, resulting in his founding Boys' Town.

Ray 6 Souls with Ray 4 Personalities of
Harmony Through Conflict

Their Souls' Purposes are to uplift humankind, devotedly and idealistically, through Personalities which bring harmony to others.

Mother Teresa's Ray 6 Soul's Purpose is helping the poor and sick in a truly idealistic, devoted way. Her Ray 4 Personality of Harmony through Conflict gives her the energy to ideally bring them harmony through her care and unconditional love.

Author James F. Cooper has a Ray 6 Soul whose Purpose was uplifting people with dedication. He manifested it through artistic work afforded by his Ray 4 Personality.

Raphael's Ray 6 Soul's Purpose was to uplift others in an idealistic manner. His Ray 4 Personality enabled him to manifest his Purpose in helping people attain harmony by viewing his religious paintings.

Ray 6 Souls with Ray 5 Personalities of the Concrete Mind

Their Souls' Purposes are to uplift humankind, devotedly and idealistically, with Personalities that accomplish this in practical ways, such as research.

George Washington Carver, a Ray 6 Soul whose Purpose was to work with devotion and one-pointedness, achieved it through his Ray 5 Personality of the Concrete Mind in researching the industrial use of peanuts.

Biologist R. Carson and professor of chemistry S. Cristal have Ray 6 Souls and Ray 5 Personalities which foster dedication on a Soul level for their scientific research.

VII

RAY 7 SOULS AND PERSONALITIES
OF ORDER AND RHYTHM

———⟨ϕϕϕ⟩———

Gives Order and Rhythm
Color—Violet
Libra Sun Sign—Ray 7 Personality
See Introduction for Possible Ray 7 Soul for Aries,
Capricorn or Cancer Ascendant

Ray 7 energy gives organizational and leadership ability par excellence. It bestows the capacity for a high level of order and rhythm, enabling one to be a leader of a government, a group, an organization or a business with ease, efficiency and success. Ray 7 gives great power in thoughts, in the spoken word and in rituals.

The Lord of Ray 7 is the Master Rakoczi; the divine principle is creative energy; the element is earth; the sense is hearing; the stone is amethyst. Ray 7 has affinity with the etheric body—the energy field which penetrates, surrounds, and gives vitality to the physical body. Ray 7 Souls and Personalities can best approach the Spiritual Path through rules, rites and rituals.

Because seven is an odd number, this Ray is aligned with masculine qualities—power, will, intellect and action. It bestows the ability to think, create and cooperate on a high level. It is mental power—the power to build new forms and new conditions with the mind.

Ray 7's energy is a bridge between matter and Spirit. It is the power that can change physical forms through Spiritual means of certain thoughts and words. Power to build strong thought forms, which combines matter with Spirit, is an attribute of this energy. Intense and one-pointed thoughts, which can be a source of help to many, can be built easily by Ray 7 people. Because of the rhythmic and orderly way they think, speak and act, they can easily bring order and rhythm out of chaos and disorder.

Ray 7 energy brings dualities together, such as Spirit-matter, man-woman and conscious-unconscious. All of us have the capacity to bring dualities together because, no matter what our Soul and Personality Rays, each Ray has all Rays as sub-rays. It is just that the energy of one's Soul and Personality Rays is more potent than the energy of sub-rays.

One of the most helpful uses of Ray 7 energy is the ability of the conscious mind to penetrate the unconscious which stores guilt feelings, repressions and undesirable attitudes, causing untold suffering. Any found can easily be brought to the conscious mind to eradicate through understanding (see Chapter IX).

The color of Ray 7 is violet which should be used, especially by Ray 7 persons, in clothing and home furnishings to bring order and rhythm in one's life. It is no surprise that astronauts found violet to be the color of Uranus which is the ruler of Ray 7.

Because Uranus is also the exoteric ruler of Aquarius, Ray 7 energy is increasing its potency as we are now entering the New Aquarian Age of the Soul. It is this Ray 7 energy with the energy of its ruler, Uranus, so strongly in rapport with the Aquarian Age, that is mostly responsible for the unusually swift changes in government, giving many people the freedoms they deserve and urging them to be who they really are.

These energies are beginning to advantageously affect many

government leaders. An example of these new thoughts is found in the December 1988 speech that former Soviet president Mikhail Gorbachev gave to the United Nations Assembly. He said that human principles take preference over class analogy and ideology and are working toward "respect for the views and positions of others, tolerance, willingness to perceive something different as not necessarily bad or hostile and an ability to live side by side with others while remaining different and not always agreeing . . . What we are talking about is unity in diversity."

Because matter and Spirit are easily combined with Ray 7 energy, its ruler, Uranus which is a planet of instant changes, has the power to quickly bring the chaos of a government, a group, a business or an organization to order. It is through the instantaneous changes of the mind that Spirit can unite with matter, which is why Ray 7 people make excellent organizers and presidents.

Uranus and Aquarius stand for unattached universal love and humanitarian service for all, regardless of religion, race, ethnic origin, sex, age or level of evolvement. Both help change our self-centered personality desires to Soul aspirations.

Divine Ageless Wisdoms, ruled by Uranus, which have been undercover for long periods of time, are again surfacing now at the dawning of the Aquarian Age. This is the reason for esoteric Transpersonal Psychology and esoteric Ray-Centered Astrology to emerge at this time. As the Aquarian Age progresses and Ray 7 energy increases in strength, Ray-Centered Astrology along with other esoteric wisdoms will be in mainstream.

Like all Ray energies, Ray 7 can be used unwisely or wisely, resulting in either difficult lesson-teaching or rewarding experiences. Rays 7 and 1 are the most powerful of all Rays because Ray 1 is will and power and Ray 7 is power between Spirit and form. Therefore, their energies can either harm or help people immensely.

Black magic, (the use of one's thoughts and words to harm

others), is a very serious misuse of Ray 7 energy. On the other hand, white magic uses Ray 7 energy with thoughts and words to help and uplift others. Few people realize the power of the mind for good or evil. Black magic is the results of selfishness. White magic is concerned with Soul evolvement.

You also use your energy unwisely when you are rigid and impose order on others in a dictatorial manner. Bigotry, pride, arrogance, narrowness of vision, untruth, poor judgment, superstition and over stressing routine are additional weaknesses of Ray 7.

The unwise use of this energy has created many problems, such as drug and alcohol abuse, violence, killings and homelessness. Those young Souls who do not yet know how to use this energy properly receive the urge for freedom, but it is manifested without responsibility. Karmic lesson-teaching results come swiftly because children of this Age grow up quickly and therefore they soon learn to use these new energies optimally. Aquarian and Ray 7 energies which are much in rapport are ever-increasingly entering the minds of all humanity, but you have a special part to play in helping yourself and then others to use this energy wisely.

This is a time in the history of the race when the emerging of completely different energies of a new Age which happens every 2160 years demands a big change in perceptions and actions because of a step up in the evolvement of earth inhabitants. The essence of this particular New Age, being Aquarius, are strong thoughts and urges for freedom of the individual. One wise use of this energy can uplift humankind by changing governments from dictatorial to supplying the needs of individuals. Another is by giving people freedom to know who they are, to be who they are, and to know why they are here and what their unique Purpose is of service to others.

Strengths of Ray 7 are courage, self-reliance in organizational ability, meticulousness, perseverance, creativity and stamina. You also have the ability to do the right thing and say the right word at the right time to establish order and rhythm in a family, group or organization—the potential to be a successful leader You can also stimulate and refine, with strong thoughts, the physical bodies of people, animals and plants.

Following is a list of character strengths, some of which you now have or can have through transmutation and the weaknesses you are prone to. It is unwise to repress flaws because this energy will then cause serious problems from your unconscious mind. Instead, because energy follows thought, transmute the energy of your weaknesses into specific strengths by visualizing often the following strengths, along with self-discipline so your life becomes more successful, enjoyable and fulfilled.

RAY 7 SOUL & PERSONALITY ENERGIES

UNWISE USE	WISE USE
Black magic and sex magic	White magic
Dictatorial	Self-confidence
Pride and arrogance	Harmlessness
Power used selfishly	Power used helping others
Rigid and overly formal	Meticulous, extreme care in details
Over-stressing routine	Perseverance
Poor judgment and superstition	Creativity
Untruth	Finding truth from Universal Laws
Disorder and chaos	Rhythm, order and physical stamina
Freedom without responsibility	Freedom to be who you are

RAY 7 SOUL OF ORDER & RHYTHM

Capricorn, Aries or Cancer Ascendant may give a Ray 7 Soul (see Introduction)

Your Soul's Purpose is to establish rhythm and order in a group, organization, business or government.

RAY 7 SOUL AND YOUR ASCENDANT SIGN

Although the primary indicator of your Soul's Purpose is shown by your Ray 7 Soul as described in previous paragraphs, there is a secondary indicator which is your Ascendant Sign.

Ray 7 Soul with Aries Ascendant

Your Soul's Purpose to organize and lead others should be done in a pioneering way with enthusiasm, optimism, direct action and sincerity. Mars, the exoteric ruler of Aries and a ruler of Ray 6 of Idealism and Devotion, gives you much energy, idealism and courage in serving others.

When you begin to eradicate your character flaws and prepare for your Soul's Purpose, you also receive the energies of Mercury, the esoteric ruler of Aries and a ruler of Ray 4 of Harmony through Conflict. This activates your mental capacities, inducing you to help others attain harmony.

When you are ready to manifest your Soul's Purpose with the motivation of love toward all people and desire to help them evolve, Uranus, the hierarchical ruler of Aries and the ruler of Ray 7 of Order and Rhythm, is also released to you. Uranus here strongly attunes you to Aquarian Age principles, increases your intuition and gives original creative ideas along with strong leadership capacities which can elevate the minds and hearts of those you serve.

Ray 7 Soul with Cancer Ascendant

Your Soul's Purpose to organize and lead others is enhanced by your sensitivity of knowing what and when to speak and how and when to act for the optimal benefit of others. The Moon, the exoteric ruler of Cancer and a ruler of Ray 4 of Harmony through Conflict, induces you to use your energy mostly for those who are down-trodden—who cannot fend for themselves—in bringing them to a higher level.

The energies of Neptune, the esoteric ruler of Cancer and a ruler of Ray 7 of Idealism and Devotion, are also released to you when you acknowledge your flaws and begin to eradicate them and prepare for your Soul's Purpose, enhancing your inspirational capacity.

Neptune is also the hierarchical ruler of Cancer and is activated in this higher level when you begin to manifest your Soul's Purpose with love toward all beings. Here, Neptune gives excellent inspirational capacity and also brings you in close contact with The God within (God Immanent—your Higher Self) and the God without (God Transcendent—those entities in the higher Spiritual planes more evolved than you).

Ray 7 Soul with Capricorn Ascendant

Your Soul's Purpose of organizing and leading others will be accomplished with sustained hard work, self-discipline and stability. Saturn, the exoteric ruler of Capricorn and a ruler of Ray 3 of Creative Intelligence, gives you the ability through contemplation to become aware of difficult and rewarding Karma resulting from your thoughts, words and actions.

Saturn is also the esoteric ruler of Capricorn. In this capacity, its energy is released when you acknowledge and began to eradicate character flaws and prepare yourself for your Soul's Purpose by inducing you to work hard and persistently with a high level of self-discipline and by giving details for your life work through contemplation.

When you are ready to serve others consonant with your Soul's Purpose and with the proper motivation of love toward all beings, Venus, the hierarchical ruler of Capricorn and the ruler of Ray 5 of the Concrete Mind, is also released to you. Here Venus grants the ability to take the creative ideas you receive in meditation with Saturn's energy and bring them down to earth through research or in some practical form to benefit many.

RAY 7 SOUL WITH YOUR PERSONALITY RAY

Your Soul's Purpose as found by your Ray 7 Soul and colored by your Ascendant has help of your Personality Ray energies to carry it out (see Introduction for the chapter number of a detailed interpretation of your Personality Ray). Following are introductory statements of your Ray 7 Soul with each of the seven Personality Rays:

With a Ray 1 Personality of Will and Power, you are able to establish order and rhythm by making sweeping needed changes in government or any discipline.

If you have a Ray 2 Personality of Love and Wisdom, you can use your capacity to establish order and rhythm by teaching humankind that right thoughts, words and actions scientifically bring good health while wrong ones do not.

With a Ray 3 Personality of Creative Intelligence, you can establish rhythm and order in an original and unusual fashion.

A Ray 4 Personality of Harmony through Conflict induces you to use your ability for establishing rhythm and order by helping others attain harmony through counseling or artistic pursuits.

As an artist, you could combine order and structure with beauty, attaining excellent form and color—excelling in sculpture, painting, music, design and literature. You might carry out your Ray 7 Soul's Purpose also by establishing right human relations between men and women, employers and employees, and minorities and majorities.

With a Ray 5 Personality of the Concrete Mind, you can use your ability for establishing rhythm and order in proving or disproving, through scientific research, a concept in the area you have chosen for your Soul's Purpose. This might be the science of chakras, the study of electricity, the radiation of minerals or that Spiritual evolvement improves the health of the physical body (see the paragraph on Ray 2 Personalities who might teach this while you might prove it).

If you have a Ray 6 Personality of Idealism and Devotion, you can establish rhythm and order by uplifting others in showing, through a Ray 7 career, how rhythm and order in peoples' lives reduce tension and make not only for efficiency in the work place, but for better health and more success.

With a Ray 7 Personality of Order and Rhythm, you can use your Ray 7 Soul's Purpose with great power and an exceptional degree of rhythm and order. Your Soul's Purpose and your personality in carrying it out are so much in rapport that your success and joy should be great. You can be a true white magician by sending strong good thoughts to others.

RAY 7 PERSONALITY OF ORDER AND RHYTHM

If you have a Libra Sun Sign, you have a
Ray 7 Personality

Your Ray 7 Personality shows that you can best carry out your Soul's Purpose, whatever it is, in establishing rhythm and order, whether it is between persons, groups, or as a government official or leader of an organization or business.

Your greatest challenge is to use this immense power, not in pride and self-centered reasons, but with love for the common good.

RAY 7 PERSONALITY AND YOUR SUN SIGN

Because you have a Ray 7 Personality, your Sun Sign is Libra. Just as your Soul's Purpose is indicated primarily by your Soul Ray and secondarily by your Ascendant, so is the type of personality you have to carry out your Soul's Purpose indicated primarily by your Personality Ray and secondarily by your Sun Sign.

Average Libra Sun Sign Person

You are ruled by Venus, the exoteric ruler of Libra and the ruler of Ray 5 of the Concrete Mind, indicating that both socializing and logical thinking are natural and enjoyable to you.

Because you want everyone to like you, you try to be all things to all people and sometimes do not know where you stand. Although you are able to see both sides of a problem or issue, it is difficult for you to form an opinion and to take a stand—vacillation is your key word and your downfall.

When this position has caused you enough trouble because others find it hard to know where you stand, you begin to adopt some of the characteristics of Aries, your polar opposite, in that you tell yourself how you really feel and think, not that this has to be in stone but at least for the present. You no longer have an unquenchable need for everyone to like you, but instead you get in touch with your Soul and realize that it is more important to be true to yourself. You are now ready to advance to the next category.

Advanced Libra Sun Sign Person

You are ruled primarily by Uranus, the esoteric ruler of Libra and the ruler of Ray 7 of Order and Rhythm, giving you great intuitive capacity and a natural sense of order and rhythm. You also receive the energies of Venus but on a higher level than the average Libra Sun Sign person. Here, Venus not only gives you enjoyment of being with people, but your motivation is changed from self-centeredness to how you can best help others in a practical way.

Together Uranus and Venus make you charismatic because others sense both your lack of self-centeredness and your capacity for good will. While vacillation and indecision was a part of your essence in the past, now you study deeply both sides of a problem or issue and take a stand on that which you believe is better.

Very Advanced Libra Sun Sign Person

You are ruled mainly by Saturn, the hierarchical ruler of Libra and a ruler of Ray 3 of Creative Intelligence. This gives you the capacity for original thoughts along with self-discipline, persistence and hard work to overcome character flaws as well as to serve others consonant with your Soul's Purpose. You are influenced also by Venus and Uranus but on a higher level even than the advanced Libra Sun Sign person. When combined with Saturn, this not only makes you charismatic, but more importantly inspires you with creative ideas which you are able to bring down to earth in both a practical and leadership fashion in carrying out your Soul's Purpose, whatever it is.

More information for Ray 7 Souls and Personalities is found in Chapters IX, X, XII and XIV.

SUCCESSFUL RAY 7 SOULS

Following are examples of Ray 7 Souls who have established rhythm and order in their lives and in the lives of others through business, esotericism, government, communication, astronomy, music, the civil rights movement, films, banking and the stock exchange:

Ray 7 Souls with Ray 7 Personalities of Order and Rhythm

Their Souls' Purposes are leadership and organizational work and have Personalities in rapport with their Souls' Purposes.

Lee Iocca's Ray 7 Soul's Purpose is to establish rhythm and order which he definitely has been doing with help of his Ray 7 Personality as president of Chrysler. He successfully turned around this failing corporation.

Annie Besant had both a Ray 7 Soul and Personality, manifesting her Soul's Purpose of leadership and organizational work with the help of her Ray 7 Personality by becoming president of both the Theosophical Society and India's National Congress.

Ray 7 Souls with Ray 1 Personalities of Will and Power

Their Souls' Purposes are leadership and their powerful Personalities can make needed changes in businesses, organizations or governments.

Rupert Murdock, a Ray 7 Soul whose purpose is organizational leadership, changed a failing newspaper in London into several successful ones with the help of his Ray 1 Personality of Will and Power.

Andrew Jackson's Ray 7 Soul's Purpose was to be a leader and organizer. He manifested it with his Ray 1 Personality of Power and Will as president of the United States.

Julian Goodman, whose Soul's Purpose was to establish rhythm and order, used his Ray 1 Personality of Will and Power to make astounding needed changes in radio and TV.

The Duke of Wellington, the General who defeated Napoleon at the Battle of Waterloo and became Prime Minister, was in tune with his Ray 7 Soul's Purpose. His Ray 1 Personality gave him power to make astounding changes, being known as "The Iron Duke."

Albert Einstein, with his Ray 7 Soul energy, was able to establish rhythm and order in his thoughts about the universe. With his Ray 1 Personality of Will and Power, he changed radically the thinking of scientists when he developed the Theory of Relativity.

Ray 7 Souls with Ray 2 Personalities of Love and Wisdom

Their Souls' Purposes are organizational leadership and their Personalities teach and/or heal.

Lech Walesa's Ray 7 Soul's Purpose is to be a leader through establishing rhythm and order. With help of his Ray 2 Personality of Love and Wisdom, he manifested his Purpose by organizing a successful strike against a state-run factory to heal citizens of Poland and later became its president.

Yasir Arafat also has a Ray 7 Soul and Ray 2 Personality who is manifesting his Purpose as leader of the Palestine Liberation Organization, bringing about a healing for his people similar to what Walesa is doing for Poland.

Robert Haack, also a Ray 7 Soul and Ray 2 Personality, is manifesting his Soul's Purpose as a stock exchange official in a teaching capacity.

Alfred Adler, whose Ray 7 Soul's Purpose was to establish rhythm and order, accomplished it through his Ray 2 Personality of Love and Wisdom by teaching and healing others as a pioneering leader in psychology.

Ray 7 Souls with Ray 3 Personalities of Creative Intelligence

Their Souls' Purposes are to be leaders, having personalities to manifest their purposes in original ways.

Earlyne Chaney, a Ray 7 Soul and Ray 3 Personality, is co-founder of "Astara", a metaphysical group very different from other Spiritual organizations.

Helena Rubinstein, also a Ray 7 Soul and Ray 3 Personality, founded, with her original ideas, the huge cosmetic firm named after her.

Clara Barton, Ray 7 Soul and Ray 3 Personality, founded "Red Cross" and was its first president.

Mohandas Gandhi, also a Ray 7 Soul and Ray 3 Personality, was a leader for independence in India which he accomplished in an original fashion—non-violence.

Rudolph Bing manifested his Ray 7 Soul's Purpose of leadership with the help of creative ideas which his Ray 3 Personality afforded him. He was an opera and concert manager in Germany, England and Scotland and general manager of the Metropolitan Opera Association in New York from 1950 to 1972.

Organizational official Allard Lowenstein, business executive Alexander Trowbridge and director of films and commercials Joseph Losey had Ray 7 Souls and Ray 3 Personalities who were leaders expressing their original ideas.

Dr. Martin Luther King, true to his Ray 7 Soul, became a successful leader of the Civil Rights Movement. His Ray 3 Personality supplied him with creative ideas.

Nobel Prize winner Rudyard Kipling manifested his Ray 7 Soul's Purpose of establishing rhythm and order with his Ray 3 Personality giving him original ideas for writing.

Astrologer/psychic Michel Nostradamus found his Purpose was making predictions with the help of his Ray 7 Soul which gives expertise in contacting the Spirit realm. He manifested it with his Ray 3 Personality of the Creative Mind.

Ray 7 Souls with Ray 4 Personalities of Harmony Through Conflict

Their Souls' Purposes are leadership roles through Personalities which help others attain harmony, such as in counseling or art.

William Quan Judge carried out his Ray 7 Soul's Purpose as president of the Theosophical Society and with his Ray 4 Personality helped himself and others attain harmony.

Ray 7 Souls with Ray 5 Personalities of the Concrete Mind

Their Souls' Purposes are leadership roles, manifesting through Personalities with logic, reason and practicality.

Robert S. McNamara found his Ray 7 Soul's Purpose was head of the World Bank and the first Ford president outside the family. In both these capacities, his Ray 5 Personality helped him use practical methods.

Ray 7 Souls with Ray 6 Personalities of Idealism and Devotion

Their Souls' Purposes are leadership roles with personalities of idealism and devotion.

Southern Baptist evangelist Billy Graham, with his Ray 7 Soul's Purpose of leadership and his Ray 6 Personality of Idealism and Devotion, is spreading his teaching to millions in his crusade.

Frederick Flick discovered his Ray 7 Soul's Purpose was being one of the most important industrialists in West Germany. His Ray 6 Personality gave him devotion and one-pointedness for his enterprise. John Wanamaker, a Ray 7 Soul, co-founded a clothing business which became one of the largest in the United States. His Ray 6 Personality supplied him with devotion to his work.

Henry Perot, a Ray 7 Soul and Ray 6 Personality, founded his company with devotion and one-pointedness.

John D. Rockefeller Sr., with his Ray 7 Soul, founded Standard Oil Corporation and his Ray 6 Personality gave him devotion to his organization.

The above Rays and those given in the previous six chapters were calculated as described in the Introduction.

To evolve Spiritually and benefit from its Karmic rewards, it is necessary, not only serve others consonant with your Soul's Purpose, but to work on transmuting your weaknesses into strengths. The following second half of this book is dedicated to that purpose—acquainting you with the Universal Laws of Reincarnation and Karma which can show how to eliminate all anger and guilt in your psyche, various proofs indicating the validity of the system of finding one's unique Soul's Purpose through Ray-Centered Astrology and much else.

VIII

ASTROLOGY

PAST, PRESENT AND FUTURE

—◠◡◠—

What about those who made history in the past? Did they benefit from the wisdom of astrology? Most of the great minds of the past, especially scientists, did study and use astrology. Astrology is our oldest science. In fact, it is considered the mother of all sciences by the scientific leaders of the past.[1]

The quote which went back in time the furthermost was written in the second century BC by Ssu Ma Ch'ien, the first historian of China, "Since man's earliest existence, through succeeding generations, was there ever a time when the rulers failed to observe the Sun, Moon and Planets, record their motions, and expound their meanings? Raise the head, and contemplate the vastness of the Heavens, look round and marvel at the manifestations on earth! Theirs is the primeval force, and such was related by the sages of long ago."

A forefather of modern science. meteorologist-philosopher/astrologer, Johannes Keplar, wrote, " . . . characteristics of that configuration is preserved, namely the configuration that was in the heavens when the life of the human being was ignited at birth and was, so to speak, poured into the mold . . . Somehow, the images of celestial things are stamped upon the interior of the human being by some hidden method of absorption . . . Nothing exists nor happens in the visible sky that is not sensed in some hidden moment by the faculties of earth and nature." Kepler's Book IV of his principal work, *Harmonices Mundi*, is entitled, *Book on Metaphysics, Psychology, and Astrology.* He also wrote two papers called, "De Fundamentis Astrologiae Certioribus" and "De Stellal Nova."

Albert Einstein said, "Astrology is a science in itself and contains an illuminating body of knowledge. It taught me many things and I am greatly indebted to it . . . Astrology is like a life-giving elixir for mankind."

Ralph Waldo Emerson wrote, "Astrology is astronomy brought to the earth and applied to the affairs of men."

"Go forth under the open skies and list to nature's teachings." philosophized William Cullen Bryant.

Karl Jung, considered by many to be the greatest of all psychologists, said he never began to treat anyone until he drew up and studied his or her horoscope. In a letter to Freud, he confided, "My evenings are taken up very largely with astrology. I make horoscopic calculations in order to find a clue to the core of psychological truth." He wrote, "Anyone or anything born of a moment has the qualities of that moment."[2]

So that humankind could now become more aware of the history of astrology and because relevant quotes have been deleted from most published works of the past, Astrologer Robert Hand and others began in 1993 to work on "Project Hindsight." This is a collaboration between the "Association for the Retrieval of Historical Astrological Texts", founded at the United Astrology Conference, and the Golden Hind Press, a publishing company which has done work in the recovery and translation of scientific and philosophical heritage. This group aims to translate into English all surviving astrological literature from ancient times through the Renaissance. Their work covers the Greek, Medieval Latin, Arabic and Renaissance Latin. These books will be sent to scholarly journals for review and sold to university libraries all over the world.

At present, there are many great minds who are devoting all their talents, time and energy to astrology but their number is too large to list their names here.

Even though the great scientific minds of the past were aware of the validity and benefits of astrology, it has not yet been accepted by certain scientists. But the wise and courageous intellectuals who were originally skeptical of its validity have looked into it deeply before making any pronouncements and later published their findings.

The best known of these researchers are Franceau and the late Michel Gauquelin, statisticians/psychologists, who set out to statistically disprove the validity of astrology. Instead, they found, through tens of thousands of birth charts, that astrology is valid. Their research methods have been reviewed and no one has found any errors in their work.

"Daft as they seem, there seems to be nothing wrong with the Gauquelins' results," said Alan Smithers, professor at the University of Manchester, England.

Hans Eysenck of the London University Institute of Psychiatry stated, "Emotionally, I would prefer the Gauquelins' results not to hold, but rationally I must accept that they do."

A psychiatrist wrote, "Gauquelins' careful replication suggests that scientists must take the effect seriously—as some are beginning to do—rather than dismiss it as supernatural and therefore necessarily untrue."[3]

"If the Gauquelins' planetary effects are real, they are truly astonishing and lie beyond anything that science can at present understand. Like many of my colleagues, I remain skeptical," said Dr. George Abell. "Nevertheless, the Gauquelins' work has attracted worldwide attention and needs to be examined carefully."[4]

Even though astrology has a scientific basis, it is difficult for some scientists to understand because true research scientists have enhanced logical, reasoning concrete minds (left brain), while the understanding of astrology requires wholistic thinking, well-developed intuitive minds, (right brain).

Once in a while we find scientists who have both enhanced right and left brains. One of these was Michel Gauquelin who wrote, "It is worthwhile abandoning for once the 'scientification' of my results in order to examine the 'symbolic' hypothesis. At the beginning, I had little belief in it and wrote to this effect. But certain pieces of empirical evidence have shaken my antipathy for this way of seeing things. Along side the theory of the celestial bodies as physical causes, we shall discover that the doctrine of the heavenly bodies as signs or symbols is full of enigmatic indications which cannot be blindly ignored simply because we wish to remain 'scientific'."[5]

Another scientist is the noted British astronomer and fellow of the Royal Astronomical Society Percy Seymour who says that astrology is astronomically sound and has a basis in scientific fact. He holds that the magnetic Sun activity, enhanced by planetary motions, contacts the earth through the solar wind. He maintains that this magnetic activity is sensed through the earth's magnetic field and that genetic make-up determines which magnetic signals a person will respond to.

Best-selling author Thomas Moore stated, "Astrology, based on one of the most fundamental of human experiences—the feeling of wonder occasioned by celestial movements—is among the few self-contained symbol systems that can help make sense out of the chaos of life. When we feel confused and lost, we can use the sky for guidance."[6]

Just as in any other profession, not all astrologers who practice or are published are competent and ethical. But some who are have been treated unfairly. One such astrologer who received notoriety because of a suit against her was Evangeline Adams who was tried for fortune-telling in New York at the beginning of the century. After the judge heard all complaints against her, Adams, who brought no defense lawyer, was asked if she wanted to speak. She replied she would like to prove the authenticity of her work if the judge would give her the date and place of his son's birth. Adams knew nothing of the boy. Having brought with her the books for setting up charts, she quickly determined the positions of the planets and then proceeded to elaborate the character traits of the judge's son—his abilities, strengths, weaknesses and the tendencies he was showing at the present time. She not only went free, but from that period on no astrologer in New York State has been tried for practicing astrology.

Astrology is a science and an art which finds the positions of the planets and other indices at the birth of a person or thing and interprets its qualities. For the purpose of this book, only the astrology of individuals is dealt with. Each of you came into this life when the prevailing horoscopic energies were the ones needed for your special evolvement. When you took your first breath at that exact moment, all the cosmic energies were synchronized and imprinted in your consciousness. Astrology is truly the study of human consciousness.

Willis Harmon, the president of Noetic Science wrote, "A few years ago two Nobel Prize Winners—in physics and in chemistry—were asked what would be the most significant award to be made in the year 2000. Without hesitation, they both replied, 'For the study of human consciousness'."

The future of astrology is indeed bright. There is now a four year college devoted to the study of astrology—The Kepler College of Astrological Arts and Sciences in Seattle.

Is astrology in tune with the evolutionary status of the human race? As time goes on, there is a gradual evolution of humankind and all disciplines which serve it must also progress if they are to survive. But at the beginning of every New Astronomical Age which occurs every 2160 years, the changes must be monumental to equate with the new energies of the in-coming Age. That time is now! We are in the dawning of the Aquarian Age. The changes in all disciplines must be consonant with the specific energies that the New Age brings to the consciousness of humankind. (See Chapter X).

How is astrology in rapport with the new Aquarian Age energies? Aquarius is a mental Sign and because the mind is the bridge to the Soul and because Aquarius stands for unconditional love and humanitarian service, Aquarius is actually the Sign of the Soul. To be in rapport with these energies, astrology must be concerned with Soul.

Astrology in the past Age of Pisces, called Traditional Astrology, was focused toward personality concerns, such as money and love life.

The astrology of the present Age of Aquarius is Ray-Centered Astrology whose focus is Soul evolvement. The Masters of the Ageless Wisdoms have released to humankind certain Universal Truths—knowledge of the Seven Ray energies. This knowledge helps one find his or her unique Soul's Purpose for serving others, the main reason for coming into this life.

Proofs of the validity of Ray-Centered Astrology are found at the end of Chapters I through VII, the Introduction and in Chapter XVI.

The next chapter is an introduction to Universal Laws, paramount to the understanding and wise use of Ray-Centered Astrology.

Notes

1 Galileo, Copernicus, Johannes Keplar and Sir Issac Newton

2 *Synchronicity*, Karl Jung

3 *Psychiatric News*

4 *Psychology Today*, Dr. George Abell, professor of astronomy at UCLA

5 *Written in the Stars*, Michel Gauquelin

6 *Re-Enchantment of Everyday Life*, Thomas Moore

IX

UNIVERSAL LAWS
AND INSIGHTS

To understand the meaning of life and your place in it—your Soul's Purpose—knowledge of the Universal Laws is paramount.

How do most people become acquainted with the Universal Laws? It usually begins with a searching for peace. Nations all over the globe are trying to achieve peace. Government officials are sometimes able to bring this issue to the table and make initiatory progress. But there can be no lasting peace in any nation until a large number of its people has acquired peace within.

The Dalai Lama said, "We cannot achieve world peace without first achieving peace within ourselves."

Pericles, ruler of Athens, asked Socrates how to improve the city-state. Socrates answered, "When you are better, the state will be better." Socrates, as well as the Dalai Lama, knew that to have a better more peaceful government, it must begin with individuals.

Around 2000 years ago, Pantanjali, an Indian sage, wrote that to have peace of mind, four attributes are necessary: compassion for the unhappy, indifference toward the wicked, friendliness toward the happy and delight in the virtuous. This has been true down through the ages and very much true still today.

It is comparatively easy for most of us to follow the last two attributes. But how many of us can feel compassion for the unhappy without the thought that they deserve it? It is harder yet to be indifferent toward the wicked, especially when we or those we love are the victims!

The Great Ones, such as Patanjali, never suggest impossible answers to problems. Understanding is the key word. With understanding, it is impossible to hate those who commit crimes or be insensitive to the unhappy. The big question is how to acquire that understanding. The answer is found in the Universal Laws of Reincarnation and Karma.

REINCARNATION

This Universal Law holds that we have opportunities for many earth lives in order to grow Spiritually. Each earth life gives the experiences we need to transmute character weaknesses into strengths and to serve others consonant with our unique talents and abilities. What urges us to grow Spiritually? It is our Soul which knows that as we progress, less and less difficult karmic experiences will be our lot and more joy will be our reward.

Many people wonder why some children are born with certain talents. Deep thinkers know that God does not show favoritism by passing out these advantages only to certain individuals. These abilities and talents were developed in their past lives. They were not handed out to them.

Although Reincarnation is accepted by Eastern religions and three-fourths of the world's population, the West is notoriously backward in accepting it because its major religion is Christianity.

The Christian church, up until 1400 years ago, recognized and preached Reincarnation. But, in 553 AD, even though the Pope did not approve, Emperor Justinian removed the concept of Reincarnation from Christian doctrine for political reasons. Many verses were taken out of the Bible, yet a few were missed. Some are mentioned by Paul, Jeremiah, Malachi and Jesus. Others are found in "Genesis" and "Revelations." One example is in John 1:21: Jesus said that John the Baptist was a Reincarnation of Eliza.

Another proof of Reincarnation is past life regression. Hypnotists have regressed many people to past lives, some of which have been validated by historical records. Psychiatrist Brian Weiss is one such hypnotist.

Still another proof of Reincarnation has been found by Ian Stevenson, MD. He interviewed twenty children who remembered details of past lives. A full investigation proved what the children said to be true.[1]

The great minds of the past accepted this law, such as Pythagorus, Plato, Plotinus, Origin, Hume, Kant, Tichte, Goethe, Schopenhauer, Renouvier, McTaggert, Ward, Broad and Benjamin Franklin.

"When I see nothing annihilated and not a drop of water wasted, I cannot suspect the annihilation of Souls; I believe I shall, in some shape or other, always exist. I shall not object to a new edition of mine hoping, however, that the errata of the last may be corrected," said Benjamin Franklin.

Philosopher Goethe stated, "I am certain that I have been here, as I am now, a thousand times before, and I hope to return a thousand times . . . Man is a dialogue between nature and God . . . On other planets, this dialogue will doubtless be of a higher and profound character. What is lacking is self-knowledge. After that the rest will follow."

The aim of this book is to increase the readers' self-knowledge. It is not only necessary for one to become aware of Reincarnation, but also Karma to understand the justice and love of God to allow, for example, some babies to be born under the most undesirable conditions and others with the most fortunate of circumstances.

KARMA

A deeper understanding of what life is all about is found in the Universal Law of Karma. It holds that for every wrong thought, word or action of a past life or the past of this life, difficult experiences result until we have learned our lessons, and that for every right thought, word or action, rewarding experiences follow because we deserve them. There are no accidents. There is only the Law of Karma working out for our good. Our karmic experiences are the result of our past.

This Law is not an eye-for-an-eye or a tooth-for-a-tooth. God is not a god of punishment, but a God who helps us attain divinity which is our heritage. As soon as we learn a certain lesson to the depth of our beings, that difficult Karma is lifted from us. This is often referred to as the Grace of God.

How do we know that Karma is a Universal Law? Christians can find the Law of Karma in the Bible: St. Paul said, "Whatever a man soweth, that shall he also reap." (Galatians 6:6)

All people, whether Christian or not, who believe in God, a Higher Power, a Universe of Justice, can become aware of the validity of Reincarnation and Karma. They know that God does not play favorites, does not bestow unusual talents to some and not to others for no reason. They know that a just and loving God cannot let some babies come into this world with deformed bodies, retarded minds or with parents unable to love and care for them, while others have healthy bodies and minds and good parents, unless it is for their ultimate good. They know that those who many call unfortunate are working out their karmic debt. They also know that geniuses worked for many lifetimes to develop their so-called gifts; they have not inherited these capacities from their ancestors, although they may have chosen to be born in a family which excels in their expertise so they could be better understood, accepted and thus sooner manifest their capacities to serve humankind.

What is so beautiful about the works of God is that all abilities, talents and character strengths we develop in each lifetime are never lost. It is only the character weaknesses that we lose as we progress.

Because individuals make up countries, the Law of Karma operates for nations as well as individuals. We are a global community. When any nation, like an individual, is concerned only with its own welfare and ignores the problems of other nations, it brings upon itself difficult lesson-teaching Karma. The success of any nation is determined by the degree to which its people think and act, not in a national way, but in a global fashion for the common good of all countries.

With the understanding of Reincarnation and Karma, we are better able to attain the following two most difficult attributes that the sage Pantajali deems necessary to experience true peace:

INDIFFERENCE TOWARD THE WICKED

We must be aware that the wicked are young Souls who have had few earth lives and are taking first steps toward evolvement. Each of us, no matter how highly evolved we are, were young Souls in certain earth lives and were also wicked. Although it is normal to hate the crimes these young Souls commit, when we truly understand the Laws of Reincarnation and Karma, we cannot hate these people. Hatred cannot give one peace. Understanding can.

Some people may say, "How can I be indifferent to a murderer or a rapist, especially if my loved one or I am the victim?" With understanding, you will know that the wicked will suffer difficult karmic experiences until they learn their lessons. Further, you will be aware that you or your loved ones were victims to learn certain lessons. Revenge and feelings of hatred toward criminals will only bring you more lesson-teaching Karma. Understanding and compassion will help both you and the criminals evolve.

While it is necessary to incarcerate criminals to protect society, it is also a matter of prudence to aid them in their Spiritual evolvement. The best way is by helping them to know what life is all about by aiding them to understand the Universal Laws of Reincarnation and Karma.

COMPASSION FOR THE UNHAPPY

This attribute can be attained when we become aware that unhappiness, as a result of lesson-teaching Karma, is a catalyst for making necessary changes. Compassion for the suffering, rather than angry or revengeful thoughts and words, can bring peace to them and to us. While we might look down at them knowing they are unhappy because of past transgressions, if we are evolved enough to rightly judge another, it would be with loving help, not unkind criticism. No one is given more difficult karmic experiences in one lifetime that he or she is evolved enough to handle. Those who have the most severe disadvantages are not invariably the least evolved. Often they are just the opposite because they have taken on a lot of lesson-teaching Karma in one lifetime. A less-evolved Soul might require two or more lives.

The most persuasive reason for trying to attain unconditional love toward all might be that when you hurt someone, you are actually hurting yourself because your Soul is a part of the Souls of everyone.

Henry Palmer, founder of the Avatar Movement, said, "When you adopt the viewpoint that there is nothing that is not part of you, that there is no one who exists who is not part of you, that any judgment you make is self-judgment, that any criticism you level is self-criticism, you will wisely extend to yourself an unconditional love that will be the light of the world."

PEOPLE NOW READY TO BENEFIT
FROM UNIVERSAL LAWS

Humankind is slowly being informed of these Universal Laws which are part of the Ageless Wisdoms.

An example of the readiness of the public to profit from these teachings is my personal experience when my husband was suffering from Alzheimer's disease. I attended a support group and listened to the horrendous difficulties each caretaker expressed. I sensed how deeply each suffered, watching and caring for loved ones whose brains were deteriorating, causing them to act like spoiled children.

As I listened to how the words and actions of their loved ones affected these care-givers to the extent that it was almost unbearable, I wanted to help lessen their pain. I wasn't sure they would accept what was helping me, so I prayed for guidance.

I was impressed to share some of my thoughts at one meeting when I said, "I've done a lot of meditating and have come up with something that is helping me. I believe that everything that happens to us is for our ultimate good. I'm not saying it is easy, because we all are suffering immensely. Each of us is learning certain lessons from this difficult experience. None of us is perfect. We all have lessons to learn. The lessons I am learning are patience and unconditional love. It's so easy to love someone when he or she returns that love, but an Alzheimer's patient is incapable of giving love. I am reminded of what St. Francis said, 'Change what you can, and accept what you can't change, and ask God for the wisdom to know the difference.'" After I spoke, every care-taker clapped, which had never happened at any other sessions I attended. Their response told me it was well received and helped to change their attitudes.

WHY CERTAIN PEOPLE COME INTO OUR LIVES

Many people believe our difficulties are the result of the way we were mistreated by our parents. This is not true. Before we came into this life, our Souls actually chose our parents, mainly because they have the same fault or faults that we have not yet overcome. To know how it feels to be the recipient of the same wrongs we perpetrated on others in a past lifetime is the catalyst for change.

How many times have you heard teenagers say that when they have children they will never mistreat them the way they were mistreated by their parents? These youngsters have learned their lesson this time around. Some young people are not so fortunate, because it takes more difficult experiences for them to learn these lessons; they are the ones who harm their children the way they were harmed by their parents; they do not understand the Universal Laws.

It is not only our parents that we choose to help us grow Spiritually, but also our mates, children, co-workers and friends, those who have the same weaknesses we have not yet overcome. When one first meets the husband or wife-to-be, the Soul rejoices. The personality falls in love because it has an opportunity for Soul growth. But, too often, even though our Souls are happy with the union, we wish to separate when our personalities become aware of the faults in our mates. That often happens to those who do not understand the workings of the Law of Karma.

We have free will and can evade unpleasant people for a time without making any effort to resolve our problems. If we do, our Souls will attract to us the same people or others who may wrong us more deeply in that particular negative trait until we have learned the lesson of overcoming it in the depths of our psyche. This may happen in this lifetime or in a future one.

Earth lives are times of great opportunities for Soul growth.

We must come back time after time on earth to have difficult experiences until we overcome our weaknesses. Yet, all the people who our Souls attract to us do not result in lesson-teaching. Some are those who we are much in tune with us and who help us evolve.

FREE WILL

God is very patient. We can go as slow or as fast as we want in our Soul evolvement. The choice is ours. We have free will. If we drift along, using no effort to grow Spiritually, we will suffer many difficult karmic experiences, over and over. However, if we make a concerted effort to overcome our faults and serve others consonant with our Soul's Purpose, we will begin to receive more rewarding experiences, leading to joy, success and better mental and physical health.

We are our own creators. Everything that happens to us, we have set into motion from the past. Everything, no matter how difficult, happens for our ultimate good. Every unpleasant experience that our Souls attract to us is a blessing in disguise, a chance to learn needed lessons to minimize future karmic sufferings and experience more joy. It is wise to accept what happens and learn from it. We cannot evade what we have created. The sooner we learn from our difficult karmic experiences, the sooner they will no longer be a part of us. Until we do learn, they will hit us time and time again, life after life.

BLAMING OTHERS

The following understanding is not only needed by the average person but also by those suffering severe mental illnesses. On the May 1, 1995 Donahue show, a multiple personality said that cure happens when one no longer carries any hate toward parents. But, she didn't know how to eradicate it. Whether we are in pleasant or difficult circumstances, we must realize that wherever we are is the result of our own creation. When we understand this, it is impossible to blame others for our difficulties. It may be true that others are wronging us, but the fact they are wronging you or me and not someone else, means our Souls attracted them to us for needed lesson-teaching experiences. These difficulties are not punishments; they are opportunities for Spiritual growth. How can we be angry at those who wrong us if we truly understand these Universal truths? Isn't it enough to know that we are all under the Law of Karma and that difficult karmic-teaching experiences will be their lot until they have learned their lessons?

GUILT

Knowing that we are our own creators and no longer blaming others for our problems does not mean we should blame ourselves or feel guilty when we experience unpleasant circumstances or ill health. Isn't it enough to know that we are under the Law of Karma, which will give us the difficult experiences we need until we have learned a particular lesson?

I tell my clients: When you were in second grade, you didn't feel guilty or blame yourself because you didn't know sixth grade arithmetic, so why should you blame yourself because you are not yet perfect? Each earth life is like a grade in school. Each teaches us many things to reach a higher level of Spiritual evolvement. In some earth lives, like some grades in school, we become lazy and self-indulgent and may have to experience another earth life to learn lessons that particular life meant to teach. Other earth lives may be like a grade in school in which we apply ourselves and do a good job. We may then learn from this life what normally would take two lives. With this conceptual thinking, my clients are able to accept and love themselves wherever they are on their level of Soul evolvement.

Even though it is unwise to blame ourselves and feel guilty when we wrong others, it is imperative to recognize our wrongs, ask forgiveness from those we have hurt (if they are no longer on the earth plane, they are only a thought away), to make restitution if possible and to overcome that flaw. But with these understandings, we will no longer need forgiveness from those who wronged us.

REPRESSIONS

Given we do this, how about all the times in past lives and in this life when we wronged someone and felt guilty but decided we would do nothing about it? Also, how about all those instances when others wronged us and we became angry but decided we would forget about our anger without resolving it? In both cases, the guilty feelings toward ourselves and the anger toward others are repressed. These feelings go into our unconscious minds and stay there, causing physical and/or mental problems until we deal with them.

All of us at some time have been upset because of some wrong or imagined wrong directed toward us, often happening in childhood. Because we didn't know how to handle it successfully, we tried to put it out of our minds. Often we were successful in releasing it from our conscious minds, but since we did not deal with it successfully, it normally went into our unconscious causing various problems, such as nervousness, depression, anxiety, poor physical health, insomnia and so on.

To think and talk about the wrongs others have done to us causes much suffering. There *is* a way to rid oneself of repressions without experiencing one's suffering over again. It is through understanding how the Universe operates for the ultimate good of all. That understanding can wipe out all repressions from the unconscious mind without any pain. The understanding of the Universal Laws of Reincarnation and Karma will help to release repressions. When the conscious mind thinks deeply and often about the nuances of the Universal Laws of Reincarnation and Karma, it changes that which is in the unconscious mind, releasing repressions of blame and also guilt that have been there for many lifetimes. It is accomplished through our thoughts.

POWER OF THOUGHT

Energy follows thought and builds thought forms which can rid us of guilt and anger. Also, thought can either help or harm others to the degree of the strength and duration of the thought. For example, if we have thoughts of anger, revenge or any undesirable thought toward others, this energy will pull them down further if they, at the same time, have undesirable thoughts. In this case, our lesson-teaching Karma will affect us at a later time. If, on the other hand, we have wrong thoughts about others when theirs are loving and kind, our thoughts cannot touch them, but will bounce right back to us and make us doubly miserable. This is called instant Karma.

It takes hard work with our thoughts to make these concepts a part of our total essence, but it is worth the effort. With each deliberate undertaking, happiness can be substituted for pain, success for failure and love for fear. The tools are understanding of the Universal Laws, visualization (imagining we have the character traits we presently lack) and discipline.

DESTINY

What about the future? Is it destined or do we have free will? Just as we created where we are now from our past thoughts, words and actions, so do we create our future from our present thoughts, words and actions.

Famous author, lecturer and healer, Louise L. Hay, says, "I believe that all of us are responsible for every experience in our lives—the best and the worst. Every thought we think is creating our future."

Our present destiny (fate) has been determined by our past, and our future is determined by how we handle our present conditions. How can we better handle our present conditions to promise a better future? It is basically through understanding Reincarnation and Karma. With this understanding comes love.

We cannot love others unless we love ourselves. We cannot give something we do not have. Some of you may wonder, "How can I love myself if I have never received love from anyone?" It is possible to have love in your heart without receiving it from others. It comes from your Soul. It is a love you can always depend on, which is always there for you. How can your Soul, which is your true Self, not love your personality, especially when you are going though difficult karmic experiences? To receive this love, you must go into the silence by relaxing your entire body and asking your Soul for the love you need.

I had a recurrent dream for years: I lived in the house in which I had actually lived from birth through high school. In every dream, I walked to another area of the city, sometimes visiting friends, sometimes going to church and sometimes shopping, but in every dream, when it was time to go home, I could not find my house. In some dreams, I could not even find the street. In the dreams that I found the street, my house was not there. In analyzing these dreams, I became aware that I was still looking for the love of a mother or father. I had no more of these disturbing dreams when I was introduced to the Laws of Reincarnation and Karma. I knew then that I had chosen my parents because of certain lessons I needed to learn. In this awareness, I no longer craved love from them or from others, but felt a love in my Soul which I am now able to share.

Once you love and accept yourself wherever you are, no matter what your level of evolvement, knowing that none of us is perfect, you can accept and love everyone else wherever they are, even criminals knowing they are young Souls and have a difficult road to hoe for possibly a number of earth lives.

The next chapter deals with the powerful Spiritual energies that are increasingly entering the minds of humankind now, at the dawning of a new Age.

Note

1 *Twenty Cases Suggestive of Reincarnation*, Ian Stevenson, M.D., American Society for Psychical Research, NY, 1966

X

THE DAWNING OF
A NEW AGE

⎯⎯ೲೲ⎯⎯

In the Universe, there are cycles within cycles. The smaller cycles are the earth rotating on its axis causing night and day, and traveling around the Sun giving spring, summer, fall and winter.

One of the greater cycles is the sun and its planets moving from one zodiacal constellation to another. This happens once every 2160 years. It is especially interesting and exciting at the beginning of every Great Age. That time is now! We are in the dawning of a New Age. In this cycle, the earth is tuned to high-frequency transmissions of cosmic energy from the Aquarius constellation.

Each zodiacal Age has particular cosmic energies, which are needed for the continued evolvement of humankind at that time. Every Age brings with it the attributes of its essence, which it showers upon the minds and hearts of humanity.

The energies of the past Piscean Age helped humankind to develop the emotional nature: to feel what others are experiencing and to induce compassion and kindness toward others. The highly evolved were leaders of the race, who helped the masses in their evolvement. A high percentage of inhabitants in the Age of Pisces were children, Spiritually speaking.

Now, in the Age of Aquarius, most of us are Spiritual adolescents. We no longer need leaders to tell us what to do. Our blind faith in them, so helpful in the past Age, is now a deterrent to our progress. The Aquarian energies are inducing freedom in us: freedom to be who we are supposed to be, freedom to think and ·act, not with blind faith in a leader, but according to the conscience within us. This does not mean we should break the laws of the land, but that we have the inducement and capacity to change those which are outdated and unfair.

While the Piscean Age was The Age of the Emotions, the Aquarian Age is the Age of the Mind—the Age of Enlightenment. It is the Age in which we are able to find answers within ourselves, even to find God within ourselves. We are now induced to find the Purpose for which we came into this life.

It is no accident that Ray-Centered Astrology, which helps people find their Soul's Purpose, surfaced on earth during the dawning of the Aquarian Age.

At the outset of any new Age, people must be open to great changes so they can become attuned to and profit from new energies. Yet, changes taking place in this Age are multitudinous and so different from the energies of the past Age of Pisces. The reason for this is that the essence of Aquarius is revolutionary, inducing quick, sweeping, and sometimes explosive changes.

These swift changes which the Aquarian Age energy induces are basically changes in our thinking because Aquarius is the Age of the Mind. Because the mind is the bridge to the Soul, the Aquarian Age is actually the Age of the Soul. Humanity is always given from the cosmos whatever is needed at every period in its evolvement. In this, the dawning of the Aquarian Age, the need is helping us reach our Souls. One way this need is being fulfilled was the discovery of the comet Chiron in our solar system. Another way was the releasing of certain Ageless Wisdoms by Masters so that I could write *Ray-Centered Astrology* and this book.

Chiron was sighted in 1977, the same year I began writing about Ray-Centered Astrology.

Both Ray-Centered Astrology and Chiron are considered to be the Rainbow Bridge from the personality to the Soul. The Rainbow Bridge symbolically portrays the energies to help people reach their Souls. Ray-Centered Astrology does this through the understanding and beneficial use of the Seven Rays of energy, which are similar to the seven physical rays of a rainbow. The energies of Chiron help us contact our Souls by also teaching us to use the Seven Rays wisely, as Chiron is found between Saturn, the planet of the materialistic personality, and Uranus, the planet of the Soul.

When we begin to contact our Souls to make changes which the Aquarian Age energies induce us to do, we begin to feel that independent Spirit within us. This tells us we are much more than we ever imagined, that we are divine beings who will live forever, and will some day, in some earth life, have overcome all character weaknesses and will no longer need to come back on earth.

The Aquarian energies are strongly impressing our minds and hearts to serve others with unconditional love, regardless of color, religion, sex or level of evolvement.

AQUARIAN AGE CHANGES FOR EQUALITY IN RACE AND SEX

Great strides are being made in equality for people of different color. Also, women have greater acceptance in society, although the male still is regarded in a superior light by many, such as employers who pay them higher wages.

Thousands of years back in history, the matriarch society existed in certain cultures. It was believed that the female was superior to the male, and the male characteristics of each individual, male or female, were repressed.

Then more recently, the reverse was true. The male was considered superior and the female characteristics of both sexes were repressed. This is where we were a few years ago. This cycle is ending.

Everyone suffers, whether male or female, when there is no equality of the sexes because everyone has both male and female characteristics, both of which should be owned and expressed.

There is a law that, before an equilibrium is attained, situations will first swing toward one end, and then the other. Now, the Aquarian energies inducing equality in all aspects, including the sexes, are helping us attain that equilibrium.

Eventually, it will not be a swinging to the other side of the fulcrum with the current women's movements—humankind has already gone through that and has grown beyond. It is an effort induced by Aquarian energies to strike the middle way, in which not only the male and female are considered equal, but the female characteristics which have so long been repressed will blossom forth in both the male and female without negative cultural interference.

Equality is a trademark of the Aquarian energies, not equality of the level of Soul evolvement, but equality in supplying the needs of others. All of us are equal in the eyes of God, but some have had more earth lives and some have worked harder in their Soul progress. While some people are more evolved than others, the color of the skin or the sex of the physical body is no barometer. It is impossible to determine the level of evolvement of any one person by his or her skin color or sex. Most of us have had earth lives with various skin colors and in both sexes.

AQUARIAN AGE CHANGES IN DISCIPLINES

Not only are the equality of the sexes and the various races seeing initial progress, but substantial changes are also being made in all aspects of human life, as shown by the disciplines that serve it, such as government, astrology, psychology, healing, Spirituality and science.

Disciplines, as well as individuals, must make the necessary changes that the New Age energies induce. It is not a simple task for humankind to relinquish the concepts and ideas fostered in disciplines for so long a period. When we realize that most of these concepts and ideas, which once were a source of upliftment, are no longer needed and must be eradicated to make room for ideas of the New Age, progress is made.

In healing, the changes are the integration of the reductionist theory of allopathic medicine with the holism of the ever-increasing healers in tune with Aquarian Age energies which induce each individual to become responsible for his/her own health. While allopathic medicine has made great progress in surgical procedures in saving many lives, it has done much harm in prescribing most drugs and certain other agents. Medical Doctor Elliott Dacher[1] says, "Today, we find ourselves living in an extraordinary in-between-time—an uncertain transition in history between two sets of values. On the one hand, the decline of previously unquestioned optimism and faith in modernism (the dominant paradigm of mechanism and reductionism) and, on the other, we seem to be witnessing a slow, unsteady emergence of a new postmodern worldview. In this 'in-between time' more people are reaching for new values—such as holism, intentionality and personal autonomy."

In government, Aquarian energies have brought about drastic changes. The Berlin Wall came down; East and West Germany were reunited; the Soviet economy is drastically changed; Hungary and Czechoslovakia have held free elections. It looks like the Royal Family of England is becoming dissolved. Governments of country after country are being toppled over and changed from dictatorial to democratic in which the will of the people is foremost. The will of the individual is taking preference over the will of leaders, in line with Aquarian principles.

Many leaders, such as the past leader Michel Gorbachev, are much in tune with Aquarian energies. Julius Stutman of the World Institute also indicated his attunement in evaluating the New York City financial problems when he said that it is unwise to relate everything to the past. "We cannot cope until we think differently," he said.

How can we think differently? Help comes in the changes of the disciplines which serve us. Because of the enormous changes induced by the New Aquarian Age energies, disciplines must evolve if they are to survive. Yet, not all practitioners of each discipline are in tune with these new energies. Some are hanging on tenaciously to the outworn concepts, methods, ideas and structures of the Piscean Age.

At the onset of every New Age, there is always an overlapping of the old Age energies with the new, the Old Age energies gradually decreasing as the New Age energies accelerate. We have to be careful that we are not among the laggards, those leaders in various disciplines who will not release the outworn ways of the Piscean Age.

On the bright side, there are ever-increasing numbers of practitioners of various disciplines who are making necessary changes consonant with Aquarian energies to better serve the public, as detailed in future chapters.

Not only are disciplines that serve humankind changing swiftly, but there is an interdisciplinary practice forming. In the Piscean Age, it was normal for practitioners of each discipline to believe that their contribution was the end-all. Now, the best practitioners in each discipline are referring people to practitioners in other professions who can better help them.

To be in tune with Aquarian energies, not only must practitioners of every discipline make needed changes but they must recognize the good that those in other fields offer and then link their expertise with them for the optimum benefit of clients or patients.

It is imperative for interdisciplinary status to occur now because the Aquarian Age stands for the freedom of everyone to be the best he or she is capable of becoming. No longer can practitioners of any discipline continue to downgrade other professions and expect success. Only when they attune themselves to their Souls and work together when necessary, instead of downgrading all other helpful disciplines, can they continue to be successful. Because the Aquarian Age is the Age of the Soul, each discipline must change its focus from the personality to the Soul to survive.

Just as the Aquarian energies are inducing the linkage of the matriarchal and patriarchal cultures to produce equality, so do these energies induce the linkage of disciplines that are basically male (of the left brain—logic) and female (of the right brain—intuition). When the left and right brains of a person do not work together, the whole person suffers. Likewise, when quantitative disciplines, such as research and mathematics are not linked with qualitative disciplines, such as psychology and astrology, the whole of humankind suffers. There has been some successful research done proving the validity of astrology and psychology, but more is needed so that those who are left-brain oriented can accept the benefits of astrology and psychology.

We are fortunate that there is a number of leaders in various fields who are making necessary changes to help humankind through this great transformational period.

Willis Harmon, the president of Noetic Sciences, said, "This is indeed a special moment in history. We are undergoing a fundamental transformation, the extent and meaning of which we who are living through it are only beginning to grasp."

"I am convinced that at this point," wrote noted psychologist

Carl Rogers, "we are going through a transformational crisis, from which we and our world cannot emerge unchanged."

Famous psychiatrist Jean Houston noted, "Societal transformation will be based on the human species coming alive and awake to its purpose."

My field of service is astrology, specifically in aiding people to find their Soul's Purpose and helping them become aware of character weaknesses along with guidance in their eradication. Also, my Soul's Purpose includes linking Ray-Centered Astrology with several other disciplines to better serve humankind.

The next chapter is a discussion of Traditional (Piscean Age) Astrology versus Ray-Centered (Aquarian Age) Astrology. Ideas and explanations show how Ray-Centered Astrology can help humanity optimally use Aquarian energies for its evolvement.

Note

1 *Healing Values*, Elliott Dacher, M.D., Noetic Science Review, Summer 1997

XI

CHANGES IN DISCIPLINES BEGINNING WITH ASTROLOGY

All disciplines, to be successful, must transfer their focus from the personality to the Soul in these changing times. Yet, the changes in Astrology are a priori because all the Seven Rays of energy make up Ray-Centered Astrology, while each discipline described in subsequent chapters is composed of only one of the Seven Ray energies, except Psychology which receives three of the Seven Rays. It is as though Ray-Centered Astrology has the big picture and sees how other disciplines can use their specific Ray energies optimally.

The focus of Ray-Centered Astrology is leading humankind from the personality to the Soul. While part of its work is to discover a person's strengths and teach how to use them in overcoming weaknesses, it primary job is to find one's unique Soul's Purpose.

While changes in each discipline must be concerned with helping people reach their Souls, Ray-Centered Astrology has the where-with-all to pinpoint the particular discipline which is the Soul's Purpose for each person.

For every discipline to survive, it must make changes in rapport with the dawning Aquarian Age energies. In astrology, it is the switch from Piscean Traditional Astrology to Ray-Centered Astrology.

Traditional Astrology is personality-centered. It helps individuals become integrated personalities, a necessary step at a certain stage of development. One who has an integrated personality is able to use his or her body, emotions and mind for one concentrated purpose. A growing number of people have attained this stage and are ready for the next step: contact with the Soul and Ray-Centered Astrology.

While Ray-Centered Astrology uses the zodiacal Signs of Traditional Astrology, it goes far beyond the zodiac as its basis to the Great Bear Constellation. This constellation resides in that section of the universe whose energies are on such a high Spiritual level which we on earth cannot comprehend. Each of the seven stars of the Great Bear originates one of the Seven Ray energies, all of which lose some of their purity and potency as they pass to Sirius to the Pleiades to the zodiac to planet earth. If we were subjected to the Seven Ray energies directly from the Great Bear, it would probably kill all of us because we are not evolved enough to withstand the Seven Ray energies in their pure, potent form. When these energies reach us, they are in the ideal range of power to help us reach our Souls.

What is Ray-Centered Astrology? As you took your first breath, your consciousness was imprinted with one of the Seven Ray energies as your Soul Ray and with one of the Seven Ray energies as your Personality Ray.

Each of the Seven Ray energies bestows certain abilities, strengths, tendencies to weaknesses consonant with your evolvement level, and your Purpose of service for this life. Each person has a unique niche in the scheme of things that no one else can fill as well because no one else has had the same past lives and developed the same abilities as each of us has. Just as every part of the physical body of a human performs a function separate from the other parts, but all parts together work in unison for the optimal functioning of the physical body, so does every human being have as its Soul's Purpose a function separate from all other members of the human family, yet all people together work in unison for the optimal functioning of the human race.

Each of us has an important function to perform so that the continued evolvement of the race progresses smoothly. Our task is to find that function. It is written in a Ray-Centered horoscope and can be found in this book. In God's Plan, there is a special place for each of us to serve. When we find our place in the scheme of things, we begin to live in harmony and rhythm with the Universe. In rhythm and harmony there is not disease, only ease of manifestation.

The Soul's Purpose of each person is found predominately in one's Soul and Personality Ray energies and in a lesser degree in the zodiacal energies of one's Ascendant and Sun Signs in the natal horoscope. These energies are the ones needed for evolvement this time around. How we use these energies are up to us and determines our future. We can use them unwisely, thus building difficult lesson-teaching Karma, or wisely, resulting in rewarding Karma.

Ray-Centered Astrology is a product of the New Aquarian Age. Because we are now in the transition period of the two Great Ages of Pisces and Aquarius, it is only normal that some people will adhere more to the Piscean energies and thus Traditional Astrology while those more advanced are ready for the Aquarian energies and Ray-Centered Astrology.

As time goes on and the Aquarian energies increase, the number of persons interested solely in their personalities and material concerns and can benefit only from Traditional Astrology will become less, while the number of those interested in Soul evolvement and the New Age Ray-Centered Astrology will become larger.

It is not easy to have an earth life during the transition stage between two Great Ages, but we chose to be here at this period of time because we have something to contribute to this momentous cycle.

Extra cosmic help is always given humankind at the difficult, yet exciting time when opportunities for much Soul growth present themselves at the dawning of a New Age. One way is through combined powerful energies of certain planets. The most powerful and helpful was the conjunction of Uranus and Neptune in Capricorn in 1993 and 1994. This planetary energy induces swift desirable changes in one's Spiritual evolvement and affects us for many years to come. Because in Capricorn, the planets' power provides for initiation (the raising of the consciousness level of individuals).

Another example of the cosmic help given us at this time and for many future years are the energies of Comet Chiron, sighted in 1977. Every heavenly body is discovered at a time when humanity is ready to benefit from it energies. Chiron induces us to search for our unique Life Purpose through the science and art of astrology. Chiron also increases the power of a "wounded healer"—one who has suffered difficult experiences, has learned from them and is thus able to heal others.

Another way this cosmic help is given is through certain books, such as this one, which are the result of parts of the Ageless Wisdom released by certain Masters and dropped as precious little jewels when humanity is ready to benefit.

The 24 volumes of the Alice Bailey books were were released by the Master DK who wrote, in the first half of the century, "I have laid down the basis of an inner esoteric astrology which must govern this ancient science in the future. In the latter part of this century, what I have given to you will be demonstrated to be true. In the discussion upon the zodiac and its relation to the Seven Rays, the new and deeply esoteric astrology will gradually supersede the present astrology. By the end of this century, it will have won its place in human thought."

The next four chapters deal with Psychology, Healing, Spirituality and Science—how Ray-Centered Astrology can help bring them safely from personality focus to the Soul in rapport with the burgeoning Aquarian energies.

XII

PSYCHOLOGY AND
RAY-CENTERED ASTROLOGY

◈◈◈

Present psychology is a help to many, but in its infancy has yet great strides to make in serving humankind more optimally.

MAINSTREAM PSYCHOLOGY

There are a number of mainstream therapists who adhere to the "Child Within" theory. They say one must go back to one's childhood to relive difficult experiences in order to be healed.

A psychiatrist appeared on television, leading an audience through the process of reliving difficult childhood experiences. The pain that showed on their faces seemed to be almost unbearable. After reliving these difficult experiences through meditation, it was suggested that they say "good-bye" to the parents who wronged them.

Some psychiatrists who practice the "Child Within" theory even do more harm than taking clients back to re-experiencing childhood problems. As a matter of fact, they cause their clients to suffer imaginary childhood traumas, by suggesting problems that may never have been there, leading to severe illness.

The "Child Within" theory originated from the fact that problems which are not dealt with successfully recede into the unconscious mind creating physical and mental suffering. The "Child Within" theory of dealing with this is not only painful, but relieves the patient only temporarily of neurotic symptoms by placing the blame on other people or on God. Sooner or later these symptoms will resurface until clients take responsibility for where they find themselves.

Psychiatrist James Hillman believes that not only is the "Child Within" theory bad for the Soul, but that most mainstream therapy is bad for the Soul, in relieving clients of symptoms and neuroses. He states, "Most therapy is usually antagonistic to Soul. Its very premise—to relieve patients of their symptoms and neuroses—would remove the ore from which the Soul is made." He adds that symptoms are opportunities for doing Soul work. "The puzzle in therapy is not how did I get this way, but what does my angel want with me."

Some psychiatrists say that, even through Hillman's ideas are aesthetically and intellectually stimulating, they are not much help in therapy. Once these psychiatrists link Ray-Centered Astrology with their practices, they may change their minds.

There is no need to re-experience these difficulties to be cured. Ray-Centered Astrology is a successful, painless way of dealing with unresolved problems. This is accomplished in two steps.

The first step is to acquaint clients with the Universal Laws of Reincarnation and Karma so they will know that everything happens for their ultimate good. They will learn such things as the fact that they chose their parents, before they came into this life, to learn needed lessons, thus aware that they created their own reality. They will then no longer blame others for their problems, but may have a tendency to feel guilty for the wrongs they perpetrated, which could delay their future progress. In fact, some psychiatrists are aware that we do create our own reality, but fail to use this concept in their practices, for fear of instilling harmful thoughts of guilt in their clients. But this need not happen if therapists explain that none of us is perfect. That is why we had to come back to learn needed lessons. Every earth life is like a grade in school. When we were in second grade, we didn't feel guilty because we didn't know sixth grade arithmetic, so why should we feel guilty because we are not yet perfect? (See Chapter IX). This step induces clients to work diligently in overcoming their weaknesses.

The other step which Ray-Centered Astrology espouses is finding one's unique Soul's Purpose for serving others and manifesting it. As people work on these two steps, they progress to a higher Soul level which enables symptoms to just go away on their own. I have used these steps for years in my astrological counseling with excellent results.

Another prevalent treatment of mainstream therapists which is not helpful concerns treating certain nervous breakdowns caused from a neurosis. These psychologists are erroneously trained to get clients back to a personality level, when the reason clients became ill in the first place was a longing for contact with the Soul, and are ready to evolve to a much higher level. Even though the conscious mind is seldom aware of this, the unconscious is and does its best to bring about the Spiritual changes for which they are ready.

For mental health, it is necessary for the conscious and unconscious minds to be in harmony. The unconscious mind is much stronger than the conscious and always wins out finally because it has a direct pipeline to the Soul. An example of this from my own experience: one morning when my husband and I were to go to a conference in New Jersey, I became very nervous and could not go. After my husband canceled our reservations, I felt fine. Later, we found that a certain bridge, that we intended to cross, collapsed and at the very time that we would likely have been on it, killing ten people. My unconscious mind kept us home the only way it knew how.

With nervous breakdowns caused from readiness for a great deal of Spiritual progress, the unconscious rebels against conscious thoughts fed it of anger, blame, guilt, wrong values and so on and is no longer willing to accept them. So what happens? Either the person consciously makes the changes that the unconscious demands, or the unconscious will not let the person continue to function as in the past, resulting in a nervous breakdown.

It is sad that few psychiatrists are aware of their clients' achievements when they suffer this type of breakdown. Most think of them as inferior instead of their actual highly- evolved status. These therapists try to get clients back to where they were before becoming ill. If there is a remission, it does not last long because the conflict of self-centered personality desires and Soul aspirations has not been solved.

Two pioneers in Psychology are doing magnificent on-line work helping those who are suffering nervous breakdowns because of "Spiritual Emergence" (a term they coined). Christina and Stan Grof, MD. believe that mainstream psychiatry considers "Spiritual Emergence" as a mental illness, instead of "challenging stages in a potentially life-changing process." As Stan worked with traditional methods, he realized that many of the states that psychiatry calls symptoms of mental disease are important and necessary processes of healing. Christina founded SEN (Spiritual Emergence Network), a large organization which helps those suffering from nervous breakdowns caused from urges for Soul progress. People can contact this group and be directed to someone to guide them. See their book, *Stormy Search for the Soul*, for details.

Mainstream psychiatry is slowly becoming aware of the importance of Soul contact for successful treatment. Since 1993, Spiritual problems, including various forms of "Spiritual Emergency", are now in the mainstream diagnostic manual used by health care professionals and included in medical and psychology training. While this is only a beginning, pioneering psychiatrists are continuing to make their thoughts heard.

So is a growing number of mainstream psychiatrists becoming aware, for mental health to take place, of the necessity of clients to serve others with their unique talents. One such, the renowned best-selling author, Scott Peck, now believes that, to be cured, clients must know and manifest their Souls' Purposes. Some colleges are also beginning to change the focus of their psychology programs to Soul evolvement. Salve Regina College in Newport, Rhode Island has a counselor education program which prepares therapists to realize that certain symptoms do not indicate illness but are necessary for Spiritual growth.

FIRST THREE "FORCES" OF PSYCHOLOGY

Psychology has experienced a number of desirable changes since its birth. These transformations have been called "Forces" by Anthony Sutick. He, with Abraham Maslow, founded the Journal of Humanistic Psychology in 1963 and the Journal of Transpersonal Psychology in 1969. A "Force" number was given to various psychological theories—a higher number signifying a theory more advanced than the previous one.

He gave "First Force" to Pavlov Behaviorist Theory. Skinner was the first psychologist to use this theory in which external conditions—the environment—is considered, such as rewards, punishments, failures and successes instead of inner reality.

"Second Force" was given to Classical Psychoanalytic Theory, pioneered by Freud and others which is focused in the unconscious, with childhood experiences thought to be powerfully formative in development.

Sutick gave "Third Force" to Humanistic Psychology, pioneered by Maslow and Carl Rogers, in which interpersonal relationships, political activities and development of the personality are stressed, with the premise that people can choose their thoughts and actions.

"FOURTH FORCE" PSYCHOLOGY AND
TRADITIONAL ASTROLOGY

Sutick's "Fourth Force" was given to Transpersonal Psychology, also pioneered by Maslow, which focuses on manifesting the Soul's Purpose, but also on visualization, symbols, meditation, ethics, myths, hypnosis and channeling. The thinking of Transpersonal Psychology is that when one gives more attention to one's Spirituality than personal concerns of health, money and so on, personality needs are better fulfilled.

Maslow stressed peak experience (that euphoric feeling when time stands still), knowing that, when people manifest their Souls' Purposes, peak experiences often happen.

Transpersonal psychiatrist Frances Vaughan says, "Transpersonal education, like science, is concerned with knowledge and discovery of truth. It does not, however, limit the truth to objectively verifiable measurement, prediction and control. It is also addressed to questions of value, meaning and Purpose which have traditionally been the province of religion or philosophy."

The questions of value, meaning and Purpose are the provinces of both Transpersonal Psychology and Astrology. Both are beginning to focus on the Spiritual, instead of the personal. Many Transpersonal Psychologists and Astrologers are working together for the optimal benefit of clients. Also, certain colleges of Transpersonal Psychology are adding Astrology to their repertoires.

The C.G. Jung Foundation for Analytical Psychology, Inc. links astrology with psychology in its repertoire of teachings. Carl Jung said that anyone born of a moment has the qualities of that moment. He would not begin to treat a client until he drew up his or her horoscope and studied it.

"Astrology can show us a way to find deep guidance;" remarks psychotherapist Thomas Moore, "I would rather turn to astrology to expand psychology than reduce astrology to the psychological."

Richard Tarnas, a professor of philosophy and psychology at the California Institute of Integral Studies, says, "Psychology textbooks of future generations will look back on modern psychologists working without the aid of astrology as being like medieval astronomers working without the aid of the telescope."

The renowned psychotherapist Stanislow Grof states, "Astrology is, in my opinion, the only system that can successfully predict both the content and the timing of experiences."

Transpersonal psychologists have made great progress in shifting from personality concerns to the Soul. They are aware of the necessity of knowing one's Purpose in life, but have no tools to find it.

E. J. Gold states, "What I question is the ability of transformational psychology, as it exists in the United States, to actually accomplish the end of transforming the walking wounded into people dedicated to their Spiritual path. In other words, the idea and the concept make for a wonderful beginning and a great first step of hope and promise, and initial results are very good. But then, after the very first step, psychology falters! Psychology, as it is known in the United States, transformational or otherwise, falters because, right after that first step, it doesn't have the tools . . . It doesn't have the tools for transformation."

"FIFTH FORCE" PSYCHOLOGY AND RAY-CENTERED ASTROLOGY

Ray-Centered Astrology has the tools! It has the tools to find one's Purpose in life. As the next step is taken to "Fifth Force" psychology, I believe it will be linked with Ray-Centered Astrology, which has as its basis the Seven Ray energies and Universal Laws.

Ray-Centered Astrology holds that each of the Seven Ray energies confers certain abilities, strengths and tendencies toward weaknesses. At the time of birth, each person receives a Soul and Personality Ray, whose energies, when combined with those of the Ascendant and Sun Sign, are consonant with his or her abilities, strengths and weaknesses of past lives, and defines one's unique Purpose in Life.

The tools which Ray-Centered Astrology offers psychology are, first and foremost, its ability of finding each person's Life Purpose. Transpersonal psychologists are well aware that this is the a priori premise for mental health. Ray-Centered Astrology also finds one's Personality Type needed to carry out one's Purpose. In addition, it identifies and shows how to eradicate innate character weaknesses. Ray-Centered Astrology accomplishes all of this with the understanding of Universal Laws and with the new energies of the Aquarian Age.

The Universal Laws that are a priori for "Fifth Force Psychology" are those that are part of Ray-Centered Astrology, such as the importance of no longer reaching back to the past to experience the wrongs others have done which often transfers the blame for one's present problems to others. Ray-Centered Astrology holds that each of us is responsible for where we find ourselves. (See Chapter IX)

Another concept of Ray-centered Astrology which can be a salient part of "Fifth Force" psychology is the awareness that none of us is perfect, which can eliminate all guilt. (See Chapter IX)

The destiny of Ray-Centered Astrology is to be linked with psychology to uplift humankind. Just as humanity progresses step by step, so do the disciplines that serve it. "Fifth Force Psychology is" a big step up from "Fourth Force Psychology" as Ray-Centered Astrology is from Traditional Astrology.

Famous Jungian Analyst Marion Woodman knows well the importance of the cosmos to the successful practice of psychotherapy. In her book, *Leaving My Father's House*, she explains how one must manifest the masculine qualities for the strength and courage to take a trip into the feminine qualities to reach the Soul. She allegorizes this process as a princess wearing first a golden dress expressing the masculine part of her being, and then a silver dress for the feminine part, and finally a dress of stars opening up to the cosmos. Then, from the cosmos and Ray-Centered Astrology, I believe that the princess will be aware of both her masculine and feminine qualities and will know who she is, why she is here and her special niche in the scheme of things shown by her Soul Ray and how she can best manifest it, according to her Personality Ray.

The first half of this century, in an Alice Bailey book, the Master Djwal Kuhl wrote, "The true psychology will only appear and right techniques be used when psychologists ascertain, as a first and needed measure, the Rays, the astrological implications and the type of consciousness of the patient . . . The emphasis in the future will be laid upon the determining of a man's life purpose. This will be brought about through a study of his horoscope . . . Psychologists will be concerned with the revelation of the fact of the Soul and with the new psychology which will be based upon the Seven Ray types and the new esoteric astrology. The psychology of the future will direct attention to the discovery of the two Rays which govern the Soul and Personality . . . In the latter part of this century, what I have given to you will be demonstrated to be true."

Esoteric spiritual leaders are well aware of the near marriage of astrology and psychology in the use of the Seven Rays. Esotericist Torkom Saraydarian says, "The psychology of the future is the science of the Seven Rays."

Ray-Centered Astrology is helping people know who they are and why they are here with phenomenal success. Many clients say that their Ray-Centered delineations have helped to turn their lives around, from frustration and hopelessness to joy and fulfillment. One said that, before reading *Ray-Centered Astrology* and receiving Ray-Centered astrological counseling, she was so unhappy that she felt she couldn't go on any longer. Now, she is happier than she has ever been. She no longer blames her husband for her problems or feels guilty because of her flaws, but accepts where she is and loves herself. At the same time, she now accepts others and loves them. She uses all her energy, previously wasted in blame and guilt, in overcoming weaknesses and in serving others consonant with her Soul and Personality Rays.

At this stage in the evolution of the human race, it is necessary to awaken the Soul and Personality Rays in each individual to raise his or her level of consciousness, thereby contributing to the evolvement of humankind. In addition to helping individuals evolve to a higher level, Ray-Centered Astrology has another task. It is to help other disciplines evolve from personality focus to Soul and to foster interdisciplinary status.

The Master DK stresses the importance of Ray-Centered Astrology combined with psychology for Spiritual evolvement and better health of clients. He says that disease can be avoided if correct psychological training is given from youth up based on the Seven Rays and esoteric astrology with emphasis on Spiritual evolvement by overcoming undesirable habits.

A psychotherapist, who is well aware of the necessity of bringing all disciplines together, trains and educates groups, including psychotherapists, physicists, economists, judges and healers in Holland and Germany. After becoming mindful of his Soul and Personality Rays, their interpretations and insights, Hans Kortwag said, "I realize that the teaching of the Rays was of the greatest importance to my training groups. Here was the ultimate framework in which all the other systems could find their place— the connective tissue that would bring them all together."

The next chapter deals with Healing and how Ray-Centered Astrology linked with it can bring the healing profession to greater heights.

XIII

HEALING AND
RAY-CENTERED ASTROLOGY

—◦◊◦—

Mind is the healer. Our thoughts can make us ill and our thoughts can make us well. We are our own creators (see Chapter IX). Because we are not yet perfect, we sometimes harbor wrong thoughts which bring avoidable suffering. We have the power to correct our thoughts and when we do, everything becomes better. The degree of understanding and love in our thoughts determines our state of health, our level of Soul evolvement and our degree of success and joy.

There is no need to feel guilty when we have an illness. None of us is perfect or we wouldn't be here this time around. But the awareness that we create our own environment can help to change things we don't like.

It must be said at the outset that one's physical health is not always a measure of one's Spirituality. Some highly evolved Souls choose to be born with less than perfect bodies to work out much lesson-teaching Karma in one lifetime. Also, when a person is ready to change from a self-centered personality to a Soul-infused one, he or she sometimes has a nervous breakdown, signifying a highly evolved Soul.

A number of case studies has proven that wrong thoughts do make us ill. A convincing case conducted by two San Francisco cardiologists, Meyer Friedman and Ray Roseman, proved that type A behavior can increase the risk of developing coronary heart disease. These researchers found, over an eight and one-half year period, that type A men were about twice as likely as other men to develop coronary disease. They found that type A men secreted more testosterone, which contributes to disease, especially arteriosclerosis by lowering the level of "good" cholesterol HDL. They also found that the hormones epinephrine, norepenephrine and cortisol pour out when one becomes angry, which can lead to coronary heart disease.[1]

They make no distinction between type A men who used their high energy level unwisely and those who used it wisely. Type A people have high energy levels. When used unwisely, are always in a hurry, impatient, angry, hostile and mistrustful of others. When energy levels are used wisely, Type A individuals work rapidly, are enthusiastic and sincere, have positive thoughts and vigorous speech, and achieve career goals.

Though the results of this study show how one's thoughts can precipitate illness, it would even be more convincing if they had used only Type A men who manifested their energy unwisely. However it may have been difficult to determine how their energy level is used, as no astrologer worked in this study. Astrologers can identify those with a high energy level from their horoscopes and pinpoint the ones who have a tendency to use it unwisely.

Another study focused on medical students at Ohio State University who underwent psychological testing and blood tests indicated declines in their immune systems during a stress-filled exam week.[2]

Just as studies have been done by medical researchers to prove that the mind can make us ill, studies also have been conducted proving that the mind can make us well.

Growing numbers of physicians and psychiatrists are using knowledge of the power of the mind to heal their patients, with amazing results. These practitioners are proving that the mind can heal many illnesses which failed to be cured with drugs and surgery.[3]

Two healers, Drs. O. Carl Simonton and Stephanie Simonton Atchley, have had startling results in teaching cancer patients to cure themselves with their minds. They found, using group support, stress management and visualization on 159 "incurable" cancer patients that, after two years, 63 were alive—22% cured and 19% with shrinking tumors.

In another case, Stanford University Medical Center proved that women with breast cancer who participated in discussion groups, led by a psychiatrist, to change their thoughts were less depressed, felt less pain, were more positive and lived twice as long as other patients. Leader David Spiegel said, "Believe me, if we'd seen these results with a new drug, it would be in use in every cancer hospital in the country today."[4]

Cancer is caused by Type C behavior—the suppressing of feelings such as anger, hostility and mistrust. Whether one suppresses these traits as in cancer patients, or expresses them as in type A coronary disease sufferers, the only real cure is through the mind. When undesirable thoughts are changed to ones of understanding and unconditional love toward wrong-doers, healing can take place. Healing can be attained through understanding the Laws of Reincarnation and Karma, which are part of Ray-Centered Astrology. These teachings can even be helpful as a preventative measure and a means of further Soul progress to those who are not at present suffering from a serious illness.

When we wholly accept the Universal laws of Reincarnation and Karma, we will no longer feel anger toward the woman who drowned her two young sons, or the man who killed his wife. We will know they are young Souls who will have difficult karmic experiences ahead of them. We will also know that those who have progressed by having more earth lives did commit crimes in some past lives and have learned from karmic suffering. Anger and hostility toward criminals only deter their progress and our own, while understanding, prayers and unconditional love help us and them to evolve.

Acceptance of Reincarnation and Karma can avoid illness caused also by guilt from wronging others, whether on a conscious or unconscious level. The mind is also the healer here, in understanding that none of us is perfect and that every earth life helps us evolve.

Whether people suffer from anger and hostility or guilt, expressed or repressed, the good news is that a number of practitioners in the medical profession is aiding these sufferers by helping them change their thought patterns.

Endocrinologist Dr. Deepak Chopra is successfully curing patients of cancer and other diseases which traditional medicine cannot. He does it through quantum healing, which he describes as "the ability of one mode of consciousness (the mind) to spontaneously correct the mistakes in another mode of consciousness (the body) . . . It suddenly dawned on me how infinitely beautiful the immune system is and how terribly vulnerable at the same time. It forges our link with life and yet can break it at any moment. The immune system knows all our secrets, all our sorrows . . . It knows every moment a cancer patient spends in the Light of life or the shadow of death because it turns those moments into the body's physical reality."[5] He said the mind can spontaneously correct mistakes in the physical body and that a change in our thoughts can cure us. Because more people are being helped by alternative healing, the National Institute of Health created an Office of Alternative Medicine.

The mind has the power to reach every cell of the physical body because all cells have a form of consciousness. Every cell in the body can be chemically changed by the mind. Nobel Prize winner Sir John Eccles, English neurologist, said, "Consider the feats of mind over matter performed in the brain. It is quite astonishing that with every thought, the mind manages to move the atoms of hydrogen, carbon, oxygen and other particles in the brain cells."

The brain is not the mind. The brain is only the physical house in which the mind often resides. The mind can even go far beyond the physical body to every part of the cosmos; witness thoughts received from out-of-body and near-death experiences. The physical brain dies when one passes away, but the mind lives forever and is brought to the physical body at the next incarnation.

Why does the mind have the power to heal? The explanation lies in our various bodies.

The physical body is the most dense. It is the only one made of matter and the only one which can be seen with physical eyes.

Interpenetrating and surrounding the physical body is the etheric body—the energy body in which the chakras are located. The chakras are energy vortices—bridges from the higher vibrational bodies, reaching the physical body through glands and hormones. The quality and quantity of the secretions of the various hormones affecting the physical body, either undesirably or beneficially, are dependent on the quality of all bodies surrounding the etheric body. The quality of these bodies is dependent on our level of evolvement.

Surrounding the etheric body is the emotional body. When one engages in undesirable emotions, such as anger, jealousy, guilt and so on, the emotional body affects the etheric body whose chakras affect the glands, pouring hormones into the physical body which can make one ill in direct proportion to the strength and duration of the undesirable emotions. On the other hand, when one feels understanding and love toward others, the kind of hormones secreted increases the health of the physical body.

The farther from the physical body each additional body is found, the higher its vibration and the power it possesses.

Surrounding the emotional body is the mental body. This explains why mind is the healer: it has the power to change any undesirable emotion to one of understanding and love. The mind not only has the power to heal through good thoughts by secreting desirable hormones from the etheric body to the various parts of the physical body, but is the bridge from the personality (sometimes referred to as the emotional body) to the Soul.

The body which surrounds the mental body, whose vibration is even higher, is the Soul body. It is Spiritual, having the power to aid in our evolvement by helping us change character flaws into strengths and guiding us to serve others consonant with our Soul's Purpose.

A number of physicians and psychiatrists are delving deeply into the study of the glandular system, the various bodies and chakras, trying to discern how they are connected and how the mind affects the physical body. One was the late Shafica Karagulla. Another is scientist/healer/therapist Barbara Ann Brennan, who writes, "Our thoughts affect our energy fields, which in turn affect our bodies and health. We then find we can direct our lives and our health . . . We create our own reality."[6]

A plan which focuses on the use of the Soul body and the emotional body to attain physical health is the 12-Step program of Alcoholics Anonymous (which includes other addictions), pioneered by Bill Wilson. AA has helped many.

Recently there has been a number of addicts who weren't helped by this program. Although most adherents try to follow the Steps the best they can, many have relapses. Perhaps, this is because AA does not focus on developing the mental body, especially to understand the Laws of Reincarnation and Karma.

Some say the reason for relapses is that it is difficult to forgive people for wronging them, especially if they have been seriously harmed. Ray-Centered Astrology holds that forgiveness is not necessary; only understanding is, which when accomplished makes forgiveness superfluous. In fact, some people can even go beyond understanding, to sending thoughts of love to their wrongdoers for giving them the opportunity to grow Spiritually.

The AA program must now add, to the faith in a Higher Power of the Piscean Age, the working of one's mind through understanding Aquarian Age principles of the New Age. While the

12 Steps worked more successfully in the past Piscean Age of Emotion and Faith, we are now in the Aquarian Age of the Mind. We have progressed from being guided only by our emotions and faith to the urge of being guided mainly by our minds.

Other adherents of AA who have had relapses say it is because religions other than Christianity are not included, that it is not universal. The major focus of Ray-Centered Astrology is the mind which speaks of the God power within us. This God power tells us that it makes no difference what religions one adheres to or whether one is an atheist. The same principles of Ray-Centered Astrology apply to all people.

It is not only necessary to overcome our character weaknesses which AA strives toward to attain physical health, but even more important to manifest one's unique Purpose for serving others.

Best-selling author Dr. Joan Borysenko says that we heal by becoming aware of who we are really meant to be.

To attain good health, we must use our minds to contact our Souls. We must ask ourselves who we are and why we are here in these revolutionary and exciting times.

Physical health is a result of self-actualization, of doing what we came on earth this time to do—the Soul's Purpose of serving others. To attain good health, we must become self-actualized, that is manifest our Soul's Purpose. The late renowned psychologist Abraham Maslow stated that people become sick when self-actualization is blocked. Illness is the result of our failure to manifest our unique Soul's Purpose.

One who knows this well is Dr. Rachel Naomi Remen, scientific advisory board member of the Institute for Advancement of Health, who wrote, "How we live is not as important to me as why we live, why we are here in these bodies . . . Health is not an end. Health is a means. Health enables us to serve purpose in life, but it is not the purpose in life . . . There is a general lack of meaning and purpose and significance that seems to underlie illness."

Dr. Deepak Chopra relates a study by scientists at Harvard School of Public Health who checked risk factors of heart attack. They found that the majority of people who died of heart attacks before age 60 do not have any one of the major risk factors which are considered to be smoking, hypertension, cholesterol and family history. They found that the number one predictor was job dissatisfaction. When one is dissatisfied with one's job, it is not one's Life Purpose.

Following is an example of how one person who became "terminally ill" was cured by finding and manifesting her Soul's Purpose. Singer and dancer Lola Filano contacted muscular dystrophy. She couldn't move her head, arms or legs. Filano was told by her doctor that she had a short time to live. She decided otherwise and dedicated her life to finding and manifesting her Soul's Purpose. In two month's time, she found it. She was able to walk then. Her Purpose was to found a "help network" in television, named "Call-a-Thon." With the help of experts, she intends to dedicate her life to solving problems of any kind that are called in. Physical death occurs when one can no longer evolve Spiritually in this lifetime. Lola's Soul made her physically ill, because dancing and singing were not her Life Purpose.

Practitioners in many disciplines believe that the a priori requisite for good health is manifesting one's Life Purpose. There is a burgeoning number of professionals who are now trying to cure people by helping them find their Souls' Purposes.

Scientist/healer/therapist Barbara Ann Brennan, who is dramatically healing others through working on their etheric, emotional, mental and sometimes Soul bodies, maintains that "the first important principle for good health is maintaining a deep connection to self and purpose in this life."

Even though many people are becoming aware of the importance of expressing their Soul's Purpose, few are able to find it.

Best-selling author Bernie Seigel M.D. states, "The blueprint for you to be your authentic self lies within. In some mystical way the microscopic egg that grew to be you had the program for your physical, intellectual, emotional and spiritual development."[7]

This blueprint can be found in Ray-Centered Astrology through interpretation of one's Soul and Personality Rays, Ascendant and Sun Sign.

The Master DK stated that the astrology of the past concerned the personality, but the astrology of the future is of the Soul and its Purpose as indicated by one's Soul and Personality Rays and that Ray-Centered Astrology will completely change medicine as well as other disciplines. He added that the basic energies pouring into the etheric body condition the physical body from the Ray energy of the Soul and the Ray energy of the Personality.

Soul evolvement is the reason each of us is here on earth, yet how few are aware of this! How many waste precious days and years seeking self-centered desires which give no lasting joy— only pain, suffering and poor health. As more people find and manifest their Soul's Purpose, not only will they enjoy good health, but the earth will then become closer to a place of light, love, joy and beauty.

The next chapter discusses the linkage of Ray-Centered Astrology and Spirituality.

Notes

1 *The Trusting Heart*, Redford Williams, M.D., Times Books, 1989

2 *Hippocrates* magazine

3 *Healing and the Mind*, book and television documentary, Bill Moyers, 1993

4 *Hippocrates* magazine, David Speigel

5 *Quantum Healing*, Dr. Deepak Chopra, Bantam, NY, 1990

6 *Hands of Light*, Barbara Ann Branan, Bantam, NY, 1988

7 *Love, Medicine and Miracles*, Bernie Seigel

XIV

SPIRITUALITY AND RAY-CENTERED ASTROLOGY

—∽∾∿∾∽—

To really know what Spirituality is in all its facets, we must first know what it is not. It is not religion which is a dogma of beliefs and practices, often tending to be exclusive, causing hatred and even wars in its name.

Neither is it moral/ethics (the right and wrong of certain actions) which vary from culture to culture and from time cycle to time cycle.

It is also not the sixth sense (the psychic) which is often used in a self-centered way.

It is none of these things in its average use, yet it is all of these things when each operates at its higher level of universality, understanding, love and attunement with the energies of the present Great Age.

Spirituality is the process of raising one's level of consciousness. Spirituality is not static. The consciousness of humankind elevates as time goes on. When we had earth lives in the past Piscean Age, Spirituality was very different from that of the previous Age of Aries, as it was also different from the New Aquarian Age we are now entering. Although there have been young Souls coming into the earth plane in every Great Age who have had very few earth lives, every Great Age finds a higher level of evolvement of humankind in general than the previous one.

215

Why are Spirituality and Ray-Centered Astrology so closely related? Following are some of the answers:

BOTH IN RAPPORT WITH THE NEW
AQUARIAN ENERGIES

The essence of Spirituality is always its attunement with the energies of the Age humanity is experiencing. Ray-Centered Astrology, while only recently pioneered from Ancient Wisdoms released by certain Masters, is a product of the New Aquarian Age. As each New Age comes into being, humankind takes a big step up in its Spiritual progression. This is induced by the new energies and the releasing, by certain Masters, parts of the Ageless Wisdom which the race can benefit from at that time. Both Spirituality of the present and Ray-Centered Astrology vibrate in unison with Aquarian energies stressing universality, unconditional love, service, and the freedom to be who we are and to know why we are here.

There are still some religious leaders who are not in tune with the New Aquarian energies and who are tenaciously hanging on to outworn religious ideas of the Piscean Age—ideas such as preaching eternal hell and damnation for those who have not overcome certain weaknesses. Perhaps this was necessary for the spiritual children we were in the past Age to protect us from each other. But we now know that none of us will suffer eternally, but that our karmic suffering is lessened as we begin to overcome our flaws. Like parents who have strict rules for their children but gradually release them at adolescence so that their offspring will become more independent, we are leaving religious leaders who are not attuned to the New Aquarian energies so we can make our own decisions for our Spiritual progress.

Some religious leaders who are resistant to the New Aquarian

energies believe that their religion is the only true one. They are
fighting the new energies which induce unconditional love for all
people. There are certain religious sects that preach, "To be
saved, you must be a Christian." Yet we find in the Bible that
Christ, when talking to Christians, said, "Other sheep have I
which are not of this fold."

Even though we may not espouse Spiritual beliefs of others,
it is folly to disrespect them. We should know that some people
are not yet ready for higher ones. Each of us is part of the human
race, part of the whole. We cannot feel disrespect by hurting
some who are part of the whole without causing suffering also to
ourselves. As an analogy: if a pianist is concerned only with his or
her hands and if a foot is cut badly and the bleeding is not
stopped, the whole body will suffer.

Both Ray-Centered Astrology and present Spirituality hold
that there are many roads to God. The religion or path that one
takes may not be right for another. No matter what your Spiritual
beliefs, if they are helping you become a better person and you
feel good with your beliefs, they are right for you at this time. If
or when you begin to question or become dissatisfied with them,
you are ready to search for higher ones. As we progress Spiritually, we find that we turn more and more to the God within and
less to organized religions. A. Wilder in *Ancient and Modern
Prophecy* says, "A man can have no god that is not bounded by
his own human conceptions. The wider the sweep of his spiritual
vision, the mightier will be his deity."

Satya Sai Baba, one of the highest evolved entities on earth
today, said, "It is good to be born in a church, but it is not good to
die in it. Grow and rescue yourselves from the limits and regulations, the doctrines that fence in your freedom of thought, the
ceremonials and rites that restrict and direct. Reach the point
where churches do not matter . . . Pardon the other man's faults,
but deal harshly with your own . . . Today people try to find God
in religions but God is to be found not in religion but in your own

mind (heart). It is only when the mind is controlled and purified that God can be recognized."

THE ESSENCE OF BOTH ARE THE UNIVERSAL LAWS

Why does one who is working on Spiritual evolvement gravitate to Ray-Centered Astrology and why does one who is interested in Ray-Centered Astrology become more concerned with Spiritual progress? The answers lie in the essence of each which are the Universal Laws, especially Reincarnation and Karma. Spirituality is the process of raising one's level of consciousness with the aid of the Universal Laws by overcoming character weaknesses and by serving others consonant with one's unique Soul's Purpose. Ray-Centered Astrology is an excellent tool to help raise one's consciousness level in overcoming flaws and in finding and manifesting one's Purpose in life.

With the understanding of Reincarnation and Karma, we know that we will live forever—that we are divine, gods in the making. We then also know that we are given opportunities of many earth lives to progress Spiritually, and that each of us creates our own environment, our own destiny.

BOTH ARE INCLUSIVE OF ALL PEOPLES

Both Spirituality and Ray-Centered Astrology are non-separative, including all people, regardless of race, color, sex, religion or level of Soul evolvement. Neither is concerned with only one religion. They include all who either believe or do not believe in God which is the entire human race.

BOTH HOLD THAT THOUGHTS DETERMINE LEVEL OF EVOLVEMENT

Our thoughts are the index to our Spiritual evolvement. We have free will and when we become aware of an undesirable thought, we have the power to change it. Every step of this kind is a step up in our progress and also reflects in better physical and emotional health as well as success and joy in life.

Our Spiritual, mental and emotional bodies are not of the earth so we take them with us when we pass away from the physical plane. When our physical bodies have deteriorated to the extent we cannot any more change character weaknesses into strengths nor serve others consonant with our Soul's Purpose, they will be discarded in death. Our physical bodies are of the earth and will be given back to the earth when so-called death happens. The real us (our Spirit) will live forever.

Our brains may fail to function because of certain illnesses, such As Alzheimer's Disease or senility, causing our minds to be severely limited, but the brain is not the mind. The brain is only a house for the mind while on earth, and if the house deteriorates, our minds cannot function properly while our Spirits are still in the physical body. When our Spirits leave the earth, our minds return to their state before we became ill.

BOTH SATISFY ONE'S INNER SEARCHING

More and more people are becoming dissatisfied with putting all their energy into material pursuits of entertainment, wealth, power, fame, honors and sex, but are continually searching and reaching for something better, something more satisfying. They know there is more to life, yet they know not what! Philosopher Jacob Needleman says, "People are starving and they don't know why." Both Spirituality and Ray-Centered Astrology satisfy that gnawing feeling of searching for something higher that each of us has within.

BOTH STRESS UNCONDITIONAL LOVE

Both hold that unconditional love is the most important trait for Soul evolvement. The importance of love can best be described by one who has attained divinity, Sai Baba, "Love is your real nature and it is your duty to express what is already inherent in you . . . Whoever you are, whatever you do, if you do not have love in your heart, your life is virtually useless."

The Christian Bible speaks about faith, hope and love and that the greatest of these is love. It is often quoted that "God is love." While Ray-Centered Astrology speaks this same language of love as found in Spirituality, it goes a step further in explaining why love is a priori for Soul evolvement.

The explanation lies with the understanding of the Seven Ray energies and the cosmos. Just as each of you has a Soul Ray indicating your Soul's Purpose and a physical body to manifest your Purpose, so do all the very highly evolved entities have Soul Rays whose physical bodies of the stars and planets manifest their Purposes.

Because our Sun is the center of our solar system, the entity controlling it is our God, from whom we receive all substance, Spiritual as well as material. To progress Spiritually, we must strive to attain the energies of the Soul Ray of the controlling entity of the center of our solar system which is Ray 2 of Love and Wisdom. In understanding Ancient Wisdoms found in Ray-Centered Astrology and making them a part of us, we can climb the ladder to unconditional love for all people to become closer to God while living in this solar system.

If we lived on a planet revolving around a Sun in a different solar system whose controlling entity has a Ray 1 Soul, our God would be a God of Will and Power. Thus willpower would be the most important trait to develop in order to become more Spiritual.

Even though it is necessary to strive mostly for the positive specific energies of the Soul Ray of the controlling entity of our Sun, we must also make a strong effort to attain the desirable traits of the other six Rays, but in a subsidiary capacity. The explanation is that each Ray energy has all Ray energies as sub-rays.

It must be remembered that there is only one Spirit, but there is a hierarchy of evolving entities with many gradations of Spiritual evolvement. There is a spark of God within each of us and when we have attained a high level of evolvement, we, too, will become Gods, yet some Gods more evolved than others.

To get back to reality—to our planet and our Sun with a Ray 2 Soul of Love and Wisdom—how can we attain that unconditional love so necessary for Soul progress? It is through Wisdom—the wise use of knowledge, the searching for truth. The mind with its capacity for understanding is the bridge from the self-centered personality to the Soul. That mind is being enlightened by the ever-increasing Aquarian Age energies entering the consciousness of humankind by urging us to choose Soul progress rather than self-indulgence. These energies are inducing us to reap the joy promised when we no longer are satisfied with fame, honors, riches, sex, alcohol and drugs and are searching for the truth to the meaning and Purpose of Life.

BOTH SPEAK THE SAME LANGUAGE IN MYTHS & SYMBOLS

A myth is the seed of a truth handed down from generation to generation. Myths were given to humankind so that those who are not highly evolved, and therefore might misuse certain knowledge, are not able to understand them. The more highly evolved and intuitive one is, the better he or she is able to interpret the true meaning of myths.

An example of a myth is found in the *Tao Teh King* in which Lao Tzu gives an intuitive explanation of the difference between those manifesting on a self-centered personality level and those on a high Spiritual one: "A lotus pond will serve as an illustration between the holy sages and the younger members of the race. Covered with broad green leaves and brilliant blooms, it irresistibly attracts child-souls. They wade into the water, sink in the slime and desperately struggle for the fragile petals; but the sages, their elder brethren, remain quietly on the bank, always alert to aid any who require assistance, content to admire, content to enjoy without desiring to possess; yet actually owning the flowers more truly than the struggling crowd in the slimy pond. We are feebled when we are grasping."

Other myths applying both to Ray-Centered Astrology and Spirituality: From the Bible—"The heavens declare the glory of God and the firmament showeth God's handiwork." From Dante—"Follow but thy star. Thou canst not miss at last a glorious haven." Both these myths indicate how astrology can hasten one's Spiritual evolvement. The former speaks of God's work in the placement of one's planets at birth to help in his or her Soul progress. The latter in which "star" signifying the Soul Purpose shows that if you manifest your Soul's Purpose, joy is assured.

Symbols are the outgrowth of myths and like myths, they, too, release greater knowledge as one becomes more evolved, thus protecting all levels of evolving humanity. A symbol is a letter, figure or a combination of letters used to represent an object or idea. Symbols are found in almost every discipline. In Ray-Centered Astrology, the Sun is symbolized by a dot in a circle with no beginning and no end, denoting the personality—there is no end to earth lives when one manifests only as a personality. This means that until we begin to manifest as a Soul, we come back to earth time and time again as personalities to experience difficult karmic lessons until we have learned them. This is a principle of both Ray-Centered Astrology and Spirituality.

Another symbol of both is the spiral, denoting the process of people pulling themselves above the circle to manifest as a Soul-infused personality The diameter of the spiral gets smaller and smaller as one grows Spiritually until it thrusts upward in a straight line, denoting one manifesting on a high Spiritual level.

BOTH TELL US WHO WE ARE
AND WHY WE ARE HERE

We are Spiritual beings who will live forever. The reason we are here is to attain our true nature. We have a physical body, an emotional body and a mental body, but we are none of these. We are Spiritual entities who use these bodies to help us become our true selves. It is our heritage to become one with God. Each of us has a spark of God within. Our Spirituality may lay dormant or the spark may have been ignited to a beautiful flame—the flame glowing at the level of our Spiritual progress.

It is not easy to live on earth at the beginning of any New Age because its energies are so different from those of the Past Age. India's Vedic Bhagavad-Gita states that in the dawning of every New Age, God will send the supreme Teacher of men and angels among us to help in our Spiritual progress. About 2,000 years ago at the beginning of the Pisces Age, it was Jesus, the Christ. Since 1977, it is Maitreya, the Christ who promises to stay with us in a physical body for all of the Aquarian Age. For details, write to: Tara Center, P.O. Box 6001, N. Hollywood, CA 91603.

Why are we here on Planet Earth? The only reason is Spiritual evolvement. Earth lives are wonderful opportunities for Soul growth because of the many experiences for karmic lessons offered and for serving others consonant with each person's unique life Purpose (see Chapter IX).

Both Spirituality and Ray-Centered Astrology are concerned with eliminating the burgeoning needless suicides and other suffering, often caused by feelings of worthlessness and guilt. Some people do not know who they are—gods in the making. Nor do they know why they are here—to help others through their unique Life Purposes and to learn needed lessons for Soul growth. Difficulties are not punishments for wrong thoughts, words and actions, but lesson-teaching experiences given us by our Souls to change what needs changing to have a better and more joyful life. They are blessings in disguise. Everything happens for our ultimate good, no matter how difficult. It is sad to see so many people giving up on life when life has so much to give them. Their Souls are eager for earth experiences in order to progress.

It may help to believe in a God Transcendent (entity in the high Spiritual plane who is more evolved than we), a God Immanent (the God within us), or both. But even if we believe in no God at all what matters the most is that we become aware of who we are and why we are here. Ray-Centered Astrology can help find the answers.

The next chapter discusses the linkage of Ray-Centered Astrology with Science.

XV

SCIENCE AND
RAY-CENTERED ASTROLOGY

—◦◦◦—

He who would study organic existence
First drives out the Soul with rigid persistence.
Then the parts in his hand he may hold and clasp.
But the Spiritual link is last, alas!
—*Goethe*

While scientists usually throw out the Soul when they originally embark on their career, there comes a time when that Soul comes back in all its glory. Examples are given later in this chapter. For any discipline to survive in this cyclic period—the dawning of the Aquarian Age of the Soul—there must be a marriage of that discipline with the Soul. Science is no exception.

To wed science with Spirituality, the first Global Conference of Spiritual and Parliamentary Leaders on Human Survival was held in April, 1988 in Oxford, England. It was attended by the Dalai lama, Mother Teresa, archbishop Runcie, Carl Sagan, members of the Central Committee of the Soviet Communist Party, the Chief Rabbi of Romania, the High Priest of the Sacred Forest of Togo, the Metropolitan of the Russian Orthodox

Church in Moscow, Sri Lankan Development Leader A.T. Ariyaratue, senators, cabinet ministers and influential members of the media from every region of the world. James Lovelock, a scientist who has been visiting professor at the University of Reading in England since 1967 and the author of many books and papers, stated at this conference, "I happen to think that although science has progressed vastly since Newton, it has also moved a long way in the wrong direction. Scientists had to reject the bad side of medieval religion: superstition, dogmatism and intolerance. Unfortunately, as with most revolutions, we scientists merely exchanged one set of dogma for another. What we threw out was Soul."

The success of science in materialistic matters has caused erroneous worship of it by many. Because scientists have been successful researching much of what is necessary for the health and comfort of the physical body, a large number of people worship science and have the false impression that scientists are experts in all disciplines. The book, *The Peter Principle*, will enlighten many that successful people in one discipline are very seldom successful in another.

Problems arise when an expert in any discipline believes he or she knows more than experts in their own disciplines. It would be folly for an astrologer to tell scientific researchers and statisticians that what they find with their logical, concrete minds is incorrect. It is also folly for scientists to tell astrologers that what they find with their intuitive, abstract minds is wrong.

Yet there are many scientists who believe that if you can't see, hear, smell, taste or feel it, it doesn't exist. In 1975, 186 scientists, none of whom studied astrology, signed a manifesto and published it in a magazine with untrue and unproven statements degrading astrology. Later, they did refute this manifesto in their magazine, but in much smaller print.

Two scientists who refused to sign the manifesto are Freemon Dyson at the Institute for Advanced Study at Princeton and the renowned Carl Sagan. Sagan said, "That we can think of no mechanism for astrology is relevant, but unconvincing. No mechanism was known, for example, for continental drift when it was proposed by Wegener. Nevertheless, we see that Wegener was right, and those who objected on the grounds of unavailable mechanism were wrong."

Out of their own ranks came another to refute this manifesto. Scientist Dr. Percy Seymour, principal lecturer at the Plymouth Polytechnic Institute in England where he teaches astronomy and astrophysics, and where before he was the senior planetarium lecturer at the Old Royal Observatory in Greenwich, presented a paper at the First International Conference on Geocosmic Relations in Amsterdam in 1989. He said, "My examination of the so-called scientific arguments against astrology had shown me quite clearly that these arguments were not scientific at all. They were merely rationalizations of pseudo-intellectual prejudices that are only accepted by some people as scientific because they reinforce their own beliefs." He holds that the scientific basis of astrology is shown by the earth's magnetic field and its interplanetary modulations through resonance within the cell and its biochemical processes.

Dr. Seymour wrote, "One of the most interesting aspects of my researches into the evidence for and against astrology has been to discover how unscientific scientists can be when addressing a problem outside of their own field of expertise . . . A scientist sets up a simple and usually quite naive model: Then he shoots down the model, and from this he often concludes that no scientific theory can be constructed to explain any part of astrology. There are normally three major flaws in arguments used to deny any validity at all to astrology. These flaws are: (1) Denial of the existence of any scientific evidence in favor of aspects of astrology; (2) Use of mathematical models of limited ranges of applicability to argue that astrology cannot work, but failing to point out the limitations of the models and the assumptions on which they are based and (3) Making scientific statements which are true under certain conditions and failing to state the conditions necessary for their validity."[1]

A second reason why most mainstream scientists believe that astrology is invalid concerns scientists' left brain versus astrologers' right brain focus. A successful scientist—one who does research, not creative work—has an enhanced left brain, denoting a well-developed concrete, logical mind, while a successful astrologer has an enhanced right brain, with excellent intuitive, creative capacities. How can the concrete mind successfully prove or disprove what the intuitive mind finds unless it is matter?

Scientists have devised research methods to prove or disprove the validity of almost anything that is matter, while astrologers use intuition to arrive at their results of those parts of one's essence that is not matter.

Scientific researchers offer a needed service so helpful to humankind in knowing which drugs, surgery, food, cars, and all other necessities for the well-being of the physical body are safe and helpful and which are unsafe. Science is a noble and definitely serving profession. How could humanity benefit from the inventions, ideas, theories and hypotheses that creative people envision for material needs if scientists were not available to prove or disprove their validity? It is only when scientists go out of their field of expertise and purport to use their present research methods, which are excellent for materialistic concerns, on professions which are not materialistic but concerned with the psyche, the Soul, that trouble begins.

Many scientists still believe that everything, including disciplines, to be valid, must be proved by the logical, analytical left brain versus Aquarian energies which tell us that the right brain of intuition, Spirit and creativity of seeing the whole picture knows that some things cannot be proven by material research procedures.

Seth, through Jane Roberts, states, "Generally, your scientific theories carry the weight of strong validity within their own frameworks . . . Common sense upholds them . . . No matter what information or data you receive as the result of animal experimentation or dissection for scientific purposes . . . the consequences of such methods are so distorted that you comprehend less of life than you did before. These methods will simply bring you pat, manufactured results and answers. They will satisfy neither the intellect nor the Soul . . . You must look with your intuitions and creative instincts . . . The poet's view of the universe and of nature is more scientific than the scientists', for more of nature is comprehended . . . Information is not necessarily knowledge or comprehension. Diagramming sentences tells you little about the spoken language, and nothing about those miraculous physical and mental performances that allow you to speak—and so diagramming the species of the world is, in the same way, quite divorced from any true understanding."[2]

A third reason for mainstream scientists' tendency to invalidate astrology is that our present culture favors masculine over feminine. Research science, a product of the left brain, is a masculine profession, while astrology, which uses the right brain, is a feminine discipline.

For a long period up until the last few thousand years, the female was considered to be superior to the male, and the right brain of feminine energies (intuition, Spirituality, love, sensitivity, wisdom) was considered superior to the male and the left brain of masculine energies (logic, courage, analysis, intellect, power). Then there came a reverse of opinion and humankind was led to believe that the male is superior and that the concrete mind should be predominantly used in guiding the race. Science then began its heyday.

We are finding ourselves at the end of this period of male dominance and left brain superiority. What we are believing now in the dawning of the Aquarian Age of Enlightenment and Equality is that there is no superiority of one sex over the other, nor one function of the brain over the other. The qualities of both sexes, and both hemispheres of the brain are necessary for one's development. The time has come for the equality of the sexes and the wise use of both hemispheres of the brain. Since the most recent culture is patriarch, it is nature's prerogative in attaining a state of equilibrium for certain people and groups to again stress superiority of female characteristics. This will be short-lived until an equality is reached.

We are beginning a period in which neither patriarch nor matriarch are acceptable and that the masculine and feminine qualities are equally important in the psyche of every individual as are the disciplines of right and left brain dominance.

It does not follow that all males have left brains superior to their right brains nor all females have right brains superior to their left brains. Whether one's left or right brain is dominant depends on what was accomplished in past lives and what one's Purpose in this life is. This can be found in Ray-Centered Astrology.

Whatever your sex this time around makes no difference to what your Purpose in Life is (whether the left or right brain is predominate). What does make a difference is what specific abilities and strengths you have brought over from you past lives. Most of us have had lives in both male and female bodies.

Those of us who are presently in female bodies are becoming aware of equality with our brothers in masculine bodies by such writers as Clarisa Pinhola Estes who is helping women to no longer be second-class citizens with her best-selling book by acknowledging and manifesting our Souls' Purposes.[3]

A fourth reason why many mainstream scientists believe that astrology is invalid is the awareness that some astrologers' work is not helpful. While it is true that there are some incompetent and unethical astrologers, there are also incompetent and unethical scientists, medical doctors, psychiatrists and practitioners in various other fields. These disciplines themselves are not invalid as the great majority of practitioners in these fields, including astrology, are productive.

Science editor of the New York Herald Tribune and Pulitzer Prize winner John J. O'Neill, said, "While I do not believe all astrology is scientific and worthwhile, there is a certain amount of good work being done in that field and it is that which makes me try to do something to help the astrologer." Likewise, not all psychology, science and medicine is valid and worthwhile but that there is a certain amount of good work in all these fields.

A fifth reason for the belief of many mainstream scientists that astrology is invalid is that zodiacal Signs are not the same as Constellations. There are two main systems of astrology, one is the Tropical which does use the zodiacal Signs, and the other is the Sidereal which bases its work on the zodiacal Constellations. There was a time during the first century AD when both were the same. But from that time on many astrologers continued to use the placements of the zodiacal Constellations as though they did not move. Constellations regress 50" per year. For example, if one has an Aries Sun in the Tropical system, it most likely would be in Pisces siderealy.

Since energy follows thought and has the power to create commensurate with the strength and duration of thoughts, and because astrologers accepted the Tropical zodiac for almost 2000 years believing it was valid, these beliefs are powerful and gained credence. Therefore the Tropical zodiac with its interpretations falls true for most people whose horoscopes are delineated. But there is a very small segment of the population—those who are very highly evolved—who find a delineation using the Tropical system does not ring true. For them, the Sidereal system does indeed work. The reason is that the highly evolved are not as impressionable from others' thoughts as are the less-evolved.

The above are my explanations, refuting five reasons for orthodox scientists' belief that astrology is invalid. A Ph.D. in physics also spent much time, in fact, six years, grappling with the question, "How could astrology possibly be valid?" William Keepin says there is scientific evidence for astrology. One argument against astrology by some scientists is that the gravitational effect of the doctor on the baby was greater than the gravitational effect of Pluto at the time of birth. Keepin says that is true, but astrology does not work by gravity. He says astrology does not contradict any of the facts of science, but that astrology is only at odds with the assumption of certain mainstream scientists, not with any established facts.

Keepin states that a physicist, who wrote a book which Albert Einstein said was the clearest exposition of quantum theory he had ever seen and who had dialogues with a number of Spiritual leaders, including Krishnamurti and the Dalai Lama, indicated the validity of astrology. David Bohm says that the electron, not only behaves as a particle, but with information about the rest of the universe as the quantum potential, a wave field. Bohm believes that the basic nature of reality is holomovement—a single unbroken wholeness in flowing movement. So everything is connected, and everything is flowing and that each part of the flow contains the entire flow. According to Bohm, the holomovement has an explicate order (manifested as the space-time universe) and an implicate order (the unmanifested, unseen, hidden and is present in what appears random). Bohm stated that reality consists of matter, energy and meaning. The consensus of mainstream science is that the universe consists of matter and energy. Bohm says, "Energy enfolds matter and meaning, while matter enfolds energy and meaning." The meaning is the a priori implicate order, while the matter-energy is the explicate order. Orthodox science is the study of order in matter and energy, but there is also order in meaning.

Keepin believes that astrology is a science of order in meaning (the implicate order, the unmanifest) and its interpenetration with the space-time universe (the explicate or manifest order). He says that astrology works in a way that is not mechanistic. It is an implicate order which becomes explicate. He believes that the process that is going on in the planets is also going on in us. And as all astrologers know, he said that a given aspectual configuration "can result in a variety of different manifestations, depending on the intentions, the being and the integrity of the person involved." He wrote, "Astrology is actually much more profound than any process that takes place in the physical realm, for which we are now gaining increasing evidence in some of the new developments in modern science."[4]

There is no doubt that science has made great strides in the material, yet it has done a disservice both to astrology—which equates with meaning, value, self worth, wisdom and Soul—and to itself when it attempts to invalidate astrology with its present materialistic research methods.

Philosopher Jacob Needlemen said, "Science is very good in certain areas of inquiry, but completely helpless in many ways when it comes to search for wisdom."

When making decisions in reference to a discipline that is outside their range of expertise or delving into research without Soul, scientists create illusions.

Psychologist Carl Jung wrote, "Science is the art of creating suitable illusions which the fool believes or argues against, but the wise man enjoys for the beauty or their ingenuity, without being blind to the fact that they are veils."

Huston Smith, former professor of philosophy at MIT, and author of *Religions of Man*, said, "Horizontally the world of nature . . . has expanded incredibly. But vertically, if we take that to symbolize the regions of value and worth, it is almost as though we have pulled the shade down on the realms of being that our forefathers believed in implicitly, but we have shut them out simply because our honored way of knowing in the modern world—namely, the scientific method—has no way of getting at those realms of worth."

It is frustrating for certain mainstream scientists who are unable to invalidate astrology with their materialistic research methods. Perhaps, in trying to validate or invalidate disciplines such as astrology, scientists, until they create research methods using Soul, might eradicate their criticisms by contemplating the Bible statement, "By their fruits, you will know them." Most astrologers are an enormous help to clients.

Science is beginning to find the source of matter and the validity of astrology. There is an increasing number of scientists who are becoming aware of the differences of present day science of matter and disciplines of the Spirit. One such is a famous scientist from Stanford, William A.Tiller of the Department of Materials Science and Engineering, who said, "Mathematics has been and will continue to be the quantitative language of science, but astrology will become the qualitative language of the human condition."

Rene Weber suggests that in interviews with scientists and Spiritual figures such as David Bohm, Krishnamurte, the Dalai Lama, Ilya Pregogine and Rupert Sheldrake, there is very likely a parallel between the search of scientists for the source of matter and the source of one's own being.[5]

When scientists make more progress in finding the source of matter which equates to finding the source of our physical bodies which is matter, they cannot help but become aware of the validity of astrology—a divine science concerned with the Spirit of each person as the real Self. Metaphysicians have said for ages that energy at its lowest vibration is matter and at its highest vibration is Spirit.

A number of mainstream scientists believes that planets and stars and also people just came into being for no apparent reason—that it just happened randomly—and that when the physical body of a star, a planet or a person dies, that is the end of it. Some scientists, especially astronomers, have not only cast out the Souls of human beings but also of heavenly bodies. It is difficult for a scientist with a highly developed concrete mind and a less than average development of the intuitive mind to fathom the true knowledge of the universe.

Fortunately, there is an increasing number of scientists who have both enhanced concrete and intuitive minds who are becoming aware of the fact that the universe was created by the consciousness of very highly evolved entities. Albert Einstein once said, "Everyone who is seriously interested in the pursuit of science becomes convinced that a Spirit is manifest in the law of the universe—a Spirit vastly superior to that of man, and one in the face of which we with our modern powers must feel humble."

The good news in science is that there has been a number of discoveries in physics, biology and chemistry that is paving the way for all of science to get back the Soul.

Pioneering leaders in various disciplines are now finding and acknowledging a divine intelligence permeating the universe. Recent discoveries are proving that there is a divine plan for earth and that the universe is run by highly intelligent and Spiritually evolved entities.

Physicist Paul Davies suggests "the existence of a progressively unfolding plan for the universe from recent discoveries in biological evolution, brain research, computer science and astrophysics."[6] He believes the universe is not the result of random energy.

Michael Talbot explored the bio-chemical findings of scientists—Nobel laureate Sir John Escles, David Bohm and others—indicating the existence of the Soul and implications by mathematical formulas that the universe was created by very highly evolved entities.[7]

David Ray Griffin interviewed Willis Harman, David Bohm, Rupert Sheldrake and Stanley Krippner and found a burgeoning movement toward a science proving the presence of a divine intelligence, described within physics, cosmology, biology, ecology, parapsychology and psychosomatic medicine.[8]

A number of physicists are becoming aware that entities not

only control the various celestial bodies, but that these entities evolve as time goes on. Physicist John Wheeler says, "The Universe is not as we thought, closed and inanimate. It is alive and continuously evolving."

Science is learning that mind is a priori. In the Newtonian theories of the past, it was thought that intelligence was only a by-product of matter—the mind was considered a part of the physical brain. Science now knows, as Physicist John Wheeler says, that mind controls matter. Research findings have proven that the mind and brain are not synonymous and that the brain is the part of the physical body which only houses the mind.

Physics is undergoing a revolution. For 300 years, physicists saw the universe as a clockwork mechanism, nature being locked in strict mathematical laws, according to Newton. With the theories of Relativity, Quantum Mechanics and Chaos, physicists are becoming aware of the unpredictability of matter and energy and of consciousness in the smallest atom. Many believe that Einstein's theory of relativity was the catalyst for radical changes in physics.

The development of Quantum Mechanics has contradicted the initial theory of the separateness of particles. It was recently thought that particles interact with one another only through certain mechanisms such as gravitational or electromagnetic fields or particle exchange. In 1930 scientists discovered a paradox in subatomic physics that light and subatomic matter can sometimes manifest as particles and sometimes as waves—a discovery of consciousness in the atom.

Since 1981 we have the Chaos Theory in which scientific pioneers speculate about determinism, free will, evolution and the nature of intelligence in looking for the whole. It is often referred to as nonlinear science, the science of complexity and the science of turbulence and disorder.

With the theories of Relativity, Quantum Mechanics and Chaos, physicists are becoming aware of consciousness in the smallest atom and the unpredictability of matter and energy. Is

not the Chaos Theory actually explained by the fact of consciousness in the atom, albeit a lower form of consciousness? Instead of
labeling the Chaos Theory a science of turbulence and disorder, it
probably could be best described as a science of interconnectedness of all parts of the universe. This could bring about a desired
change by understanding a higher level of order in the universe—
an order in which humanity becomes aware of the true relationships of everything in the universe, how each affects all others.

Science today is moving away from almost four centuries of
assuming that there is an objective universe, independent of the
observer, but which must be physically observable, explainable in
reducing the complex to the elemental. The emerging science is
finding help in holism.

Physicist David Bohm and brain researcher Karl Pribram
have done work on vibratory rates and holography. They found
that by cutting an optical hologram in pieces, that each piece can
reproduce the entire image. Their work proves that people and
their minds are parts of the universe and that their minds can
contact knowledge in the universe.

Scientific research started with behavioral science at the beginning of the century. The last 20 years saw the discipline of
neuroscience, followed by cognitive science (the study of the
mind). In only the past few years has consciousness research been
recognized.

Physicist Paul Davies says, "We no longer see matter as entirely
passive and inert; in some circumstances it can behave as if it has a
will of its own . . . The universe is evolving and matter and energy
are free to enjoy some degree of spontaneity in the way they move
and change to explore different pathways of evolution."

Quantum physicist Dr. John Hagelin, the presidential candidate in 1992 for the Natural Law Party of the United States, won
the Kelby Award for 1992, conferred on him for his global efforts
to apply the scientific knowledge of the unified field for the welfare of mankind. He developed a unified description of nature,

uniting the knowledge of modern physics with the physical framework for understanding consciousness.

It is being proven that each minute particle has a consciousness. It has been found that what looks like identical atoms do not always behave in the same way. At the famous Fermi-lab in Illinois, physicists hope to uncover, within the atom, the very force that created our universe. One researcher said, "We may be on the threshold of finding God."

When science finds God, it can rightly be called Sacred Science. In the "Modern Sage" by Passage Press: "Sacred science takes us to true philosophy—philosophy in the classical and ancient sense as the deep inquiry into the nature of things, the uncovering of the Soul . . . It is our thought patterns that constrict the universe in various preconceived and self-promoting ideas and beliefs which prevent us from accessing the cosmic energy and wisdom . . . Sacred Science focuses not on the apparent maniputable or measurable aspect of reality, which is only the surface, but on the essence, the sacred being. It works, not through the visible and the known, but through the hidden dimension in things and the secret wisdom of life itself. It does not give us a theory, equation or statistics but a direct connection with the thing itself. It is revealed more by myth and symbol than by logical expression." When science becomes more sacred, there will be a happy marriage between it, with its burgeoning use of myths and symbols, and astrology.

Nobel Laureate Roger Sperry believes that science must recognize "inner conscious awareness as a causal reality." He insists that the best scientific mode of inquiry is to give scientific validity to both the analytical and the intuitive, but to the analytical in terms of the intuitive.

It is time now to give validity to analytical science in terms of the intuitive Ray-Centered Astrology. One way is to link together various disciplines with the aid of the Seven Rays.

Philosopher and inventor of the Bell helicopter, Arthur M.

Young suggests that astrology is a more comprehensive system than science and that scientists could benefit from its study, regardless of its application in individual horoscopes.

We can credit the Aquarian energies that are increasingly entering the consciousness of humankind for the monumental change in science. These energies are helping us understand that everything is connected to everything else—the seven Ray energies of the cosmos to mind, mind to matter, each discipline to every other discipline and so on.

British biochemist Rupert Sheldrake's theory is that there exists a field that is the entire universe and space/time is a subset of this field called the morphic field which connects everything to everything else. He wrote: "A natural extension of the morphic field approach would be to regard living ecosystems as complex organisms with morphic fields that embrace the communities of organisms within them, and indeed to regard entire planets as organisms with characteristic morphic fields, and likewise planetary systems, galaxies and clusters of galaxies."[9]

Sheldrake found that traditional science cannot detect "morphic resonance"—fields that govern certain types of learning. The world view is changing from separative emphasis to wholeness. The Aquarian Age energies and Ray-Centered Astrology have within their essence the power to speed that change. Ray-Centered Astrology is concerned with wholeness, with Spirit and with finding the unique Purpose of each person to contribute to the progress of humankind—diversity in unity.

The Master DK said that a knowledge of the Rays and their tendencies and energies will bring much illumination to practitioners in the various sciences.

Ray-Centered Astrology is not only able to bring science to a higher level, but can link science and Spirituality in helping each to understand and accept one another. Dr. Philip S. Berg says, "Science probes for the answers that religion takes on faith, and astrology is the bridge between them."[10]

How can we best change our ideas of separateness to wholeness and find the meaning of life and a celebration of it? While it must begin in the consciousness of the individual, that consciousness is swayed in most people by the disciplines that serve them. As each discipline changes its major focus from material to Spiritual, from separateness to wholeness, it finds itself recognizing the worth and differences of all other disciplines. It then becomes eager to refer clients/patients/students to other disciplines when necessary for optimal help. The linkage of disciplines is an evolutionary fact of our present cycle while Ray-Centered Astrology is the evolutionary catalyst for this linkage.

We are now in the dawning of the Aquarian Age—the Age of Enlightenment, the Age of the Mind—and because the mind is the bridge to the Soul, this Age is truly the Age of the Soul. Inducing contact with Soul, the enhanced mind of humankind is urging the linking of all disciplines. It is the higher consciousness level, our more enlightened thoughts, which is the catalyst for interconnectedness, for wholeness in all disciplines.

The following phrases depict the wholeness in various disciplines: In Spirituality—As man thinketh, so is he. In science—a burgeoning awareness of consciousness in the atom. In both psychology and healing—good, right thoughts resulting in mental and physical health. In the arts—beauty of artistic expression raising the level of consciousness (the Don Campbells are searching for an interdisciplinary study and are impressed to use music to heal the physical body and emotions, and to uplift the Spirit). In Ray-centered Astrology—knowing who we are and why we are here by finding the true meaning of life and one's unique Soul's Purpose, helping various disciplines reach their optimal expertise and teaching the wisdom of interdisciplinary status.

Astrology, being a divine science, is not only the bridge between science and Spirituality, but is the catalyst for the linkage of all disciplines to better serve and uplift humanity. Astrology has within its essence, the where-with-all to reach to the very core of one's being—that which makes one what he or she is, so different from all others, yet so important for the contribution to evolutionary development of the race. "When we do what we were created to do," writes scientist/journalist/astrologer Dennis Elwell, "without any additional effort and straining, we arrive at self-fulfillment."

It is this a priori essence of each individual that confers upon astrology the capacity to help practitioners of all disciplines recognize, not only the special expertise of their own as it relates to the Soul, but the special expertise and wisdoms of all others by referring clients/patients/students to other disciplines when necessary for their optimal help. Ray-Centered Astrology also shows other practitioners that it is not only to the advantage of their clients, patients and students when they show wisdom and courage to work in an interdisciplinary fashion, but also to their own in creating rewarding Karma (see Chapter IX).

Each discipline has much to offer humankind, but none alone can benefit the individual to the extent that all can working together. When the motivation of practitioners is not for ego satisfaction of one's discipline being superior to others, but unconditional love of humankind, the result is greater success and true joy in affording optimal help to the client/patient/student.

It seems that the two disciplines which perhaps can be the greatest catalysts for linkage are at present the most at loggerheads—mainstream science and astrology. Mainstream science believes there is no Purpose to Life, while Ray-Centered Astrology's main issue is Purpose in Life. Nobel Prize winner Jacques Monod states, "The systematic denial of Purpose is the cornerstone of the scientific methods."

Following is part of an address given at the 1988 First Global Conference of Spiritual and Parliamentary Leaders in Human Survival: Dr. Robert Runcie, the archbishop of Canterbury, said, "Our world is in danger of being pervaded by a widespread pessimism about the future of mankind. There is a diminished sense that our problems can be resolved by technology alone or political utopias alone. We are confronted by a search for meaning and the human enterprise, the need for reconciliations, for greater compassion, for justice and for a celebration of life in all its wholeness."

Professor of philosophy and comparative religion Huston Smith states that the western scientific mind is dominated by materialistic values. He says this leads to great technological progress, but often a denial of quality, meaning and Purpose in Life, leading to alienation and discontent.[11]

Scientist Benjamin Pinkel believes that there is a fundamental mystery in nature that is unassailable by traditional science, transcending the laws of physical sciences. He says that humankind has an important purpose in the cosmic scheme.[12]

In "The Modern Sage" by Passage Press, it reads, "Just as there is a mundane astronomy that aims to unlock the physical and chemical structure of the universe, so there is a sacred astronomy that holds the key to the cosmic meaning of life and consciousness, which we find hidden within the various systems of astrology."

Ray-Centered Astrology with its Seven Ray energies is that sacred astronomy which reveals the meaning of life.

Physicist William Keepin says that even though astrology is the absolute last straw for a rigorous scientist, that it is in astrology where science may have one of its greatest openings.

The next (last) chapter gives many proofs, for both left and right brain-oriented people, verifying the system found in the Introduction of calculating one's Soul and Personality Rays by Ray-Centered Astrology.

Notes

1 *The Scientific Basis of Astrology*, Percy Seymour, St. Martin's Press, NY, 1992

2 *The Nature of the Psyche*, Jane Roberts, Prentice Hall, Inc., 1979

3 *Women Who Ride With the Wolves*, Clarisa Pinhola Estes

4 *Mountain Astrologer Magazine*, William Keepin, August 1995

5 *Dialogues with Scientists and Sages*, Rene Weber

6 *Cosmic Blueprint: New Discoveries in Nature's Ability to Order the Universe*, Paul Davies

7 *Beyond the Quantum: God, Reality, Consciousness in the New Scientific Revolution*, Michael Talbot

8 *The Re-enchantment of Science: Postmodern Proposals*, David Ray Griffin

9 *The Presence of the Past*, Rupert Sheldrake

10 *Astrology, Star Connection*, Philip S. Berg

11 *Beyond the Post-Modern Mind*, video tape, Huston Smith

12 *The Existential Adventure*, Benjamin Pinkel

XVI

CONCLUSION

—◦◦◦—

We are living in exciting and swiftly changing times. It is amazing yet beautiful how everything going on in the hearts and minds of humankind is revealed in the cosmos.

Because our Sun and its planets are moving from Pisces to Aquarius, we are entering a New Age which only happens every 2160 years. These New Aquarian Age energies are inducing sweeping changes in our consciousness, thus giving us freedom to be who we are and the knowledge of why we are here—the essence of this book.

Another important change in the cosmos is the increasing Ray 7 energies by the Lords of the Seven Rays who see fit to give us more power to change from personality focus to the Soul.

Although it seems to many that civilization is falling to a dismal abyss from which it cannot pull itself up because of the increased violence, mental illness, and alcohol and drug abuse, this is not so! The increased Spiritual energies reaching us demand swift karmic lesson-teaching and though this is painful and sometimes causes temporary regression, it is the catalyst for Soul progress.

In addition to the changes precipitated by the New Aquarian Age and the waxing of Ray 7's energies, is the stepped-up power of Uranus which is the ruler of Ray 7 and the exoteric ruler of ever-increasing Aquarius Age energies and which transited into

Aquarius in 1995. All this Uranus/Aquarian energy entering the minds and hearts of humanity urge us to climb higher to reach our Souls, especially by giving us freedom to be who we are along with finding out who we are, why we are here and to serve others consonant with our unique Soul's Purpose.

If that is not enough, we found in 1993 that Uranus was in the same degree in Capricorn as Neptune, urging swift changes in Soul progress in raising our consciousness to a high level, leading to a Spiritual regeneration of humankind.

It is a metaphysical teaching that humanity discovers physical knowledge of a cosmic body at the time people are ready to profit from its energies. Only recently have astronauts found that the color of Uranus is violet, the color of the highest vibration in the spectrum and the highest Spiritual color seen with physical eyes. This indicates that humanity is evolved enough to benefit from the stepped-up power of Uranus.

Also, the discovery between Saturn and Uranus in 1977 of Comet Chiron, which is considered the Rainbow Bridge from the materialistic personality symbolized by Saturn to the Soul symbolized by Uranus, is a precursor to the wise use of Uranus. This makes it easier for us to reach the Spiritual energies of Uranus by walking the bridge of Chiron, the healer from the self-centered personality desires of Saturn to Spiritual concerns of Uranus.

It was also in 1977 that Chiron's energies induced me to write the scholarly, definitive book, *Ray-Centered Astrology*. This new astrology, like Chiron, is the Rainbow Bridge from the personality to the Soul. And in 1993 the combined energies of Uranus and Neptune in the same degree of Capricorn urged me to compose this new book for helping people with no knowledge of astrology to reach their Souls and find that peace for which they have so long searched.

So that the contents of this book reach as much of humankind as possible, the following proofs of the system for finding one's unique Soul's Purpose are given.

For any new paradigm to be accepted in large numbers by colleagues and also by people at large, it must satisfy not only their left brains (lower concrete minds of logic, analysis and statistics), but more so their right brains (higher minds of sensing the whole, of intuition and of Soul).

The left brain often states emphatically, "Prove it with logic, reason or research!" The right brain does not shout; in fact it operates optimally in a subdued, subtle, contemplative state. It can tell you if something is right or wrong, helpful or harmful and can give you additional needed information by meditation—quieting and relaxing your physical body and questioning your Soul.

My right brain instantaneously informed me of the accuracy and potential of this new Ray-Centered Astrology. It also told me that research is necessary to prove this for some. The reason is that at this period of time humanity is still entrenched in thought forms of the predominance of the left over the right brain because of the prestige that scientific research and statistics have acquired. Even though the importance of the left and right brains is slowly and rightly being equalized, research and proof are necessary for this new astrology to be accepted by large segments of the population.

LEFT BRAIN VERIFICATION OF SYSTEM CALCULATING ONE'S SOUL AND PERSONALITY RAYS BY RAY-CENTERED ASTROLOGY

Ideally, both the right and left hemispheres of the brain should have equal importance, but until there is an equal acceptance in our culture, it behooves anyone desiring to prove the validity of one's project to put more effort into the prevailing mode which at this period of time is the left brain (lower concrete mind of logic and research). That is the reason I spent much more time with left brain proof than with right brain (higher mind of intuition and psyche) validation.

For the following studies, it is important to know that one's Soul Ray is determined from the Ascendant Sign, and the Personality Ray from the esoteric planetary ruler of the Sun Sign. These studies prove that planets in Signs do indeed have statistical significance. Another who has found this to be true by deep research is the late Gary Duncan. A number of astrology researchers, including editor of *American Federation of Astrology Research Magazine* Dr. Robert Donath, assert Duncan's expertise in astrology research. President of Llewellyn Publishing, Incorporated Carl Llewellyn stated, "Gary Duncan will be remembered for his demands for mathematical accuracy in computation and rigorous statistical approaches to astrological research."

While some of the following proofs utilize both the right and left hemispheres of the brain, they use predominantly the left.

(1) Study of Personality Rays Given by Benjamin Creme Shows Significant Correlation to Those Found by Ray-Centered Astrology

This study was taken from Personality Rays of successful people given by Benjamin Creme through his Master.[1]

In a fair statistical study, it is imperative that one does not use only the information that would make one's hypothesis accepted, but all information available, which in this case was 663 persons. The year of birth was given in Creme's book, but not the month and day which made it impossible to find the Personality Rays. So I laboriously tried to find the birth dates of each of the 663 persons given. I found the horoscopes of 269 people of the 663 for which I searched in the books of the renowned research astrologer Lois Rodden.[2]

From the 269 horoscopes, I found that 203 had the same Personality Rays calculated by Ray-Centered Astrology as the ones given by Creme in his book. Because some were born centuries ago, some BC even, it could be difficult to find exact birth dates of all, even by Rodden's painstaking methods.

Regardless, this study shows very significant results. Because there are seven Rays, we divide 269 by seven which equals 38¾, the number of Personality Rays randomly expected to be similar in both Cremes's report and those found from Ray-Centered Astrology calculations. The number found, 203, minus the number expected to be found, 38¾, is 164¼ more than expected. 164¼ divided by 38¾ is 4+ which is the correlation and extremely significant. Any correlation above 0.26 is considered significant by the editors of the prestigious magazine, *Correlation—Journal of Research into Astrology.*

In all my research studies to prove the validity of the system of calculating one's Soul and Personality Rays through Ray-Centered Astrology, I found this study to be by far the most significant and revealing because of its very high correlation between the Personality Rays given by Creme's Master and those calculated by Ray-Centered Astrology. In my opinion, the reason is that Creme's Master, who is very highly evolved, chose individuals who are in the top echelon of contributors to humanity and therefore definitely served in the area of their Souls' Purposes.

(2) 226 Successful People who have Soul and Personality Rays Consonant with their Fields of Expertise

This study concerns 226 successful individuals and how their Soul and Personality Rays, as found by Ray-Centered Astrology, coincide with the specific contributions they make to society. The results of this study are found at the end of each Ray Chapter.

Two Studies Showing Significant Correlation of Ray 5
Personalities with Gemini Sun Signs

For these studies, I chose Ray 5 Personalities—scientific researchers and statisticians. I excluded inventors, scientific theorists, psychologists, astronauts and physicians because their careers are not Ray 5 but are included as scientists by some authors.

I am much indebted to research astrologer Lois Rodden and statisticians/psychologists Francoise Gauquelin and the late Michel Gauquelin for their dedicated painstaking work in finding birth dates and erecting horoscopes published in their various books. It is validating that all three of these famous researchers have Ray 5 of the Concrete Mind (scientific research and statistics) placed strongly in their Ray structure. Lois Rodden has both a Ray 5 Soul and Personality, Francoise Gauquelin has a Ray 5 Personality and Michel Gauquelin has a Ray 5 Soul, all of which verify their capacity for research. Francoise has a Ray 2 Soul and Michel a Ray 6 Personality, both of which indicate proficiency also in psychology, their twin field.

I followed two hard rules that statisticians say are a priori—do not pick out the names of only those adhering to your hypothesis and try to replicate your work.

For the first study, I used all scientific researchers and statisticians in Lois Rodden's three books. Later I replicated this study by using the Gauquelin's *Book of American Charts*.[3] I did not use Gauquelin's *Men of Science* because no indication of specific careers was given.

I chose the hypothesis that there are more successful people in research and statistics who have Sun Signs in Gemini than in any other Sign. The reason is that the ruler of Ray 5 is Venus which is the esoteric ruler of Gemini. These studies concern Ray 5 Personalities of the Concrete Mind of logic and reason.

To allow these studies more accuracy, I chose not to use Soul Rays because they are determined from Ascendant Signs which in turn are found from the clock time of birth which is often inaccurate. I chose instead, for more accuracy, to work with the Personality Rays which are found from the Sun Sign which is determined from the day of birth.

I felt initially that there would be more Sun Signs found in Gemini than in any other Sign. Yet I did not believe there would be a large number of Gemini Sun Signs for two reasons. One, some successful research scientists and statisticians would not have Ray 5 Personalities which I used in this study, but may have Ray 5 Souls which I did not use. Two, that some successful scientific researchers and statisticians may not have Ray 5 Personalities or Souls, but have Ray 5 strongly placed in their mental, emotional and/or physical bodies which is beyond the scope of this work (See Chapter V for additional information on Gemini Sun Sign Personalities).

(3) Study Showing Significant Correlation of Scientific Researchers and Statisticians with Gemini Sun Signs (Ray 5 Personalities)

For this study, the Sun Signs of all scientific researchers and statisticians from Rodden's three books were used. See bar graph of Rodden study of the Sun Signs of 82 Ray 5 scientists: Aries—5, Taurus—5, Gemini—15, Cancer—5, Leo—7, Virgo—4, Libra—4, Scorpio—7, Sagittarius—5, Capricorn—8, Aquarius—4 and Pisces—13. Because there are 12 Signs, we divide 82 by 12 equaling 6⅚ scientists, the expected number of scientists in each Sign. I was both surprised and delighted to find 15 Gemini Sun Signs, the highest number in any Sign, which is 8⅙ more than expected (15 minus 6⅚). Dividing 8⅙ by 6⅚ = 1.1+ which is a very high correlation of scientists with Gemini Sun Signs, as anything above 0.26 is considered significant.

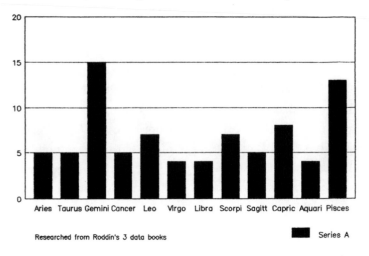

SUN SIGNS OF RAY 5 SCIENTISTS
not Psychologists Astronauts Physicians

Researched from Roddin's 3 data books   ■ Series A

(4) Replication Study of Significant Correlation of Scientific Researchers and Statisticians with Gemini Sun Signs (Ray 5 Personalities)

For this study, the Sun Signs of all scientific researchers and statisticians found in Gauquelin's *Book of American Charts* were used. See bar graph for Sun Signs of 111 Ray 5 scientists: Aries—6, Taurus—8, Gemini—19, Cancer—15, Leo—9, Virgo—10, Libra—9, Scorpio—8, Sagittarius—6, Capricorn—6, Aquarius—4 and Pisces—11. Dividing 111 by 12 gives 9.25 scientists, the expected number in each Sign. I found 19 Gemini Sun Signs, the highest number in any Sign, which is 9.75 more than expected (19 minus 9.25). Dividing 9.75 by 9.25 gives a correlation of 1.05+ which is also considered very high.

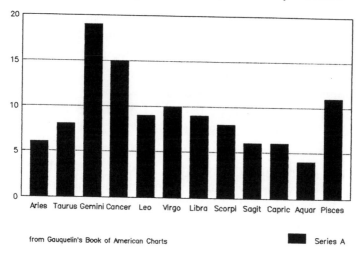

SUN SIGNS OF RAY 5 SCIENTISTS
not Psychologists Astronauts Physicians

from Gauquelin's Book of American Charts   Series A

(5) Study Showing Significant Correlation of Managers and Libra Sun Signs (Ray 7 Personalities)

Ray-Centered Astrology holds that Libra Sun Signs give Ray 7 Personalities, inducing capabilities for successful managers. This study was done by Christina Neill-Higgins which appeared in *The Astrological Journal*, March/April 1989. She received her information from 21 insurance and pharmaceutical companies to find the Sun Signs of all ordinary employees and management. I divided the 336 managers she found by 12 giving 28, the expected number of managers in each Sun Sign. The Libra Sun Sign ranked highest of all Sun Signs, receiving 38 which is 10 more than expected. Dividing 10 by 28 gives a correlation of 0.35+. Any amount above 0.26 is considered significant (see Chapter VII for additional information on Libra Sun Sign personalities).

(6) Study Showing Significant Correlation of Dictators and Taurus Sun Signs (Ray 1 Personalities)

Coralie Koonce did a study, found in the January 1994 *Horoscope* magazine, in which she searched for Sun Signs of the world's dictators. Of the 44 found, 9 had Taurus Sun Signs, the most by far of any Sun Signs. Koonce did not work with the Rays. But I divided 44 by 12 which equals 3⅔—the expected number of dictators in each Sign, and 9 minus 3⅔ = 5⅓ more dictators with Taurus Sun Signs than expected. Therefore, 5⅓ divided by 3⅔ = 1.45+, an extremely high correlation.

Unlike the previous Ray 5 and Ray 7 studies in which only one Sun Sign is involved with each Ray because each of those Rays have only one ruler, Ray 1 has two rulers and thus involves two Sun Signs. This system holds that Taurus and Pisces Sun Signs are aligned with Ray 1 Personalities of Power and Will, but while Taurus Sun Sign people have a tendency to use power in an overt, extroverted, inflexible and dictatorial manner, Pisces Sun Sign individuals direct their power inward in a subtle and introverted way, able to sense the feelings and thoughts of many before making a move. Koonce found no dictators with Pisces Sun Signs. She cites examples of two powerful men with Pisces Sun Signs—George Washington who refused to be king of the United States and Mikhail Gorbachev who "used his vast power to encourage democracy and to weaken centralized rule, although this eventually put him out of office" (see Chapter I for further differences of a Ray 1 Personality having either a Taurus or Pisces Sun Sign).

(7) Study of Sun Signs of Therapists Showing Even Rays Predominating

Ray-Centered Astrology holds that Sun Signs giving Personality Rays 2, 4, or 6 induce capabilities for successful therapists.

SUN SIGNS OF RAY 1 DICTATORS
SHOWS PREDOMINANCE OF TAURUS SUNS

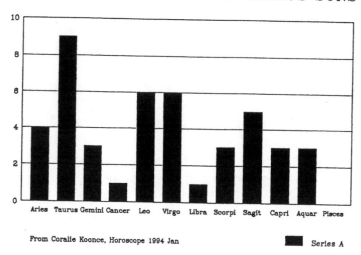

From Coralie Koonce, Horoscope 1994 Jan   ■ Series A

While each of the even-numbered Rays is different in specificity, together they have general characteristics of sensitivity, introversion, love and intuition.

This study of 412 professional therapists includes all found in the 1987 and 1988 *Listing of Professional Members of the Association of Transpersonal Psychology*. Again, I followed the hard rule in avoiding picking out only birth dates that adhere to my hypothesis, but used all. However, I had access only to the 1987 and 1988 editions because those were the only years I paid for professional membership.

In the accompanying bar graph, the number of therapists in each of the 7 Ray Personality categories is shown.

Again, I was delighted with results—the three even-numbered Rays (feminine Rays) have the highest number of therapists. Ray 6 of Idealism and Devotion (Cancer and Scorpio Sun

Signs) took the lead with 76 therapists. This Ray is the most emotional of all Rays. Therapists must deal with difficult emotions of clients, but how better to help others with emotional problems than to have successfully dealt with their own. Also Ray 6 energy gives much idealism and devotion to one's cause—therapists as a group are exceedingly devoted to uplifting their clients. Cancer gives a strong need to help those who cannot fend for themselves and Scorpio can pierce to the very depth of a problem (see Chapter VI for additional information on Cancer and Scorpio Sun Sign Personalities).

Ray 4 of Harmony through Conflict (Aries and Virgo Sun Signs) came in second with 74 therapists, trailing first place by only 2. This Ray energy gives intuition and superb counseling capacity to help clients attain harmony in resolving their conflicts. Aries gives propensity for pioneering divine ideas and enthusiasm in carrying them out. Virgo is aligned with a need for perfection. Both Signs give many karmic lesson teaching experiences which, when worked through, enables these therapists to help others the way they were helped (See Chapter IV for additional information on Aries and Virgo Sun Sign Personalities).

Next, with 68 were Ray 2 Personalities (Leo and Aquarius Sun Signs) of Love and Wisdom who have a high level of intuition and a great capacity for teaching and/or healing others, emotionally, mentally, physically and/or Spiritually. Leo gives insights for reaching the heights of the Soul no matter where one is, and Aquarius induces the freedom to be what one is supposed to be (see Chapter II for additional information on Leo and Aquarius Sun Sign Personalities).

It is validating that the four trailing Rays are all odd-numbered, symbolizing the masculine part of one's essence—power, courage, extroversion and intellect—having the smallest numbers of therapists. The highest number in this category was 62 in Ray 1 (Taurus and Pisces Sun Signs). These individuals have great power and strong wills needed to make the necessary changes in

PERSONALITY RAYS——COUNSELORS
SHOWS PREDOMINANCE OF EVEN RAYS

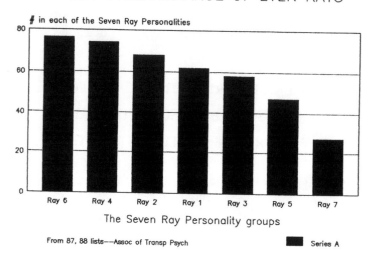

 # in each of the Seven Ray Personalities

The Seven Ray Personality groups

From 87, 88 lists——Assoc of Transp Psych   ■ Series A

therapy for the New Aquarian Age (see Chapter I for additional information on Taurus and Pisces Sun Sign Personalities).

Next in number are Ray 3 Personalities with 58 therapists (Sagittarius and Capricorn Sun Signs) who are blessed with creative potential for new psychology methods and theories (see Chapter III for additional information on Sagittarius and Capricorn Sun Sign Personalities).

Following Ray 3 are Ray 5 Personalities of the Concrete Mind, numbering 47 (Gemini Sun Signs) whose expertise is research, logic and practicality. They can easily take the creative ideas of Ray 3 Personalities to make usable in a practical way through research or logical explanations. Good examples are the works of the Gauquelins mentioned earlier (see Chapter V for additional information on Gemini Sun Sign Personalities).

Last are Ray 7 Personalities of Order and Rhythm (Libra Sun Signs) with only 27 which is understandable—they are the few therapists who are equipped to be organizers, leaders and presidents (see Chapter VII for additional information on Libra Sun Sign Personalities).

I was delighted to find the largest number of therapists having Personality Rays in a graduated scale consonant with what is expected according to Ray-Centered Astrology teachings.

RIGHT BRAIN VERIFICATION CALCULATING ONE'S SOUL & PERSONALITY RAYS WITH RAY-CENTERED ASTROLOGY

While the above research was done to satisfy the skepticism of those seekers who are predominately left-brain focused (logic, statistics, intellect), the energy for developing Ray-Centered Astrology in the first place was from the urgings of my right brain (intuition, sensitivity, Soul).

It was my intuition and Soul which impressed me to read contemplatively all 24 Alice Bailey books twice, 19 which were dictated by the Master Djwal Kuhl.[4] Without this knowledge, there would be no Ray-Centered Astrology.

In His wisdom, DK scattered clues here and there throughout His voluminous writings like precious little jewels for two reasons. One is that only the seekers of truth who studied all these volumes contemplatively would be in a position to create anything of substance. The other is His wish to develop the intuition of readers.

(1) Validating Ray-Centered Astrology By DK

While stressing the importance of developing one's intuition, He supplied the basics for this new astrology by certain statements which can prove the validity of this work to the astronomical number of readers all over the world of the Alice Bailey books.

Soul Ray Determined By Ascendant (Rising Sign)

Esoteric Astrology, p. 17: He said that the Rising Sign indicates the Spiritual goal and purpose of the present incarnation.

Esoteric Astrology, p. 497: He stated that the esoteric astrologer holds that the Rising Sign indicates Soul direction.

Esoteric Astrology, p.18: Here He repeats that the Rising Sign indicates Soul Purpose for this life-time.

Treatise on White Magic, pp. 435, 436: Again He repeats that the Rising Sign indicates the kind of energy to fulfill one's Life Purpose.

Treatise on White Magic, p. 437: Here He says that the energy of one's Soul Ray comes through a constellation, (He does not say a planet).

Esoteric Astrology, p. 28: He states that the twelve constellations embody the Soul stimulation.

Esoteric Astrology, P. 51: Here He says that the the twelve constellations are concerned mostly with Soul stimulation.

Personality Ray Determined by Planetary Ruler of Sun Sign

Esoteric Astrology, p. 16: He says that the secret of the Personality Ray is found in the Sun Sign.

Esoteric Astrology, p. 51: Here He says that the twelve planets affect potently the personality.

Esoteric Astrology, p. 28: He states here that the twelve planets relate to the external life of the human personality.

Esoteric Astrology, p. 31: He adds that disciples and initiates can be affected by the planets relating to their personalities and Sun Signs.

(2) Personality Rays given by DK to his Disciples Corresponds to those Calculated by Ray-centered Astrology

In *Discipleship in the New Age*, Vol. 1 and 2, DK gave the Rays of each of his forty one disciples. To see if the Personality Rays He gave were the same as those calculated by Ray-Centered Astrology, I tried diligently to find birth dates of His disciples. I could not find all, but two esoteric astrologers who had several birth dates shared with me all they had. One gave me fifteen and the other shared five, four of which were included in the fifteen given me by my other colleague. These four birth dates were the same from both sources.

It is significant that I received these birth dates after my first book, *Ray-Centered Astrology* which gives the system for calculating Soul and Personality Rays, was published. Therefore there was no fitting in and matching of the Rays given by DK to birth dates so that I could exoterically come up with a system of calculation for finding one's Soul's Purpose. I created this method though inspiration and intuition after studying and contemplating all 24 Alice Bailey books.

The Master DK stated that in finding one's Rays, the Tropical System should be used for the large majority, and the Sidereal System for the very advanced. *Treatise on White Magic*, p. 437: He said that the month and the Sign do not coincide at all in the Tropical System but, because energy follows thought, this thought-form which has been built up for ages by astrologers, is true for most people, but not for the highly evolved. I don't pretend to know why the Master DK believes this, but it is my feeling that the highly evolved are not as influenced by others' thoughts as are average people. Astrologers believe the Sidereal system puts the placements on the chart somewhere between 23 to 30 degrees ahead of the Tropical system.

There were six disciples, by using the Sidereal System, who had the same Personality Rays found by Ray-Centered Astrology that DK gave: Alice Bailey, Foster Bailey, Robert Assagioli, Marion Walter, Eugene Cosgrove and Harriet Richards. According to DK, these disciples are highly evolved.

Using the Tropical System, which is the one applied by practically all American astrologers, for the remaining ten disciples whose birth dates I have, eight had the same Personality Rays calculated by Ray-Centered Astrology as those DK gave. One had the same Personality Ray calculated by Ray-Centered Astrology as his past life Personality Ray given by DK. Another disciple, LUT, whose birth date was not given the author, had his Sun Sign submitted by DK. This gives a correlation of 15 out of 17 which is extremely high. Charts to find Soul and Personality Rays from one's Ascendant and Sun Sign are given in the Introduction. This study proves the accuracy of the system of Ray-Centered Astrology to find one's Personality Ray.

HIGHLY EVOLVED DISCIPLES USING SIDEREAL SYSTEM HAVE SAME PERSONALITY RAYS BY RAY-CENTERED ASTROLOGY AS DK GAVE

Name	Birthdate	Sun Sign	Ruler	Personality Ray
AAB A. Bailey	June 16	Taurus	Es. Vulcan	1
JWK-P F. Bailey	March 16	Aquarius	Es. Jupiter	2
ISGL E. Cosgrove	June 1	Taurus	Es. Vulcan	1
RSW M. Walter	Nov. 2	Libra	Es. Uranus	7
HSD H. Richards	Sept. 30	VirgoEs.	Moon veils Vulcan	1
FCD R. Assagioli	Feb. 27	Aquarius	Hier. Moon	4

OTHER DISCIPLES USING TROPICAL SYSTEM
HAVE SAME PERSONALITY RAYS FOUND BY
RAY-CENTERED ASTROLOGY AS GIVEN BY DK

Name	Birthdate	Sun Sign	Ruler	Personality Ray
LUT	Unknown	DK-Taurus	Es. Vulcan	1
LDO	Nov.	Scorpio	Hier. Mercury	4
PGC	June 2	Gemini	Es. Venus	7, past life 5
RSU	Jan. 17	Capricorn	Es. Saturn	3
DHB	Sept. 18	Virgo	Es. Moon Veils Neptune	6
RLU	March 29	Aries	Es. Mercury	4
OLRD	June 7	Gemini	Es. Venus	5
SRD	July 6	Cancer	Es. Neptune	6
GSS	Sept. 11	Virgo	Es. Moon Veils Neptune	6

(3) Hints DK gave denoting Ascendants and Sun Signs of Disciples corroborates with Soul and Personality Rays found by Ray-Centered Astrology

DK intentionally gave only hints to the Ascendants and Sun Signs of certain disciples because His purpose in all His work was to help readers evolve and develop their own intuition.

I found in *Discipleship in the New Age*, Volumes I and II of the Alice Bailey books, hints given to 24 disciples of their Ascendants and/or Sun Signs, along with their Soul and Personality Rays. Using these Ascendants and Sun signs, I calculated the Soul and Personality Rays through Ray-Centered Astrology and found them identical to those given by DK. If you read these volumes, remember that DK stated on Page 435 in *Treatise on White Magic* that the Constellation or Sign in which one is born is related to his or her Personality, not Soul.

Treatise on White Magic, p. 435: He said that the energy of the Constellation or Sign in which one is born is related to the personality. Therefore when He says "Sign in which a man is born," He refers to the Sun Sign, not the Ascendant. The following information that DK gave concerning His disciples prove that the Personality Ray is determined by the planetary ruler of the Sun Sign.

Disciple ISG-L was given a Ray 1 Personality by DK. *Discipleship in the New Age*. Vol. 1, p. 513: He said that ISG-L was born in the Sign Gemini as well as AAB. His June 1 birthday gives a Tropical Gemini Sun. The Sidereal System was used because he is highly evolved, giving him a Taurus Sun with its esoteric ruler, Vulcan, a ruler of Ray 1—his Personality Ray.

Disciple AAB was given a Ray 1 Personality by DK. From the above paragraph, we find her Sun was in Gemini tropically, born June 16. Considered very highly evolved (the leader of the group), the Sidereal was used giving her a Taurus Sun with its esoteric ruler, Vulcan, a ruler of Ray 1—her Personality Ray.

Disciple LUT was given a Ray 1 Personality by DK. *Discipleship in the New Age*, Vol. 1, p. 471: He stated that a Taurus person is on the First Ray of the personality. The esoteric ruler of Taurus is Vulcan, a ruler of Ray 1—his Personality Ray.

Disciple RSW was given a Ray 7 Personality by DK. *Discipleship in the New Age*, Vol. 2, p. 736: He said that such incarnations, as RSW has, are frequently lived under the Sun Sign of Libra or have Libra as the Rising Sign, but later the indecision ends and the Soul begins to function, and that such a life is now hers. Because Libra denotes inactivity and indecision and because DK said that she should shift from those personality characteristics to the Soul, Libra must be her Sun Sign (personality), not the Ascendant (Soul). She was considered very highly evolved, therefore her birth date of November 2 which gives a Scorpio Sun Sign in the Tropical system, gives her a Libra Sun Sign of the Sidereal System. The esoteric ruler of Libra is Uranus, the ruler of Ray 7—her Personality Ray.

Disciple BSD was given a Ray 3 Soul by DK. *Discipleship in the New Age*, Vol. 1, p. 115: He said that BSD had a sense of duty, a steadfastness sand persistance. This sounds much like a Capricorn Ascendant which could give him a Ray 3 Soul.

Disciple LDO was given a Ray 2 Soul by DK. *Discipleship in the New Age*, Vol. 2, p. 443: He said that LDO should be more discriminating. This sounds very much like a Pisces Ascendant which could give a Ray 2 Soul.

Disciple FCD was given a Ray 2 Soul by DK. *Discipleship in the New Age*, Vol. 1, pp. 143, 147, Vol. 2, p. 464: He stated that because FCD was so close with auras of other people in constantly giving, it sometimes causes a seepage of vitality, especially because the path of the world savior is a hard one and because FCD said that he had no inner confidence. This sounds very much like Pisces which could give a Ray 2 Soul.

Disciple JWKP was given a Ray 1 Soul by DK. *Discipleship in the New Age*, Vol. 1, pp. 138, 169, 170: He said that JWK is stable and responsible and should ponder on joy, happiness, gaiety and bliss. This definitely sounds like Capricorn which could give him a Ray 1 Soul.

Disciple RAJ was given a Ray 2 Soul and Ray 7 Personality by DK. *Discipleship in the New Age*, Vol. 2, pp. 475, 476, 482, 483, 487: He said that she has an inferiority complex and is a heart person and should learn discrimination; also that she is an executive and administrator. This sounds strongly like a Pisces Ascendant which could give a Ray 2 Soul. Her administrative nature could give a Libra Sun Sign with Uranus as the esoteric ruler and the ruler of Ray 7—her Personality Ray.

Disciple IBS was given a Ray 1 Soul and Ray 6 Personality by

DK. *Discipleship in the New Age*, Vol. 1, pp. 237, 242, Vol. 2, pp. 553, 554: He noted that IBS produces symbols of mist and fog, bringing fire and water together with her intensity, resentment and wanting to be the center of attraction. This sounds much like a Leo (fire) Ascendant which can give a Ray 1 Soul, and a Scorpio (water) Sun Sign with its esoteric ruler, Mars, which is a ruler of Ray 6—her Personality Ray.

Disciple RVB was given a Ray 2 Soul and Ray 4 Personality by DK. *Discipleship in the New Age*, Vol. 1, pp. 263, 271: He wrote that more coordination is needed between the inner and outer and that RVB has pose and fine efficiency but also fear. This could very well be a Pisces Ascendant which could give a Ray 2 Soul, and a Virgo Sun Sign with the esoteric ruler, Mercury, a ruler of Ray 4—the Personality Ray. Pisces and Virgo are polar opposites which are often difficult to bring together, as in this case of the Soul (inner) and personality (outer).

Disciple PGC was given a Ray 2 Soul and Ray 7 Personality by DK. *Discipleship in the New Age*, Vol. 1, pp. 342, 344: He asks if PGC will refrain from criticism and too analytical a nature and states that his Fifth Ray activity is due to being his Personality Ray in his past life. This sounds very much like a Virgo Ascendant which could give a Ray 2 Soul. His June 2 birth gives a Gemini Sun Sign with Venus as the esoteric ruler and the ruler of Ray 5. Is it possible that he was born with the Ray 5 Personality of his past life which changed to Ray 7 later?

Disciple RSU was given a Ray 2 Soul and a Ray 3 Personality by DK. *Discipleship in the New Age*, Vol. 1, p. 360: He noted RSU's inner sense of inferiority, steadfastness, persistence and sensitivity of the mystical realm. This very much sounds like a Pisces Ascendant which could give a Ray 2 Soul, and a Capricorn Sun Sign with Saturn, its ruler and also the ruler of Ray 3—her Personality Ray which is further corroborated by her January 17 birthday.

Disciple WDS was given a Ray 2 Soul and Ray 1 Personality

by DK. *Discipleship in the New Age*, Vol. 1, pp. 375, 381: He said that WDS has a lack of self confidence and a strong-willed personality. This sounds like a Pisces Ascendant which could give a Ray 2 Soul, and a Taurus Sun Sign whose esoteric ruler, Vulcan, is a ruler of Ray 1 of Will and Power—his Personality Ray.

Disciple DPR was given a Ray 1 Soul by DK. *Discipleship in the New Age*, Vol. 1, pp. 382, 387: He noted that DPR had been working for years with steadfastness and self-discipline. This certainly sounds like a Capricorn Ascendant which could give a Ray 1 Soul.

Disciple DHB was given a Ray 2 Soul and Ray 6 Personality by DK. *Discipleship in the New Age*, Vol. 1, pp. 419, 424: He noted DHB's compassionate comprehension, yet criticism of others and a glamour of depression caused by a sense of undue Spiritual inferiority. This sounds like a Pisces Ascendant which could give a Ray 2 Soul. Born September 18, corroborating with his critical nature, he has a Virgo Sun Sign with the Moon as the esoteric ruler veiling Neptune, a ruler of Ray 6, his Personality Ray.

Disciple WOI was given a Ray 2 Soul by DK. *Discipleship in the New Age*, Vol. 1, p. 446: He recommended to WOI that he not indulge in His self-analysis. This could very will be a Virgo Ascendant which could give a Ray 2 Soul.

Disciple DIJ was given a Ray 2 Soul by DK. *Discipleship in the New Age*, Vol. 2, p. 697: He said that DIJ has prejudice and criticism and suggested that he be careful that the physical body is not unduly nurtured. This sounds much like a Virgo Ascendant which could give a Ray 2 Soul.

Disciple DEI was given a Ray 2 Soul by DK. *Discipleship in the New Age*, Vol. 1, p. 497, Vol. 2, p. 704: He wrote that DEI has a tendency to self-defense and criticism of others. This very likely is a Virgo Ascendant which could give a Ray 2 Soul.

Disciple CDPR was given a Ray 2 Soul and Ray 6 Personality by DK. *Discipleship in the New Age*, Vol. 1, pp. 504, 511, 512, 516, 526: He stated that CDPR was fearful, suspicious, nervous,

foreboding, worrisome, restless, resentful, self-pitying, failed to
be detached and has an inferiority complex, yet is greatly sympa-
thetic, understanding, loyal, steadfast, humble, gentle and has a
loving, unselfish attitude. This strongly points to a Pisces Ascendant which could give a Ray 2 Soul. Because of resentment and
suspicion, a Scorpio Sun Sign is seen with Mars as the esoteric
ruler and a ruler of Ray 6—her Personality Ray.

Disciple OLRD was given a Ray 1 Soul and a Ray 5 Personality by DK. *Discipleship in the New Age*, Vol. 1, p. 554: He stated
that OLRD's higher mind is quick, intuitive and grips essentials
rapidly with power and a strong will, yet his lower concrete mind
sometimes deters him from anticipating great things. Because of
his intuitive and quick, alert mind and powerful will, this portrays
an Aries Ascendant with a Ray 1 Soul. He was born June 7 with a
Gemini Sun Sign whose esoteric ruler is Venus and the ruler of
Ray 5—his Personality Ray. Ray 5 symbolizes the lower concrete
logical mind, and Ray 1 symbolizes the powerful mind that syn-
thesizes the whole picture; DK suggested that he be more attuned to his Ray 1 Soul than his Ray 5 Personality.

Disciple SRD was given a Ray 2 Soul and Ray 6 Personality.
Discipleship in the New Age, Vol. 1, pp. 560, 562: He stated that
SRD was over-sensitive with a strong inferiority complex. This
looks like a Pisces Ascendant which could give a Ray 2 Soul, and a
Cancer Sun Sign with Neptune as the esoteric ruler and also
ruler of Ray 6—his Personality Ray. He was born July 6, the Sign
of Cancer, again corroborating DK's statements with Ray-Centered Astrology's calculations.

Disciple HSD was given a Ray 2 Soul and a Ray 1 Personality
by DK. *Discipleship in the New Age*, Vol. 1, p. 571, Vol. 2, p. 714:
He says that HSD intensively psychologizes others with a tendency to criticize and that her mind goes from one thought to another so quickly that she fails in understanding, yet has a deep,
creative mind. This certainly looks like a Gemini Ascendant with
her fleeting mind, giving a Ray 2 Soul. Because of her tendency

to criticize, she has a Virgo Sun Sign with its esoteric ruler, the Moon veiling Vulcan which is a ruler of Ray 1—her Personality Ray. She was born September 30 giving a Sidereal Virgo Sun Sign, which is another proof of the validity of Ray-Centered Astrology.

Disciple LTS-K was given a Ray 3 Soul and Ray 6 Personality by DK. *Discipleship in the New Age*, Vol. 1, pp. 609, 615, 613, 614, 732, 733: He says that LTS-K has great persistence and tenacity but there is ambition, love of power and deviousness. This sounds much like a Capricorn Ascendant (persistence and ambition) which could give a Ray 3 Soul. He has a Scorpio Sun Sign (intense vibration and deviousness) with its esoteric ruler, Mars, a ruler of Ray 6, his Personality Ray.

(4) Ray-centered Astrology is Commanding Attention across Eight Disciplines

Astrology

I was told that a number of astrologers in my area asked each other what they thought of Ray-Centered Astrology. They decided to go into the silence to touch their Souls before replying. After meditation, each said, "It is very accurate and very deep."

"Ray-Centered Astrology is an excellent work of esoteric research and study. Congratulations on a masterpiece." —founder of Susquehanna Valley Institute of the Seven Rays, astrologer Terance Sillett

"Literate, unpretentious, offers concrete techniques to help you figure out why you're here, what your Soul's Purpose is and how to use challenging aspects beneficially. Among only a tiny handful of esoteric books that offers a promise of bearing something beyond dandelion fluff as fruit. I recommend it highly."

—world renowned astrologer, reviewer, writer, lecturer Donna Van Toen

"I was almost unable to put the book down for 24 hours after I received it." —astrologer Jane Dater

"Whole new vistas are opening to view as the Wisdom of the Ages returns in the form of Ray-Centered Astrology. It is the most valuable and inspiring teaching that I found at the 1986 United Astrology Congress which, in itself, was rich with inspiration. Practical, informative and dynamic, it deserves to become a classic in counseling. It will bring astrology fully into the New Age when so many Souls are seeking an understanding of life and spiritual purpose by showing how we can best express our Soul and Personality Rays." —dedicated astrologer preferring to remain anonymous

"Your book is most thought-provoking, a tremendous task. It has unfolded for me some of the mystery in delving into the core meanings of the Bailey books. You have done an exceptional piece of work." —astrologer, lecturer, membership secretary of the National Council of Geocosmic Research Margie Herskovitz

"I have received a great deal of pleasure and insight from your book. I use it in my counseling with clients." —astrologer T. Stan Riddle

"The study and application of Ray-Centered Astrology is the highest endeavor I could imagine attaining." —astrologer Valerie Bond

"I want to incorporate Ray-Centered Astrology with the charts I do." —esoteric astrologer Pauline O'Dell

"Fascinating, highly spiritually-moving, I find a depth of understanding and love in the teachings of your Ray-Centered Astrology that I do not find in others. I was about to give up my astrology profession until I found this book. To guide people accurately would change the whole nature of the world." —Ray-Centered astrologer Pamela McLean.

Psychology

"The amount of thought, love and hard work you put into Ray-Centered Astrology is deeply appreciated by all of us who are trying to find our soul's purpose and act on what is revealed."
—clinical social worker Rita McClure Cunningham

Education

"I am so excited with your writing—this is indeed an excellent textbook for students. Alice Bailey's work is difficult reading and you have synthesized the rays with astrology beautifully." — Boulder College psychology professor Stephanie Clement

"Using Ray-Centered Astrology, we have spectacular results with understanding, learning and behavior. As educators, we are grateful for approaching this realistically, magically and understandingly." —principal Sequoia Preparatory School and Insight Child Development Center Alexandra Kolkmeyer

Philosophy

"I have been greatly fascinated and enthusiastic about Ray-Centered Astrology. It seems a much needed book with a terrific future. It is a most excellent New Age contribution for psychologists, astrologers, counselors, teachers and for everyone. I have used it for counseling with rich rewards. Many of the key ideas and words in my Ray sonnets seem to be mainly extracted from your book. Much good luck on your great book and I myself am very grateful to you as all the world should and *will* be."
—philosopher, poet, essayist William Walters

Spirituality

"Very accurate, very deep, and beautiful." —World Fellowship of Religions founder His Holiness, Acharya Sushil Kumarji Maharaj

Science

"I found Ray-Centered Astrology to be extremely enlightening, along with adding a new dimension to the more common astrological interpretive techniques." —computer technician, astrologer C. Michael Smith

Metaphysics

"My own use of Ray-Centered Astrology started about ten years ago. I was not sure I was correct in my view but having put it to the test with family and friends, I was confident enough to know I was on to something. You can imagine how happy I was to find your book at the 1986 United Astrology Congress. I missed the next lecture to read it and decided that was why I had gone to the Congress in the first place. My Virgo Moon and Ray 5 Soul have often caused me to reject many things which seem too unscientific for one of my bent . . . When I found your book, I cried for joy." —metaphysician, psychologist, astrologer Dr. Marion Blumenthal

Publishing, Literature

"The definitive work on the Astrology of the Seven Rays where Alice Bailey left off; deals with self-realization, success and joy and provides a more meaningful and in-depth delineation than does Traditional Astrology." —editor of *Considerations*, astrologer Kennett Gilman

"It is very enlightening and comprehensive and can be a goldmine." —editor of *Welcome to Planet Earth* astrologer Mark Lerner

Seekers of Truth

"Before I was acquainted with your work, I was so unhappy I felt I couldn't go on any longer, and after reading your book and listening to my delineation tape you sent, my life turned completely around. I now devote my life to helping people the way I was helped." —Irene Bouchard

"A physical illness sent me to the hospital. After your Ray-Centered counseling and reading the book, my health is good and I now accept and love myself where I am as well as accept and love everyone else wherever they are, and am helping many who are suffering as I once did." —Nancy Piccarreto

"The Seven Rays are constants in a changing universe. Just as a fine telescope enables us to see beyond the mundane, the Rays draw the mind's eye to higher dimensions which are just as real. Your book served to further my belief that you are indeed on the paths of both Logic and Spirit." —Claire Soule

(5) Cosmic Happenings

Why would a Spiritually-oriented astrology surface at this period in the history of the race? Whenever any two of the slow moving planets come together in the same degree, certain powerful changes affect humanity which last until the next conjunction when different changes will begin to occur. The last conjunction of Neptune and Pluto, occurring every 492 years, which Astrologer Mark Lerner says is the most powerful of all conjunctions, took place in 1892 giving immense power for Spiritual regeneration. Ever since, a renaissance of Traditional Astrology, which had been undercover for centuries because of certain unenlightened people, began.

Now after a century of the last conjunction of Neptune and Pluto, the time is right for a step up—the astrology of the Soul in Ray-Centered Astrology found in the pages of this book.

What cosmic happenings at this time verify this? First, 1993 finds the conjunction of Neptune and Uranus, inducing sudden changes for Soul evolvement, and located in Capricorn, the Sign of Initiation, denotes energy released for raising the consciousness of humanity.

Add to that the discovery of Comet Chiron, less than 20 years before, which induces people to want to know who they are, why they are here and to find and manifest their unique Soul's Purposes through Ageless Wisdom teachings such as Ray-Centered Astrology.

The most important reason for this Spiritual astrology to surface at this time is the releasing of the ever-increasing New Aquarian Age energies, giving people the freedom to be who they are. All these energies are entering the consciousness of humankind laying the foundation for the acceptance of this New Astrology of the Soul—to know who you are and why you are here

(6) Universal Truths as part of Ray-Centered Astrology: Details Found in Various Chapters of this Book

That we are divine beings who will live forever, but who will take on earth bodies and then discard them when they can no longer be used for overcoming weaknesses and/or serving others

That the greater the effort to overcoming weaknesses and serving others consonant with our special Purpose in life, the more we will experience that peace and joy we have always longed for

That we create our own reality, both the good and the difficult by our thoughts, words and actions

That everything that happens to us is for our ultimate good

That the "Why me?" should no longer be a question when difficult experiences surface, but instead awareness of the blessings in disguise for opportunities to learn needed lessons

That we are where we are supposed to be—our Souls attract to us relationships and experiences at the exact times needed for our evolvement

That the crises that many people are now experiencing in drug and alcohol addiction, mental illness and violence are actually times of great opportunities for change—to evolve to a higher level

That God is within us and we have the power to make all the Spiritual progress we wish

That guilt toward self and anger and blame toward others need no longer be a part of our lives—we can now accept and love ourselves and others wherever we and they are.

That none of us is perfect and that we can help ourselves and others only through understanding and love

That the Universe is wise and loving and is constantly helping us reach that divinity which is our heritage.

That it is a privilege and a responsibility to be living in these fascinating, exciting and difficult times in which opportunities for great changes in our consciousness are being offered

That we came to earth this time around for a special Purpose and that no one else can help humankind as well as each of us in our own unique capacity

That when we do what we came on earth to do, life begins to take on a special wonderful meaning which not only brings us joy and success but makes this a better world for others

That Ray-Centered Astrology can help us find that Purpose for which we came into this life, mainly through our Soul and Personality Rays, Ascendant and Sun Sign

That we are now living in the dawning of the New Aquarian Age in which faith, hope and love, as in the past Age of Pisces, are not enough for our continued evolvement, but now we also need understanding—knowing who we are and why we are here!

Notes

1 *Maitreya's Mission*, Benjamin Creme, Share International Foundation, London, 1986

2 *Astro-Data II, Astro-Data III, Astro-Data IV*, Lois Rodden, American Federation of Astrologers, NV, 1980, 1986, 1990

3 *Book of American Charts*, Francoise and Michel Gauquelin, Astro Computing Services, CA, 1982

4 *The 24 volumes of the Alice A. Bailey books*, Alice Bailey, Lucis Trust, NY Quotations from Alice A. Bailey's books cannot be reproduced without special permission from the Lucis Trust which holds copyright

Appendix

In the Introduction are charts to find your Sun Sign and Personality Ray which give your Personality Type. However, if you were born from the 20th to the 23rd of the month, your Sun Sign as shown by the chart in the Introduction could be one of two Signs. The reason is that the day the Sun changes Signs varies from year to year. Therefore it is necessary to have your horoscope erected to find your true Sun Sign.

The Introduction also gives a chart to pinpoint your Soul Ray from your Ascendant. However, if your Ascendant is not Taurus, Gemini, Libra, Scorpio or Aquarius which shows your Soul Ray, it is necessary to erect your horoscope to calculate your Soul Ray. The reason is that this chart gives two or three possible Soul Rays for each of the other seven Ascendant Signs.

The following available from Ruth Mierswa, 1092 Turk Hill Road, Fairport, NY 14450:

1. Finding your Sun Sign if you were born from the 20th to the 23rd of the month.
2. Finding your Ascendant Sign.
3. Finding your Soul Ray if your Ascendant is not Taurus, Gemini, Libra, Scorpio or Aquarius.
4. A complete Ray-Centered astrological delineation using three horoscopes—the natal (used by Traditional astrologers) and two the author created (the Soul's Purpose Horoscope and the Most Serious Problem Horoscope). Results are put on tape.
5. The book, *Ray-Centered Astrology*, which is the scholarly,

definitive book of this new Astrology with details to do Ray-Centered astrological delineations, how the author arrived at the information in *Who You Are and Why You Are Here,* and much else.

Index

—◦◦◦—

Ruth Mierswa
1092 Turk Hill Road
Fairport, NY 14450

Please send me _____ copies of *Who You Are and Why You Are Here.*

Please send me _____ copies of *Ray-Centered Astrology.*

$16.00 per copy of each book, + $3.00 shipping & handling for the first book and $1.00 for each additional book, not to exceed $6.00, payable in U.S. funds.

NY residents please add sales tax.

Checks and money orders accepted.

Amount enclosed: $ _____

Name _____

Address _____

City, State, Zip code _____

_____

—◦◦◦—